C000296504

Unfinished

The Church 40 Years after Vatican II

Essays for John Wilkins

Edited by
Austen Ivereigh

continuum
NEW YORK • LONDON

CONTINUUM

The Tower Building, 11 York Road, London SE1 7NX

15 East 26th Street, New York, NY 10010

www.continuumbooks.com

© The Tablet Publishing Company 2003

All rights reserved. No part of this publication may be reproduced or transmitted in any form or by any means, electronic or mechanical, including photocopying, recording or any information storage or retrieval system, without prior permission in writing from the publishers.

First published 2003

British Library Cataloguing-in-Publication Data
A catalogue record for this book is available from the British Library.

ISBN 0-8264-7100-5 (paperback)

Typeset by Aarontype Limited, Easton, Bristol
Printed and bound by Cromwell Press Ltd, Trowbridge, Wiltshire

Contents

Part III Signposts from Afar

Part IV Postscript

About the Contributors

LAVINIA BYRNE is a regular broadcaster with the BBC on domestic radio and with the World Service. She used to teach communications in the Cambridge Theological Federation, where she was a tutor at Westcott House. A former editor of the Ignatian spirituality journal *The Way*, she is author of *Woman at the Altar* (Continuum, 1999), and 20 other titles. She writes *The Tablet*'s internet reviews and edits its Catholic internet portal, www.cathport.com.

JOAN CHITTISTER OSB is a Benedictine sister of Erie, Pennsylvania, and a popular speaker and writer. A theologian, social psychologist and communication theorist, she is an active member of the International Peace Council and a regular columnist for the *National Catholic Reporter*. Her recent books include *Scarred by Struggle, Transformed by Hope* (Wm. B. Eerdmans, 2003), *New Designs: An Anthology of Spiritual Vision* (Benetvision, 2002) and *The Story of Ruth: Twelve Moments in Every Woman's Life* (Wm. B. Eerdmans, 2000).

JOHN CORNWELL is Director of the Science and Human Dimension Project at Jesus College, Cambridge, and an Affiliated Research Scholar in the Department of History and Philosophy of Science in the University of Cambridge. His books include *Hitler's Pope: The Secret History of Pius XII* (Penguin Books, 2000) and *Breaking Faith: The Pope, the People and the Fate of Catholicism* (Penguin Books, 2002).

SHIRLEY DU BOULAY worked for several years covering religion for the BBC. Among her many books are biographies of Teresa of Avila, Dame Cicely Saunders, Desmond Tutu and Bede Griffiths. She is currently working on a biography of Swami Abhishiktananda. She was married to the late John Harriott, for many years a much-loved *Tablet* columnist.

EAMON DUFFY is Reader in Church History in the University of Cambridge, and President of Magdalene College, Cambridge, where he has been Fellow since 1979. He has recently been appointed Professor of the History of Christianity. He is a member of the Pontifical Historical Commission and of the Theology Committee of the Roman Catholic Hierarchy of England and Wales. Among his books are *The Stripping of the Altars: Traditional Religion in England 1400–1570* (Yale University Press, 1992) and a history of the popes, *Saints and Sinners* (Yale University Press, 1997, with a revised and expanded edition in 2000). His most recent book, *The Voices of Morebath, Reformation and Rebellion in an English Village* (Yale University Press, 2001), was awarded the Hawthornden Prize for Literature in 2002. He is a frequent broadcaster on radio and television, and a longstanding *Tablet* contributor.

JULIAN FILOCHOWSKI was director of CAFOD, the Catholic Agency for Overseas Development in England and Wales, from 1982 until 2003. He was also a member of the Committee for International Justice and Peace of the English and Welsh Bishops' Conference from 1981, and co-chair of the Caritas International AIDS Task Force from 1988. In 1999 he was elected a member of Caritas International's Executive Board and a member of the Board of Caritas Europe. In 1998 he received an OBE for services to International Development.

THOMAS C. FOX is the publisher and former editor of the *National Catholic Reporter*. His books include *Sexuality and Catholicism* (George Braziller, 1995) and most recently *Pentecost in Asia* (Orbis, 2002).

JOHN HALDANE is Professor of Philosophy and Director of the Centre for Ethics, Philosophy and Public Affairs in the University of St Andrews. He is author (with J. J. C. Smart) of *Atheism and Theism* (Blackwell, 2nd edn, 2003) and of *An Intelligent Person's Guide to Religion* (Duckworth, 2003). His next book is a collection of essays, *Faithful Reason* (Routledge). He has been a frequent contributor to *The Tablet* for the last decade.

MARGARET HEBBLETHWAITE is a theologian, spiritual director and journalist living in Santa María, Misiones, Paraguay, where she teaches a Bible class at a tertiary institute for the poor. She married the Vaticanologist Peter Hebblethwaite in 1974 and was widowed in 1994. From 1991 to 2000 she was assistant editor at *The Tablet*. Her books include *Motherhood and God* (Geoffrey Chapman, 1984), *Basic Is Beautiful: Basic Ecclesial Communities from Third World to First World* (HarperCollins, 1993) and *The Next Pope* (with Peter Hebblethwaite: HarperCollins and HarperSanFrancisco, 2000). She has edited an anthology of texts which appeared in *The Tablet*'s 'Living Spirit' column: *Living Spirit: Prayers and Readings for the Christian Year* (Canterbury Press, 2000).

AUSTEN IVEREIGH is *The Tablet*'s deputy editor. A former lecturer in Spanish and Jesuit novice, he is the author of *Catholicism and Politics in Argentina* (Macmillan, 1995) and editor of *The Politics of Religion in an Age of Revival: Essays in Nineteenth-Century Europe and Latin America* (University of London, 2000).

JOSEPH KOMONCHAK holds the John C. and Gertrude P. Hubbard Chair in Religious Studies in the School of Theology and Religious Studies at the Catholic University of America in Washington, D.C. An expert in the ecclesiology and theology leading up to the Second Vatican Council, he is editor of the English-language edition of the five-volume *History of Vatican II*, the fourth volume of which is about to appear.

NICHOLAS LASH is the Norris-Hulse Professor Emeritus of Divinity and Fellow Emeritus of Clare Hall at the University of Cambridge. His books include *Easter in Ordinary: Reflections on Human Experience and the Knowledge of God* (SCM Press, 1988), *Believing Three Ways in One God: A Reading of the Apostles' Creed* (SCM Press, 1992 and 2003) and *The Beginning and the End of 'Religion'* (Cambridge University Press, 1996).

CLIFFORD LONGLEY is *The Tablet*'s editorial consultant, fortnightly columnist and leader writer, and was for six months in 1996 its acting editor. For 20 years he was religious affairs editor of *The Times*, and for a time its chief leader writer. He wrote a weekly column in *The Times* throughout that period, and continued it in the *Daily Telegraph*, from 1992 to 2000. Books include *The Times Book of Clifford Longley* (Harper-Collins, 1991), *The Worlock Archive* (Geoffrey Chapman, 2000) and *Chosen People* (Hodder & Stoughton, 2002). He is a regular contributor to BBC Radio 4's *Thought for the Day*.

MICHAEL NOVAK covered the second session of Vatican II in 1964 for the *National Catholic Reporter*. The winner of the Templeton Prize for Progress in Religion (1994), he currently holds the George Frederick Jewett Chair in Religion and Public Policy at the American Enterprise Institute in Washington,

D.C. His books include *The Spirit of Democratic Capitalism* (Madison Books, 1991), *The Catholic Ethic and the Spirit of Capitalism* (Free Press, 1993), *Belief and Unbelief: A Philosophy of Self-Knowledge* (Transaction Publishers, 1994), *The Experience of Nothingness* (Transaction Publishers, 1998) and *Catholic Social Thought and Liberal Institutions: Freedom with Justice* (Transaction Publishers, 1989). His latest book is *On Two Wings: Humble Faith and Common Sense at the American Founding* (Encounter Books, 2001).

TIMOTHY RADCLIFFE OP is a Dominican of the English Province. He joined the Order in 1965, studying in Oxford and Paris. He taught Scripture at Blackfriars, Oxford, for many years and was its Prior from 1982 to 1988. As Provincial he was President of the Conference of Religious. He was Master of the Order of Preachers from 1992 to 2001, and is now an itinerant preacher and lecturer. He is the author of *Sing a New Song* (Dominican Publications, 1999) and *I Call You Friends* (Continuum, 2000).

MICHAEL WALSH wrote the commemorative history of *The Tablet*, and was for many years its television critic. He retired as Librarian of Heythrop College, University of London, in 2001, and is now editor of the *Heythrop Journal*. He is also the editor of the *Dictionary of Christian Biography* (Continuum, 2001). Among his recent books are *Warriors of the Lord* (John Hunt Publishing, 2003), an account of the military religious orders, and *The Conclave: A Sometimes Secret and Occasionally Bloody History of Papal Election* (Canterbury Press, 2003).

REMBERT G. WEAKLAND OSB is the Archbishop Emeritus of Milwaukee and an international expert in liturgy and sacred music. A Benedictine monk of Latrobe, Pennsylvania, he was elected Abbot Primate of the International Benedictine Federation in 1967, and ten years later named Archbishop of Milwaukee by Pope Paul VI. In 1999 he received his thirty-seventh doctorate from Columbia University for his thesis on the Office Antiphons of the Ambrosian Chant. He remains active in the dialogue between the Catholic Church and the Orthodox Church in the United States.

ALAIN WOODROW, *The Tablet*'s Paris correspondent, was for 20 years religious affairs and then media correspondent for *Le Monde*. His nine books include a novel, *Le pape a perdu la foi*, and a study of the Society of Jesus published in English as *The Jesuits, A Story of Power* (Geoffrey Chapman, 1995). He divides his time between Paris and the Auvergne.

HUGO YOUNG has been a political columnist with the *Guardian* for 15 years and a *Tablet* director since 1985. He was a columnist and editor on the *Sunday Times* until it was taken over by News International. His books include a biography of Margaret Thatcher, *One of Us* (Macmillan, 1991), *This Blessed Plot: Britain and Europe from Churchill to Blair* (Macmillan, 1998) and a recent collection of his *Guardian* columns, *Supping with the Devils: Political Journalism from Thatcher to Blair* (Atlantic Books, 2003).

Introduction[1]

Austen Ivereigh

As a unit of time, 40 is a number rich in biblical resonances. Jesus was tested in the desert for 40 days, which was also the period the apostles waited in the Upper Room for the fire of Pentecost. The Flood lasted for 40 years – the same period the Israelites wandered in the wilderness. And it was 40 years ago that the Second Vatican Council (1962–65) was getting underway in Rome, unleashing a revolutionary return to the Church's sources, and setting Catholic Christianity on its still-unfinished journey of renewal and reform.

The metaphor of the journey is the right one. The Council jettisoned the historically isolated idea that the Church was outside time and history; the Church would henceforth be seen as the People of God on pilgrimage.

Every pilgrimage must at some point pause and take some bearings. The retirement this year of John Wilkins after 22 years as editor of *The Tablet* seemed too good an opportunity to pass up. Some of the leading Catholic writers of the 'Vatican II generation' were therefore invited to find positions overlooking the postconciliar route and ask: How far have the pilgrims come? What roads have they travelled? Which turnings did they miss? Which routes remain inadequately trodden?

The Council made John Wilkins a Catholic. In the first of a 2002 series of *Tablet* articles commemorating the opening of

Vatican II, he recalled how, as the son of an Anglican mother and an agnostic father, and knowing little of the Catholic Church, he could barely believe his eyes when Pope John XXIII summoned the world's bishops to Rome.

> Here was a Pope like the fisherman Peter. You could almost see him casting out his nets, you could almost feel his love for the whole world. And then this Council – the bravery of it, the confidence of it. Where did that come from? Reflecting, I could see it came from a Christian community that felt itself to be connected in a special way with the Upper Room in Jerusalem where the Church began. The Catholic Church, I suddenly saw, was attached to that Upper Room experience as by an umbilical cord that ran through the centuries up till now. And therefore it had a unique hold on the apostolic tradition, leading to a willingness to return to the sources in a transforming way.

As the Council got underway, his eyes grew still wider. First, the document on the liturgy, now to be in English as well as Latin; then the constitution on the Church, replacing the pyramidal structure with a circular conception ('a people's Church, hierarchically structured'); then the document on the Church in the modern world, which overturned the image of the Church as a lighted castle in favour of that of a people on pilgrimage. These astonishing documents were followed by still others: one on ecumenism, which recognised the baptism in the name of the Trinity for every Christian; another on religious liberty, which performed a U-turn on the question of the rights of error; and still another on non-Christian religions, which laid the groundwork for a positive view of all the world's religions. 'Before the Council ended', he recalled, 'I had become a Catholic.'[2]

2

But if Vatican II undoubtedly changed the Church, why, he asked in a following article, was there now 'a sense of short-fall, of unfinished business?'[3]

There was never one view of the Council, then or now, even within the progressive majority at Vatican II. Indeed, as Joseph Komonchak in these pages illustrates in his account of the redaction of *Gaudium et spes*, there were substantial differences among theologians otherwise united in their determination to forge a new pastoral plan for the Church. Those differences – expressed in part by the two theological journals, *Concilium* and *Communio* – would become more marked after the Council ended. Some deplored the lack of courage in implementing the Council; others regretted that it was implemented 'in the wrong spirit'; still others that the rejection of the preconciliar culture was too drastic for the health of a community founded on tradition. If it is not easy to mark the distance travelled since Vatican II, it is in part a reflection of different understandings of what the Council was *for*.

These differences are apparent in the three magisterial overviews which make up the first part ('Taking Stock') of *Unfinished Journey*. Speaking for his generation, and especially for 'those who have personal experience, as adults, of preconciliar Catholicism', the Cambridge theologian Nicholas Lash takes a characteristically clearsighted view of the directions which the Church was set to follow after the Council. He measures the extraordinary distance travelled, notably in three areas: the celebration of the liturgy, the relations of the Catholic with other Churches, and the preferential option for the poor. Lash has a correspondingly clear view of where the Church has got bogged down – birth control and priestly celibacy – or, in some cases, notably on the question of collegiality and the place of women, has actually backtracked.

3

The American writer and theologian Michael Novak also has a clear line of vision of the Church's pilgrim path, but what he sees is rather different from Lash. Novak, who as a young reporter filed with enthusiasm from Rome on the Council's second session, later came to regret 'the spirit of Vatican II' which, he says, 'sometimes soared far beyond the actual, hard-won documents and decisions of Vatican II'. His view is not that the Church backtracked; rather that it set off in great haste, then got sidetracked, hastening towards false horizons. He credits John Paul II's pontificate with 'rescuing' the Council, restoring it to its true path, purpose and spirit. In the end, because of Pope John Paul, he suggests, the Council has worked out for good, and the Church as a consequence of Vatican II is a holier, more significant presence in the world.

The historian Eamon Duffy takes up a position between the hills, with a view of both the preconciliar and postconciliar cultures. His essay is concerned with the way the Church can articulate itself to the wider culture, something he believes contemporary Catholics find it harder to do than their fore-bears. In a carefully argued discernment of why, even as things got better, they have often appeared to worsen, he nonetheless perceives the major drawback of the postconciliar era, which is a debunking of tradition, a 'psychic evacuation' which is 'a feature of any cultural revolution'. He calls for a recovery of tradition, arguing that if Catholics are to survive as a community they need to learn to explain 'to the culture at large, and to ourselves, just who we are and what we stand for'.

The main body of *Unfinished Journey* consists of 11 essays by Catholic writers who focus their sights on particular paths. The Swiss theologian Hans Küng offers a characteristic-ally provocative invitation to Catholics to have 'civil courage' in speaking truth to power, to be willing to challenge the hierarchy when conscience demands it. Such a willingness is implicit in a pilgrim Church rather than a 'perfect society' – a fundamental revisioning of the way Catholics see the Church which is charted by the emeritus Archbishop of Milwaukee, Rembert Weakland. But the equality implicit in this vision – St Paul's image of the body made up of equal parts with differing functions – remains remote. The American Benedictine writer Joan Chittister shows dramatically how doors opened for women after the Council, then firmly shut again in their faces.

The former Master of the Dominicans, Timothy Radcliffe, sees in the recent clerical sex abuse crisis a historic opportunity for the Church to embrace a truer, more gospel-based notion of its power, so freeing up its capacity for 'spaces of undistorted communication'. Vatican II was, above all, intended to enable this. But the Church's ambiguous record in dealing with the media is patchy, as two contributors argue. Lavinia Byrne describes the Church's view of the media as 'captivated ambivalence': captivated because it is seduced by reaching millions; ambivalent because it resists transparency. Alain Woodrow finds at least part of the problem in the Council's declaration on social communications, which is widely acknowledged to be one of its poorer documents. After offering some suggestions as to how the Church can now improve on its communications document, Woodrow, who has worked for both the secular and the religious media, offers solace for the Catholic journalist trapped between a Church distrusted by the media and a media distrusted by the Church. The high ideals preached by the Church need to be translated, he argues, into a clear and simple professional code of ethics for the media; to kickstart the process, he ends with his own, thoughtful decalogue.

Michael Walsh and Clifford Longley respectively treat two 'political' themes rich in philosophical conundra: religious

freedom and social rights. Walsh charts one of the most remarkable developments since the Council: how the Church
has moved to embracing religious freedom as a key universal
human right rather than an undesirable concession. But he
warns that, in privileging truth over freedom, and in his notion
that freedom exists in order that people seek religious truth,
Pope John Paul has eroded, rather than reinforced, the Council's view of religious freedom. As Walsh notes, and Clifford
Longley illustrates with a vivid excerpt from the diary of an
English bishop who was present at the debate over religious
liberty, the issue was one of the most intensely argued over at
Vatican II. Longley places that debate within the broader
context of the developing view in Catholic thinking of the role
of the state, and the relation of human rights to the modern
state. He points out that the Catholic doctrine of human rights
goes much deeper than the idea of citizen rights, for they are
not concessions of the state but are intrinsic to people by virtue
of their God-given dignity, which is why 'a refugee seeking
entry to a state has the same human rights as one born into it'.
Since the Council, the Church's voice in favour of the refugee
and the poor has, as a result, considerably strengthened.

   With a philosopher's clarity, John Haldane observes that
every gain has a cost and, therefore,

> whether, overall, the post-Vatican II Church is better or
> worse than that which preceded it is a question that
> should be felt to be difficult to answer, and even prob-
> lematic to contemplate, for it is, after all, one and the
> same Church as was founded by Christ and as will persist
> until his return.

But that does not stop him trying, with an overview of the
place of philosophy in the Church since the Council. The
aggiornamento of that place, he concludes, is incomplete,

6

and is likely to remain so; but he praises above all the greater accessibility – and therefore attractiveness – of Aquinas's Catholic/Aristotelian synthesis to rigorous non-Catholic thinkers of the day.

John Cornwell's essay might equally be called 'After Dualism', for it reminds us of how far the Church has travelled since the Council's pastoral constitution of the modern world dismissed the old demarcations of body and soul, restoring unity. Emboldened by this, he believes the Church now needs to beware of 'a vociferous group of thinkers, highly popular within the genre of public understanding of science, to reduce and distort the nature of consciousness, selfhood, freedom, in order to make a fit with closed, reductionist, computational explanations'.

The final part of *Unfinished Journey* is entitled 'Signposts from Afar'. In terms of vitality and sheer numbers, the centre of the Church's gravity since the Council has shifted to the developing world. Asia, for Thomas C. Fox, offers an exciting vision of the Church which 'has been taking shape now quietly for some 30 years, largely off-stage and out of sight'. As he lays out that vision, it becomes clear that the conciliar priorities – the option for the poor, inculturation, interfaith dialogue, respect for theologians and collegiality – are all far more characteristic of the Church in Asia than in Europe and North America. Where Asia goes, will the rest of the Church now follow?

Prayer has already opened up many paths. Shirley du Boulay's essay on the popularity of Eastern meditation shows that one of the fruits of the Council – which invited religious orders to return to their sources – was the way in which the East helped Western monks rediscover their own desert contemplative traditions, a process which has continued in spite of the Vatican's anxiety about syncretism.

Latin America, home to 40 per cent of the world's Catholics, also points to the future, although here the example is less ecclesiological than one of witness and prophecy. Both Filochowski and Hebblethwaite document examples of suffering by the Church for the sake of the poor, the first in the famous case of the saint, martyr and model of the Vatican II bishop, Oscar Romero of San Salvador, the second in the hitherto unknown case of the Agrarian Leagues of Paraguay, an early example of base communities which were snuffed out by brutal repression. Those who criticise the Council for accommodating the Church to the world – the danger which Duffy discusses in relation to Europe and America – too easily forget how, in Latin America, precisely the reverse occurred. The interpretation of the Council at the great meeting of bishops at Medellín in 1968 paved the way for the martyr Church, whose place was no longer in a privileged bunker under the shadow of wealth and power but alongside the poor, directly in the line of fire.

As Archbishop Weakland notes, the bishops at the Second Vatican Council retained the idea that the means of holiness, through the Holy Spirit, were present to the Church and its members, but that the full perfection would only come with the eschaton. For that reason the Church was always in need of reform – semper reformanda – but full of hope because of Christ's promise to remain with his Church till the end of time.

There can be little doubt that the Holy Spirit presided over Vatican II and through it has brought the world great fruits. The adventure of spiritual and pastoral renewal to which the Council called the Church has not always been accepted and has sometimes been resisted. But it remains an invitation whose depth and power continue to be revealed over time and which may only now, 40 years on, at the beginning of the new millennium, begin to be genuinely embraced by the ordinary faithful, as they awaken to their vocation, and take their place in the ranks of the priesthood of all believers.

The Council is to the Church as a marriage vow is to a couple, or a vocation to a priest or religious – assented to in faith, but whose meaning and impact are revealed gradually, over time. *Unfinished Journey* is, in this sense, like those life inventories which pilgrims make periodically in the course of their lives: a catalogue of achievements and failures, of openness to grace and resistance to it. The purpose of such inventories may be a resolve to do better, but their effect is inevitably to bring home to pilgrims how little they have gained on their own merits and by their own strengths. Therein the real virtue of taking stock: *Unfinished Journey* is an urgent reminder that it is still Pentecost, and there is much more for the Spirit still to do, and much more openness to that Spirit required of the Church.

Unfinished Journey is also a tribute – paid expressly by Hugo Young on behalf of *Tablet* readers at the end of this book – to John Wilkins in thanks for the many years he has spent patiently and gently reminding the Church of the promises it made at the Council. Nowhere are those promises more powerfully expressed than in the opening words of the Pastoral Constitution on the Church in the Modern World, that trumpet call to the Church to immerse itself in human history. The words are great favourites of John's, and implicitly a charter for *The Tablet* under his editorship. They remain as vivid today as 40 years ago.

The joys and the hopes, the griefs and the anxieties of the men [and women] of this age, especially those who are poor or in any way afflicted, these too are the joys and hopes, the griefs and anxieties of the followers of Christ. Indeed, nothing genuinely human fails to raise an echo in their hearts ... United in Christ, they are led by the Holy Spirit in their journey to the kingdom of their Father and they have welcomed the news of salvation which is meant for every man [and woman]. That is why this community realises that it is truly and intimately linked with humankind and its history?[4]

Notes

1 The editor would like to thank the directors and staff of *The Tablet* for their help and support of this project, and for keeping it under wraps. He would especially like to thank Michael Phelan and Robin Baird-Smith from the Board, and his colleagues Sue Chisholm, Mian Ridge and Robert Carey.
2 John Wilkins, 'Earthquake in Rome', *The Tablet* (12 October 2002), pp. 10–11.
3 John Wilkins, 'Unfinished Business', *The Tablet* (19 October 2002), pp. 10–12.
4 *Gaudium et spes*, 1.

Part I

Taking Stock

OV

1

Vatican II: Of Happy Memory – and Hope?

Nicholas Lash

My generation – those who have personal experience, as adults, of preconciliar Catholicism – have a unique responsibility. We who were brought up in the Church of Pope Pius XII know that it was a world neither of tranquil certainties and quiet obedience disrupted by dissent, nor a dark place of clerical oppression from which the Council set us free. But like others of this generation, for most of my adult life the constitutions and decrees of the Council, and the spirit which animated them, have been the benchmark by which to judge the reform of Catholic pastoral practice. And those of us who had personal experience of the context in which the Council came to birth, and of its dynamics as a historical event, still have a unique contribution to make to the assessment and evaluation of its outcome – not least because, in a few years' time, the Council will be nobody's living memory.

To what extent are we suceeding in implementing the programme of reform initiated by the Council? To answer that question, it is not primarily the period between 1962 and 1965 we should look at, but that from 1965 to the present day. Our concern, in other words, is with what biblical scholars would call the *Wirkungsgeschichte* of the Council – the history of its effects. How far have we realised, or failed to realise, the programme of reform which it initiated?

13

The Achievements

The identity of the vast majority of Catholic Christians is formed and finds expression principally at Mass on Sunday. It is here, in the way we celebrate the Eucharist together, and relate what we are doing there to what we do and undergo elsewhere, that the doctrine of the Church expounded in the Council's Constitution *Lumen gentium*, the doctrine of God's word in *Dei verbum* and the account of Christianity's relationship to secular society in *Gaudium et spes* do or do not take shape, find flesh. In this sense, the state of the liturgy is the first and fundamental test of the extent to which the programme, not merely of the decree *Sacrosanctum concilium* but of all the Council's constitutions and decrees, is being achieved.

In 1968, the Catholic Truth Society in London invited me to produce a replacement for its standard catechetical pamphlet on the celebration of the Eucharist, *What Is He Doing at the Altar?* I entitled the new text, *What Are We Doing at Mass?* The pastoral, missionary and political implications of that shift in the identity of Christian agency are incalculable. It is the structured community that is the Church – God's gathered people – which celebrates the Eucharist, not merely the person presiding over the celebration. There are many weaknesses in liturgy today: the banality of so much that we sing, the uneven quality of translations, the poverty of so much preaching and our failure to make the liturgy what Paul VI called a 'school of prayer', among others. But to dwell on these would risk distracting our attention from what is the Council's single most profound and significant achievement.

Notwithstanding the continued nervous isolation of Russian Orthodoxy, the transformation in our relations with other Christian traditions has been hardly less comprehensive. Although full communion and common ministries with the

14

Churches of the Reformation remain a distant dream, the depth of mutual understanding and respect, and the extent of pastoral collaboration that we have already achieved, would have seemed unthinkable a few years before the Council opened. (As recently as 1950 one of the English Catholic bishops referred, in the pages of *The Times*, to the Archbishop of Canterbury as 'a doubtfully baptised layman'.)

The third great achievement of the Council is a shift towards the preferential option for the poor. Some years ago, I was present at a lecture that the father of liberation theology Gustavo Gutiérrez gave to an enormous crowd of students at Boston College. The Peruvian spoke of the assassination of Archbishop Oscar Romero on 24 March 1980, and of his funeral a week later. 'I was at that funeral', he said, 'during which 40 other people were killed. Can you name any of them?' The students, of course, could not. 'Those', said Gustavo, 'are the poor.'

One reason why it is difficult to generalise about the extent to which the Church is becoming converted to the preferential option is that those who work with and for the poor are often as invisible as the poor themselves. But even if we cannot easily measure it, without doubt the Council's impulse in this direction has borne impressive fruit.

The phrase 'preferential option for the poor' was coined at the 1968 conference at Medellín in Colombia, where the bishops of Latin America gathered to apply conciliar teaching to that continent. Reflecting on Medellín some 20 years later, Archbishop Michael McGrath of Panama said that the Latin-American Church was committed 'not only' to 'a preferential option for the poor in economic and political terms', but that 'this option' was to be applied 'first of all to the evangelisation of the poor, so that with them and from their point of view we can carry out the evangelisation of the entire community'.

Notwithstanding the reverses in Latin America during the present pontificate, and the Vatican's attempts to curb what it regards as the 'political' errors of liberation theology, I suspect that future historians will judge John Paul II to have been committed to the notion of evangelisation 'with and from [the] point of view of' the poor.

The Council put things in the right order in other ways, too. In 1985, one of the English bishops, shortly before leaving for Rome to take part in the Synod convened to celebrate the twentieth anniversary of the end of the Council, asked me what I thought were important clues to the quality of our remembering of what the Council sought to do. I suggested that one such clue lay in the importance which people attached to the sequence of chapters in the Council's two dogmatic constitutions, *Dei verbum* and *Lumen gentium*.

In the case of *Dei verbum*, the Council treats first, in Chapter 1, of God's being and act, God's utterance, the *Verbum Dei*; and only then, in Chapter 2, does it go on to consider what we are to do about the Word that has been spoken to us, and about the responsibility of those who teach us to 'listen' to that Word, to 'guard' and to 'expound' it. (The *Catechism*, deplorably, begins, not with God, but with our 'search' for God.)

In the case of *Lumen gentium*, Chapter I insists on the irreducible diversity of biblical and patristic images of the mystery of God's gathering of humankind, the mystery of the Church. Chapter 2 nevertheless privileges one such image: that of God's 'people' on the move through history. Only in Chapter 3 does the Council consider the structures and offices that this pilgrim people need.

The Failures

In his 1966 Sarum Lectures, Bishop Christopher Butler gave a lengthy and careful analysis of Chapter 3 of *Lumen gentium*.

It is in this chapter that the Council had struggled to incorporate the narrowly juridical teaching of Vatican I on papal primacy into its own larger view of episcopacy. 'What matters in the end', said Bishop Butler, 'is the successful achievement of the Council's intentions.'[1]

In the distance between the theory and practice of collegiality, those intentions have, thus far, been dramatically frustrated. I do not believe that anybody, as the Council ended, foresaw the possibility that, only 37 years after the promulgation of *Lumen gentium*, the Church would be far more rigorously and monolithically controlled by Pope and Curia than at any time in its history. The Church has paid a heavy price for John Paul II's lack of interest in administration. And with hindsight, it was naïve of the bishops to suppose that the Roman Curia – many of whose most senior members had been key players in that handful of bishops who had resisted the reform programme, line by line – would suddenly and easily surrender power.

To have an idea of just how new is the twentieth-century centralisation of ecclesial power, we need only go back to the early nineteenth century. In 1829 there were 646 diocesan bishops in the Latin Church. Of these, 555 owed their appointment to the State, about 67 had been elected by diocesan chapters or their equivalent, while only 24 had been appointed by the Pope. Not until 1917 (in the new Code of Canon Law) was it claimed that inherent in the papal primacy was the right to appoint bishops throughout the Catholic Church. Power swiftly taken is not as swiftly abandoned.

Until the mid-nineteenth century, such centralisation was logistically impossible to achieve even if it had been desired. It took a very long time for messages to get from Rome to Paris or Vienna – to say nothing of Cape Town or Bombay. With the coming of the railways, the world became much smaller, a process which accelerated dramatically in the century that followed with the coming of air travel, television and the Internet. Centralisation and micromanagement have grown along with technology, unimpeded by a countervailing principle.

'The most striking accomplishment of the Council', noted that shrewd commentator 'Xavier Rynne', writing in 1966, 'has unquestionably been the proclamation of episcopal collegiality, the principle that the bishops form a college and govern the Church together with the Pope who is their head.' Moreover, he went on, 'the new doctrine is bound to influence the exercise of [papal] authority in practice, particularly if Pope Paul's plans for the reform of the Roman Curia and the establishment of the Synod of Bishops are fully carried out'.[2] Which, of course, they were not. The Curia remains unaccountable to the episcopate, and the Synods, in their present form, have become little more than further instruments of papal power.

There are areas today in which the Church is dangerously polarised, and the Council is often blamed for this. Is such blame justified? That a body of human beings comprising, at least nominally, one-sixth of the human race, should display a vast diversity of temperament and attitude and opinion is both inevitable and desirable. A Church in which there were no serious disagreements would be dead. Disagreement about things that matter deeply to the disputants may create tensions but does not, of itself, do damage to the bonds of charity or threaten sacramental unity. Polarisation, in contrast – the dramatised simplification of disagreement to the point where there appear to be, for all practical purposes, two and only two approaches or opinions possible (and these two locked in mutual incomprehension and distaste) – threatens truth and charity alike.

On almost every issue considered at the Council, there was, it is true, a fairly clear division between majority and minority opinion. But for all the influence it wielded, in numerical terms the minority was very small indeed. Consider the figures: *Lumen gentium* was approved by 2151 votes to 5, *Dei verbum* by 2350 to 6, and *Gaudium et spes* by 2309 to 75. These are not the acts of a polarised episcopate, nor of a Church seriously divided.

Pope John XXIII had called the programme of reform for which the Council was convened *aggiornamento*, a bringing-up-to-date. Paul VI, in contrast, preferred to speak of *rinnovamento*, or renewal.[3] The scholars meanwhile used a French word, *ressourcement*, meaning the refreshing of Catholic thought, liberating it from the arid juridicism of late neoscholasticism, drawing once again upon the richness of its biblical and patristic sources. The journalists, for their part, unsurprisingly but unhelpfully preferring political terminology (which increasingly, in the English-speaking world, meant the language of American politics), spoke of the majority at the Council as progressive or liberal, and the minority as conservative.

The confusion resulting from all this is succinctly illustrated by the following remark from a recent biography of Cardinal Ratzinger: 'To put all this into political terms, *aggiornamento* was a liberal impulse, *ressourcement* more conservative.'[4] Yet *ressourcement* is not an alternative to *aggiornamento*, but the means of its achievement. As Yves Congar said in 1966: 'True reform implies an appeal from a less perfect to a more perfect tradition, a going back to the sources.'[5] In the second place, it was misleading to describe as conservative a group of people whose principal ambitions were to sustain the thought-patterns of nineteenth-century scholasticism and the neo-ultramontane institutional innovations of the twentieth century.

19

The Problem with Open Windows

On the larger issue, those who seek to hold the Council responsible for polarisation in the Church today underestimate the extent to which the attitudes of Catholics – bishops included – are shaped behind the gospel's back, as it were, by the seismic shifts that there have been, in recent decades, in social and economic structures, attitudes and expectations.

Does this mean that the Council came too late? If what was needed in the 1960s was *aggiornamento*, when did the Church begin to fall behind the times? Bernard Lonergan's answer was: in the late seventeenth century: 'When modern science began, when the Enlightenment began, then the theologians began to reassure one another about their certainties.'[6]

Confronted by a Western culture increasingly hostile, both institutionally and intellectually, Catholic Christianity tried to pull up the drawbridge, seeking security in disengagement from the world of which it formed a part. This stance could not last indefinitely. The pressures which began building up in the nineteenth century came to a head during the beginning of the twentieth. The Modernist crisis marked the painful and often tragic beginning of a rich and fruitful renaissance of Catholic life, thought and spirituality, which came near to fruition in the 1960s.[7]

But in many ways it came too late, sowing the seeds of its own dissolution. The condemnations of 'Modernism' dangerously delayed all programmes of renewal. For decades the Church remained in a state of siege, fully alerted to the danger of attacks as much from within as without. With the forces of renewal marginalised and suspect for half a century, the official expression of the reform movement, when it came in the form of the promulgation of conciliar documents, was greeted by many Catholics with bewilderment and incomprehension.

Pointing the way, albeit hesitantly, towards an eventual transformation of structures, the documents presupposed for their understanding a transformation of consciousness which was too often lacking. Moreover, fundamental shifts of culture did not wait upon the re-engagement of Catholicism with those secular worlds which it had for so long viewed with baleful suspicion. As a result, even when the conciliar message did begin to get through to the Catholic community as a whole, it seemed not to speak to the felt concerns and expectations of increasing numbers of people.

This account goes some way, I believe, to help explain the sadness, even the bitterness, of some of those (such as Louis Bouyer and Cardinal de Lubac) who had worked tirelessly to bring about the renewal which the Council sought, only to find themselves in a situation far more anarchic and confused than anybody had expected. Culturally, ethically and politically, we live in most bewildering times; but it is not Catholicism that is, as Cardinal Ratzinger complains, collapsing, but the citadel that we erected to protect us from the tempests of a changing world.

Did the Council come too late? No, it came just in time. But it came too late for renewal to be achieved without considerable confusion, misunderstanding and distress.

The Crisis of Authority

To conclude these reflections on the failure of the Council, it is necessary to say something on two topics which were kept off the conciliar agenda: birth control and priestly celibacy.

Pope Paul VI will surely go down in history as one of the truly great popes of modern times. It is all the more painfully paradoxical that, if there is one event which triggered the contemporary crisis of authority in the Church, it is his rejection of the official report (not, as it is sometimes erroneously described, the 'majority report') of the Commission which he had convened to consider the question of birth regulation and his promulgation, on 25 July 1968, of the Encyclical *Humanae vitae*.

As with birth control, so with priestly celibacy. Many of the bishops wished the Council to consider the matter, but Paul VI insisted on reserving it to himself and, in 1967, issued the Encyclical *Sacerdotalis coelibatus*.

Whether or not Paul VI was well advised, in the circumstances of the time, and in view of the pressures to which he was subjected, to reserve these two questions to himself is for the historians to decide. The really striking thing to notice, however, is the disturbing frequency with which questions of sexual behaviour are decided, in the Church, not on the basis of doctrinal or ethical considerations, of what human beings should or should not do, but on account of problems of authority.

The point of crisis was probably reached for many, said Professor John Marshall, a member of the Commission, around 23 April 1965. It was now that 'the four theologians of the minority group acknowledged they could not demonstrate the intrinsic evil of contraception on the basis of natural law and so rested their case on authority'.[8]

In recent decades, the failure to tackle questions of sexual behaviour on their own terms – and in terms which honestly confront the damage done to men and women by the sexual misbehaviour of the clergy – has led, in many parts of the Church, to the scandal of widespread clerical concubinage and, most recently, to damaging revelations of the extent to which ecclesiastical authorities have covered up and condoned the sexual abuse of minors.

If ever there were a time when the Church needed to treat questions of sex and gender honestly, it is surely now – not simply for its own sake, but for the sake of the society in which the gospel of God's friendship is to be proclaimed. In a culture increasingly corroded by destructively egocentric individualism, a culture which finds lifelong commitment not simply unsustainable but well-nigh unintelligible, the Catholic tradition of the primacy of relations, of the centrality and possibility and fruitfulness of the gift of lifelong friendship – both in the form of love given and exchanged in marriage and in the form of celibacy freely undertaken in witness to the kingdom – has so much to offer that we surely dare not squander it by preoccupation with the fear of change.

Unfinished Business

Questions concerning how the gospel of the crucified and risen one is effectively to be proclaimed, in solidarity with and from the standpoint of the poor, the weak and the disadvantaged, are vastly more important than questions of Church structure. Nevertheless, inappropriate structures frustrate appropriate evangelisation. There are, at present, few more urgent tasks facing the Church than that of realising the as yet unrealised programme of Vatican II by throwing into reverse the centralisation of power which accrued during the twentieth century, and restoring episcopal authority to the episcopate.

The need for collegiality is crucial to the vision of the Council. When we speak of the 'universal' Church, the 'Catholic' Church, we refer, in the first place, to that gathering, by God's redeeming grace, of all the just 'from Abel, the just one, to the last of the elect'.[9] What we usually call 'the Church' subsists as a kind of sacrament or symbolic enactment of this

23

eschatological gathering, this assembly, *congregatio* or *ecclesia*. More concretely, as *Lumen gentium* puts it: 'This Church of Christ is truly present in all legitimate local [gatherings] of the faithful ... united with their pastors.' Each celebration of the Eucharist, each parish or diocese, are not, therefore, merely fragments or small parts of some vast multinational corporation. They are the universal Church in its particular existence – in this time and at this place. Thus it is that, where episcopal office is concerned, *Lumen gentium* insists that every bishop is 'the vicar of Christ', and that bishops are not 'to be regarded as vicars of the Roman Pontiff', as branch managers of 'Church International PLC'.[10]

But, of course, the universal Church in each particular place will be a community of limited experience and resources. It can only draw on so much holiness, scholarship and wisdom. It will necessarily be a fragile group of sinful men and women in continual need of strengthening and enrichment, of education and correction, from all those – of every age and race and culture – with whom it exists in communion. In other words, the strengthening of bonds of solidarity, of *koinonia*, at every level – local and regional, national and international – is indispensable for the health and liberty of each particular instance and expression of the Catholic Church.

It is worth bearing in mind that the initial impulse behind the Ultramontane movement in early modern Europe was to strengthen the bonds of union between German and French dioceses and the See of Peter in order to ensure the freedom of the Church from state control. To the extent that, in our own day, the bishops of the Church succeed in taking back their own episcopal authority (within, and not 'above', their Churches, I need hardly add) through the development, at every level, of appropriately collegial instruments, the indispensable vocation

24

of the Holy See will become clearer: as 'sheet-anchor', 'rock' or 'court of last appeal'. This vocation of the See of Peter is (as Luke's Gospel says) to 'strengthen [his] brethren' (Luke 21:32). It is to facilitate and enable, not to control and dominate through power over all appointments and the issuing of endless streams of 'orders' and 'instructions'.

One of the most striking developments in Catholic life since the Council ended has been the flourishing of 'movements' such as Opus Dei, the Neo-Catechumenate, Communion and Liberation, and so on.[11] According to one commentator, Cardinal Ratzinger has said that these movements 'cannot be reduced to the episcopal principle, [but] represent a new justification for the Petrine ministry'.[12] In view of the enthusiasm with which Roman support for the movements, thus rationalised, is being prosecuted in the closing years of the present pontificate, it is impossible not to fear that they are being used as instruments subversive of that recovery of episcopal authority for the importance of which I have been pleading.

The ministry of women remains, quite evidently, seriously underdeveloped. If one sets aside the question of women's candidacy for the sacrament of order,[13] it is sometimes unclear whether the underdevelopment in question is specifically of women's ministry or, more generally, of the ministry of the laity. Suppose, for example, someone were to argue that there should be women nuncios or women in charge of Roman congregations. If such suggestions were resisted on the grounds that the nature of these offices is such as to require their exclusive occupancy by priests or bishops, then it would be clear that the opposition was to these offices being held by laypeople, rather than specifically by women.

For most of the Church's history, it has been maintained that women cannot hold high office in the Church because (to put it at its simplest) running things is what men do. It is instructive, in this regard, that when the Declaration *Inter insigniores* of October 1976 stated that 'the Church desires that Christian women should become fully aware of the greatness of their mission: today their role is of capital importance both for the renewal and humanisation of society and for the rediscovery by believers of the true face of the Church', the only vocations through which this mission might be exercised were specified as martyrdom, virginity and motherhood. Moreover, the evidence of the patristic and medieval authorities appealed to by recent pronouncements asserting the impossibility of ordaining women suggests that almost the only arguments adduced against their ordination in the past were variants on two themes: we cannot do it because Our Lord did not do it, and we cannot do it because running things is what men do.

Church history tells another story. Consider Fontevraud, in whose great abbey church lie Eleanor of Aquitaine, her husband Henry II of Anjou and England, and their son Richard Coeur de Lion. Fontevraud, for centuries the largest monastic complex in the world – containing priests, lay brothers, lay sisters, contemplative nuns, invalids and social outcasts – was, from its foundation in 1101 until its dissolution at the French Revolution, uninterruptedly governed by the abbess of the community of contemplative nuns.

The question of the ordination of women – as the Pontifical Biblical Commission advised Pope Paul VI when he sought their advice on the matter – cannot be decided on the basis of New Testament exegesis. The historical evidence is if anything even more fragile. The question has never previously been raised on the assumption (now agreed on all sides) of the social equality of men and women. It is a new question, and new questions need time, attentiveness, sensitivity and careful scholarship; they cannot be foreclosed by fiat.

In 1979, Karl Rahner argued that the fundamental theological significance of the Council lay in the fact that it marked 'the beginning of a tentative approach by the Church to the discovery and realisation of itself as world-Church'.[14] He saw three great epochs in Church history, the third of which has only just begun. There was a short period when Christianity was still a form of Judaism; another period, lasting nearly two thousand years, when it was (with few exceptions) the Church of what became European culture and civilisation. The third period was now beginning, 'in which the Church's living space is from the very outset the whole world'.[15]

Rahner's argument was not about geography, but about culture. At Vatican I, there were bishops from Asia and from Africa, but these were missionary bishops of European or American origin. Vatican II, in contrast, really was a first assembly of the world-episcopate.

In order for the Church truly to be a world-Church, on this account, it has to become a Church which – while never ceasing to keep alive the memory that it grew from Jewish roots and flourished, for many centuries, in European soil – will be genuinely at home in all the diverse cultures of the world.

Such genuinely pluralist inculturation of the gospel will, of course, profoundly influence not only liturgical styles and forms of theological argument but also patterns and structures of Church order and of ministry. There will, as Rahner sees it, be no future Christendoms: he saw the Church of the future as a Diaspora-Church, a little flock, *pusillus grex*. This situation, he insisted, must not be interpreted – either in practice or in theory – in sectarian terms, in attempted insulation from the contexts in which the gospel is to be proclaimed.[16]

At least in its broad outline, Rahner's argument seems to me persuasive, and it raises two issues of immense importance for the future of the Church. In the first place, there is the question of the relations between Christians and (for example) Jews, Muslims, Buddhists and Hindus. In Western culture, since the seventeenth century, it has been customary to see these peoples as specific variants of the genus called religion. There are many reasons for believing this interpretative framework to be misleading,[17] but the question raised by Rahner's argument is this: do these other peoples now also find themselves required, on their own terms, to understand themselves as, and to live as, world-peoples? I simply raise the question, the answers to which would, I suspect, be very different in each case, with very different implications for the pattern of our quest, as Christians, for deeper mutual understanding and collaboration.

In the second place, it is clear that a Church becoming a world-Church, increasingly diverse in structure, in thought-forms, in liturgical expression, would need to sustain, with even more attentiveness and energy than has been the case thus far, the bonds of common faith, and hope, and charity. But, if the Church is truly to be a world-Church, a Church that is equally at home in every corner of the world, then the principal instrument for sustaining *koinonia*, for deepening the global bonds of faith, and hope, and charity, will be the collegiality of the worldwide episcopate (*sub et cum Petro*, by all means). Such communion of the world-Church can certainly not be sustained by structures of control from a single Roman centre, aided and abetted by movements of (for the most part) parochially Mediterranean origin and character.

In 1995, John Paul II, through the encyclical *Ut unum sint*, asked bishops to engage with him in dialogue about the reform of the papacy. One of those who responded was John Quinn, the former Archbishop of San Francisco. In the Conclusion to his study on *The Reform of the Papacy*, the archbishop said there were two great problems above others: centralisation and the need for reform of the Roman Curia.[18]

My own view is that these two problems in fact boil down to one. There is not the slightest possibility that the Roman Curia will reform itself to the extent of surrendering its control and rendering itself accountable to the episcopate. Only the world-episcopate, with the pope, can effectively instigate and supervise the necessary reforms. It would be premature to convene a general council for this purpose. A renewal of regional councils, as a regular feature of Church life, would be a great step forward. But the history of synods in Rome since Vatican II and the sustained campaign to rein in the authority of episcopal conferences demonstrate that the curial stranglehold is at present so complete that there is no serious possibility, without curial reform, for effective worldwide recovery of the ancient tradition of regional councils.

What we need, and what (in my judgement) it is not unrealistic to hope for, is the election of a pope who, broadly sharing Archbishop Quinn's diagnosis of the problem, establishes a commission, which the pope would chair, whose members would be perhaps 40 or 50 diocesan bishops, drawn from every corner of the world, and which would be advised by officials of the Roman Curia, and by historians, theologians and canon lawyers from outside Rome (many of whom, of course, might be laypeople, women as well as men). The task of this commission would be to draw up proposals for the transfer of governance in the Church from pope and Curia to pope and bishops, through the establishment of a standing synod whose members would be diocesan bishops and whose work would be assisted by the offices of a curia so reformed as to function, not as an instrument of governance, but as a service of administration. The work of this commission, when completed, would then be submitted to the worldwide episcopate for comment and, presumably, revision, before receiving from the pope its final ratification. The centralised control from which we suffer, and which has contributed so greatly to the present crisis of authority, was built up in less than 100 years. It could be put into reverse in less than 10.

Notes

1 Christopher Butler, *The Theology of Vatican II* (London: Darton, Longman & Todd, 1967), p. 113.
2 Xavier Rynne, *The Fourth Session* (London: Faber & Faber, 1966), p. 257. Xavier Rynne was later identified as F. X. Murphy.
3 Rynne, *Fourth Session*, p. 258.
4 John L. Allen, *Cardinal Ratzinger* (New York: Continuum, 2000), p. 57.
5 See *Informations Catholiques Internationales* (1 January 1966), p. 55.
6 Bernard Lonergan, 'Theology in its new context', in William Ryan and Bernard Tyrrell (eds), *A Second Collection* (London: Darton, Longman & Todd, 1974), pp. 55–67 (55).
7 Nicholas Lash, 'Modernism, aggiornamento and the night battle', in Adrian Hastings (ed.), *Bishops and Writers* (Wheathampstead: Anthony Clarke, 1977), pp. 51–79 (52).
8 From a 1968 article in *The Times* by John Horgan, 'The history of the debate', in Peter Harris et al., *On Human Life* (London: Burns & Oates, 1968), pp. 7–26.
9 See *Lumen gentium*, art. 2, quoting from a homily by Gregory the Great.
10 See the debate between Cardinals Kasper and Ratzinger, especially Kasper's article in *Stimmen der Zeit* (December 2000), translated as 'On the Church', *The Tablet* (23 June 2001), pp. 927–30.
11 See series of reports on the movements in *The Tablet* (March–April 1997 and January 2001).
12 Gordon Urquhart, 'A dead man's tale', *The Tablet* (22 March 1997), p. 367.
13 See Nicholas Lash, 'On not inventing doctrine', *The Tablet* (2 December 1995), p. 1544.
14 Karl Rahner, 'Basic theological interpretation of the Second Vatican Council', *Theological Investigations*, vol. XX (London: Darton, Longman & Todd, 1981), pp. 77–89.
15 Ibid., pp. 82–3.

16 Rahner, 'Structural change in the Church of the future', *Theological Investigations*, vol. XX, pp. 115–32 (128–9).
17 See Nicholas Lash, *The Beginning and End of Religion* (Cambridge: Cambridge University Press, 1996), pp. 3–25.
18 John R. Quinn, *The Reform of the Papacy* (New York: Herder, 1999), p. 178. See also Lash, 'A papacy for the future', *The Tablet* (11 December 1999), pp. 1678–9.

2

The 'Open Church' 40 Years Later: A Reckoning[1]

Michael Novak

My account of Vatican II, *The Open Church*, had a model in the long journalistic account written by Lord Acton at the First Vatican Council in 1870. Acton recreates what it felt like in Rome during those days, the sentiments as well as the ideas, the rumours and suspicions and the hopes; and, while clearly partisan in his own leanings, he made a mighty effort to see things truthfully. Despite all this, Acton misread the events of Vatican I quite dramatically. He could not foresee how, in the cataclysmic world of the twentieth century, the Church would badly need a strengthened papal leadership, and even suffer for papal weaknesses. Notwithstanding this failure, Acton awakened in his readers an *eros* of honesty and truth; and that saved Acton, too.

How history will come out is not known to those living through the heat of the present, and much that they may have missed may turn out to have been crucial, while events that seemed to them decisive would be smothered by later twists and turns. As a historian of vast erudition, Acton opposed the declaration of the infallibility of the pope – at least at that time, when the Vatican's struggle to keep papal states on the one hand and rampant positivistic rationalism on the other lent the occasion exactly the wrong connotations. But he eventually came to see (after the papal states were definitively lost) that the conditions placed upon the exercise of infallibility by the Council might actually restrain later popes and chasten them, and thus narrow the channels of papal power, not broaden them.

In my account, too, I tried to be aware of irony and tragedy – themes which the antiquity and tangled passions of the history of Rome impose upon the mind with every mocking jester of every fountain. How they laugh at the passing generations, those fountains! How they laughed at ours. I meant most seriously such passages as these in my Introduction of 1963, in which I wrestled with the problem of foresight and interpretation. I felt keenly the irony inherent in our hubris in those days, our pride of life, our sense of being special:

As the Council Fathers gathered in Rome in the last week of September, 1963, it was difficult to understand the exact meaning and direction of the work that had been begun in the first session the year before. As the weeks of October passed and then of November, it became even more difficult to understand. It will take a century perhaps, or two centuries, before the event is put in sufficient focus for men to grasp it simply. From our position, while the Council is still going on, we grope more in darkness than in light. It is not that we lack for theories about what is going on; it is rather that our theories are inevitably partial, and probably partisan. The facts which seem important to observers caught up in the events may prove in the perspective of time to have been insignificant; small things which occur unobserved may one day prove to have had a great effect upon subsequent history.

Despite the manifest faults, sins and weak minds of many of us during and after Vatican II, the Holy Spirit did preside over it, and brought the world immense fruits through it. Without the Council, we could never have had the enormously important pontificate of Pope John Paul II, and perhaps not the long hidden but energetic stirrings of Eastern Europe that erupted so magnificently in 1989, that year that will reverberate throughout history, the year that showed international Communism to be tinkling brass, whistlingly empty. The year 1989 was the year in which Joshua blew the horn, and the Wall again came down.

And yet the very pope who presided (brilliantly, by the way) over the final three sessions of the Council, Paul VI, said publicly some few years afterwards that 'the smoke of Satan' had filtered into the work of the Council, and blown up a mirage of 'the spirit of Vatican II' that had subverted the letter of what the Holy Spirit had wrought, and blown the barque of Peter far off course and tossed her about on stormy seas. Many inhaled a spirit of self-intoxication from the air they breathed from 'the spirit of Vatican II'. A spirit of radical individualism and hatred for the way things had been swept through religious community after religious community, through colleges and universities, through the ranks of priests (and even some bishops, although the latter were more constrained by their close ties to Rome), and eventually through the educated laity. Thus, 'Vatican II Catholicism' was born. It was much celebrated by its proponents.

It has not yet been dispassionately evaluated, and its colossal failures have not been weighed against its much-praised successes. This is not the place for such an accounting. But it is worth indicating at least where the events I began to record in 1963 had led by the beginning of the following century.

The Growth of Collegiality

In a chapter fittingly called 'October 30', I wrote as follows in 1963: 'On the evening of October 30, a nearly full moon bathed St Peter's Square in such brilliance, such serenity, as was worthy of the greatest day in Roman Catholic history since 1870.' On that day the central vote of Vatican II was taken, indicating a powerful consensus of the assembled 2,100 bishops in favour of a renewed emphasis on the supreme authority of the entire college of bishops, united around the world with the pope, and thus stressing the 'collegiality' of all bishops, including their centre, their servant, and their leader, the Bishop of Rome, rather than (as Vatican I had seemed to many to have done) the authority of the pope in solitude. How has that final sentence in that crucial chapter held up over these last four decades?

Very well, I think. Without that emphasis on the collegiality of the bishops around the world, there would scarcely have been the effort to select a non-Italian bishop – a Pole, from the Eastern bloc – in those dangerous years of the late 1970s, when the Soviet Empire still seemed to be expanding (in Angola, Afghanistan, Nicaragua, El Salvador, Yemen and elsewhere) and the world feared 'nuclear winter'. The internationalisation of the Roman Curia, and the regular participation of bishops from around the world in international synods, commissions and committees would not as likely – or at least so quickly – have occurred. Again, even as Pope John Paul II has dramatised the international *pastoral* role of the Bishop of Rome by a steady, relentless round of visits to his brother bishops in country after country, each of his public Eucharists in every country he visits is celebrated in a highly visible *collegiality* with all the bishops of that country, and of many other countries besides. There the pope and bishops are visibly united as the grains of wheat in the one bread, the grapes in one wine. This ecclesial body of bishops is visible for all the world to see, in the dramatic moments of the internationally televised Eucharists. The theology of collegiality first signalled by the consensus of the Fathers of the Council in five dramatic votes on 30 October 1963 has been witnessed in highly dramatic visual symbols by billions around the world.

Thus, in public perception the Catholic Church at the beginning of the twenty-first century is in many ways more vital, more dynamic and more important than it ever was at the beginning of 1700, 1800 or 1900. One sees this in the number of stories about the Catholic Church appearing on the front pages of major newspapers and the covers of popular magazines. The US Ambassador to Italy wrote to Washington *circa* 1864, and with morose delectation, that he was most assuredly witnessing the last days of the Roman papacy. By the end of the twentieth century, US Presidents, the most consequential of world leaders, were eager to be televised with the Pope, and as frequently as possible in order to bask in his moral authority and the aura of dynamism that surrounds him. None of this is likely to have happened apart from Vatican II.

Why an Open Church Needs Borders

On still other fronts, what has happened to the grand project of the 'open Church'? Pope John Paul II's work with and in frank dialogue with Jews is one good evidence of solid accomplishment, and even more sweeping is his boldness regarding human rights around the world. His visits to the Synagogue in Rome and to Israel, his words at Auschwitz and at Yad Vashem, his conversations with Jewish survivors from his boyhood home, Wadowice – all these touched many Jewish friends of mine and writers in the public press quite deeply. So did his appeals for human rights to Pinochet in Chile and Marcos in the Philippines. John Paul II has not hesitated to upbraid the powerful, including the United States and its presidents. In Cairo, Beijing and elsewhere he has opposed the cultural elite of a communications age – journalists, commentators, feminists, secularists and anti-Christians of all stripes and formidable powers – in calling abortion and euthanasia moral evils of a horrifying sort, and in refusing to budge on his duty to uphold the considered practice of Jesus, namely, that only males, weak and unworthy as they are, may be ordained as priests. Most of all, the Pope has urged truth within the Church, and repentance for many heretofore unadmitted sins of its members, including bishops and popes. His appeals for repentance have sometimes drummed down like rain, they have come so often – for Galileo, the Inquisition, the Czech martyrs, the massacre of Huguenots, and many more. The Church is a very human institution, whose vocation is to *incarnate* Christ in history, and it has not been afraid to dirty its hands in that task, as it must. If it is always to be calling the world to repentance, it must lead in that path every day.

Moreover, there is lively, not to say furious, argument *within* the Church (and between the Church and the surrounding culture) on almost everything. The Church in America is not dying of terminal indifference; passions run very high, and arguments cut even deeper. If there has been a failure of openness, it lies in the paucity of fora in which intelligent representatives of otherwise hostile points of view can engage one another in the same room. Richard John Neuhaus, a convert from Lutheranism, has attempted to make the scholarly seminars around the journal *First Things* one such forum. On a less intellectually rigorous level the Common Ground Initiative, launched by Cardinal Bernardin before his death, is another. More are needed, variously conceived.

Most Catholics, left and right, really do love the Church. They have, alas, learned to be fearful of one another from abuses by one side and the other during the past 40 years. The reformers were far from generous toward the conservatives, whom they roundly defeated when they took over virtually all the institutions within the American Church. In addition, they are sometimes the last to recognise their own intolerance, since in their own self-image they are by definition tolerant. From Vatican II onwards, most liberal Catholics abandoned the practice of tolerance, towards conservatives at least, having learned to refer to 'conservatives' in tones of mockery. By contrast, the besetting sin of conservatives, now that after generations of dominance they find themselves a defeated minority, is a peculiar sort of resentment born of a feeling of powerlessness. These besetting sins feed each other's worst tendencies.

The very conception of the open Church, like that of the open society according to Karl Popper, requires a falsification procedure, a test for being found out to be wrong, and being rejected on that account. Not everyone who claims to be speaking for the Catholic faith is actually doing so. It is quite important for the community to have methods for ascertaining the falsification of the witness. (Is racial segregation compatible with Catholic faith? Is it Catholic to encourage the practice of abortion, or to have one? Do Catholics still believe in purgatory?) Down the ages, in matters of faith and morals the method protected by the Holy Spirit has been to defer to the judgement of the Bishop of Rome, when the latter is in conformity with the faith as it has been taught 'always and everywhere' (in other words, not solely because it is his private opinion). To be Catholic means to be in communion with Rome.

In cases of irresolvable dispute, the noble Christian's course is, in the end, having made his case to the best of his ability, to defer to the Bishop of Rome, and in silence and peace to await

38

the decision of history. It is not unusual for an intellectual to be in a greater hurry than the Holy Spirit. If his position turns out, actually, to be correct and that of the Bishop of Rome wrong, his willingness to have deferred for the good of the whole community will be all the more honoured, and his original opinion given the priceless sanction of a position held firm at great personal cost. Meanwhile, it sometimes happens that public understanding moves more slowly than that of the learned, so that even a delay in the public presentation of an advance position may work to the good and the equanimity of the whole body of the faithful. It will sometimes secure, as well, the rounding out and deepening of the initial advance position. 'For those who love God, all things work together unto good.'

In no other period in my life have so many theological disputes been conducted so broadly and openly in the secular press, in the religious press, and in public debates as in the years from 1961 until now. In such an era, theologians need to develop their own mechanisms for guarding the data entrusted to them. They themselves should mark out of bounds opinions that falsify the data. If theologians watch over their own ranks, bishops and Rome will not have to intrude. An open Church cannot be built if those with the crown jewels – the data of revelation – do not hold these life-giving data precious. The truths of the faith are essential for a true humanism. To treasure them, many in our blood-soaked time have given up their lives.

Three Scarlet Threads

Vatican II was a call to holiness sent out to hundreds of millions of hearts. It will be a success only if that call is heeded many times over, in critical mass. God sheds abundant graces among us. The task is hard, but not impossible. That is what John Paul II has been calling us to, in his own vision of opening up the Church to the world, so as to open the world to God's gracious mercies.

Many who do not understand the language of theology – who are flummoxed by theological terms (much like the spell checker in my computer) – may find it easier to grasp a philosophical model of the same. That model is not entirely adequate, but it does accustom the mind to making some fruitful moves, like a child learning to ride a bicycle with training wheels.

If you try to become conscious of the driving urgency within you to pursue questions to their conclusion – sometimes, for instance, to get to the point of a joke, or to hear the end of a story, or to solve a nettlesome puzzle – you have some clue about the yawning hunger of a woman or man to come to an understanding of all things. To see it all whole. To grasp every detail. And it might seem to you that such an understanding would be so far beyond any of your limits of time and ability that it would require an insight that is infinite, as infinite as are the questions to be raised. To pursue such an insight is what it means to love the truth, to be in the grip of the *eros* of understanding, restless until you rest in the full light of a limitless understanding.

To pursue that light day by day you need to be free, free to test out putative theories and hypotheses – first approximations, as it were – and to drive on to better-grounded ones; free to acquire your own insights and make your own judgements. You need, as well, a certain degree of self-command, a sobriety of purpose and equanimity of judgement, a fearlessness in the face of uncomfortable findings. You need a certain detachment from other passions, in deference to the passion for seeing things straight. In all those senses, you would come to see the meaning of the line: 'Ye shall seek the truth, and the truth shall make ye free.' Our love for truth nourishes in us the self-command of free men. By contrast, other loves can deflect us from following the light. They can twist our judgement and undermine our courage, as in the case of the scientist who falsified data for the sake of advancement. Oddly enough, the profoundest characteristic of free women and men is their love for truth. That is the love that makes them free.

If you are reflecting along with me about your own love of truth and willingness to bear the burden of asking questions, you have available in your own consciousness much of the classic evidence for assertions about the nature of the human person, human community and God, according to the traditions of the Catholic Church. The infinitely restless drive of inquiry, the appetite for truth, the discomfort with anything less than truth – all these are best nourished in community, with friends with equal (or even superior) love for truth, who keep you honest and inspire you through times of great difficulty, because they have also known dry and painful times.

If you follow me so far, then you can understand why Bishop Wojtyla wrote even before the Second Vatican Council assembled that the most important word for the Council to tell the world concerns Everyman's answer to the question: Who am I? Who are we? What is the meaning and sense of the human project? In formulating this answer, three terms seemed to him crucial: *freedom*, the *person* and *community*. These three are tied together by the active energy that drives through all of them: love of the truth about man. Freedom is for truth, and is built up, constituted, by fidelity to truth. The search for truth is communal, not only personal, and it requires for its exercise the open society – open in its polity, its economy and its culture. It is the vocation of the Church to keep this vision before the human race, in part by living out this vision in advance of the human race, through its own constant repentance, reform and starting again.

I am here sticking, as I said above, to merely philosophical language. But the Bible also speaks richly of these three realities, as does the liturgy and the whole of the theological tradition. The excruciating experience of our own bloody century and the exhaustion of so many competing ideologies has, perhaps, fashioned for us a more precise language for articulating this tradition than was available to earlier ages. We have acquired a sharper historical consciousness, and perhaps an even fuller sense of collision with all the different cultures of earth, such as individual bishops felt in St Peter's. In greeting those who sat near them during the Council, they struck up friendships with men from entirely different continents and cultures. (In his letters to his diocese, Bishop Wojtyla described his amazingly diverse seat mates, as did Bishop Tracy of Baton Rouge in his, not failing to note the at times incommensurable cultural distances they encountered. One could find unity in faith and love, they learned, even when in the eyes of the other one saw a totally different world of experience.)

Perhaps, too, these searing times have taught us a richer language of interiority and consciousness than the tradition had felt need of before. Thus, Wojtyla found in phenomenology richer terms for expressing *interior* dimensions of the person and community than are to be found in Aquinas. He had needed to draw on such terms to understand his own inner life during the Nazi, then the Communist, occupation of Poland.

All these points Vatican II wrestled with, for instance in its debates about the meaning of the liturgy (public worship) of the Church, its most vital, inmost source of connection with God's action in the world, for this connection is at once communal, personal and free. And then wrestled with them again in its discussion of the meaning of the Church. *Person, community* and *freedom* were important red threads coursing

42

through all its debates. They were woven into worldly contexts in the later debates in later sessions, first raised in this Second Session, in such documents as those on Religious Liberty and, as it was at first called, 'The Church in the Modern World'. In both these documents, Wojtyla played leadership roles in committee, not always in the very front rank, but by making intellectual contributions at crucial intersections.

Although he was only 42 when the Council opened, Wojtyla made 8 oral interventions in the Council hall, a rather high number, and often spoke in the name of large groups of bishops from the East. (Altogether he made 22 interventions, oral and written.) He was an unusually active member of various official drafting groups for *Gaudium et spes,* and even a chief author of what was called the 'Polish draft'. His voice was crucial to the passage of the document on religious liberty and to the deepening of its philosophical and theological dimension, in line with the necessities of the non-free nations behind the Iron Curtain. No one, perhaps, was more influential in persuading the Americans and Europeans that their own views on liberty needed to be deepened, in order to account for questions arising from other cultures. In later memoirs about the Council, such world-class theologians as Yves Congar and Henri de Lubac praised Wojtyla's acumen in committee work as well as his magnetic presence.

All in all, the Council met for four sessions across four consecutive autumns from 1962 through 1965. It reached agreement on 16 major documents. All these were published in official form in the languages of the nations and have been subjected to a stupendous amount of commentary. Still, it is surprising how few Catholics, even well-educated ones, have actually spent time reading the documents themselves. (Those most fond of the 'spirit' of Vatican II seldom sent students to study the 'letter'.) These 'Declarations', 'Decrees' and

'Constitutions' are for the most part splendidly poised and balanced, and quite nourishing to the inquiring soul. They were written as if with devotional purposes in mind, to move the heart as well as intellect.

Rescuing Vatican II

I can remember the smells of burning chestnuts in the streets of Rome; the taste of Sambuca after dinner with my wife Karen; the excitement of the press conferences every early afternoon; the perfect October air in St Peter's Square with the great dome glinting in the sunlight. It was a wonderful time to be alive. Since an Ecumenical Council happens only once in a century, I am glad to have been present at this one, a great and history-changing outpouring of the Spirit, and just plain fun.

But it was much easier to portray the sheer novelty of the Council than to portray its continuities with the past. The news business is in the business of *news* – novelty – and the public does not go to the press for solid scholarship. In a delicious irony the media bring us the opposite of 'non-historical orthodoxy' – non-orthodox novelty.[2] Important realities are often distorted, and history itself is significantly falsified. For instance, the era before the Council was more like a Golden Age in Catholic history than like the Dark Age described to an eager press by the post-conciliar 'progressives'. There were many glaring deficiencies in it and yet it was in many respects healthier and more faithful to the Gospels than much that came later in the name of 'progress' and 'openness'.

Once the passions of those participating in the Council rose, the victorious majority (the 'progressives') acquired a vested interest both in stressing new beginnings and in discrediting the leadership and the ways of the past. That emphasis shifted the balance of power in the Church into their hands. To them accrued the glory of all things promising, new, and not-yet-tried; to their foes accrued the blame for everything wrong. The more power wrested from the 'old guard', the more massive the power acquired by the reformers. The more the past was discredited, the greater the slack cut for new initiatives and new directions. The politics of the post-conciliar Church in the United States and some parts of Northern Europe became an unfair fight.

Within a decade of the end of the Council, every major institution in the American Church and in many others was dominated by the progressives, under the sway of 'the spirit of Vatican II'. That spirit sometimes soared far beyond the actual, hard-won documents and decisions of Vatican II. Some seized the right to go *far* beyond those. It was as though some took the Church to be dis-incarnate, detached from flesh and history – detached, that is, from Rome and the Vatican, and so far as possible from any concrete local authority. Detached, too, from past tradition and the painful lessons of the past. It was as though the world (or at least the history of the Church) were now to be divided into only two periods, pre-Vatican II and post-Vatican II. Everything 'pre' was then pretty much dismissed, so far as its *authority* mattered. For the most extreme, to be a Catholic now meant to believe more or less anything one wished to believe, or at least in the sense in which one personally interpreted it. One could be a Catholic 'in spirit'. One could take *Catholic* to mean the 'culture' in which one was born, rather than to mean a creed making objective and rigorous demands. One could imagine Rome as a distant and irrelevant anachronism, embarrassment, even adversary. Rome as 'them.'

One way of putting this is that 'non-historical orthodoxy' was driven out from the centre of the Church, only to be replaced in not a few hearts by 'neodoxy', the love of the latest thing, the cult of the new. Thus, those we used to call at Vatican II 'the prophets of doom', 'the School of Fear', turned out to have had in some respects prudent foresight. As world-weary Romans say, 'To bet on pessimism is always safer.'

It is not that way in America, and not in the breast of Karol Wojtyla, activist young bishop at Vatican II and, in due course, 13 years after the Council's conclusion, the pope who took as his papal name the names of the two popes of Vatican II, John XXIII and Paul VI. Wojtyla's key word is not pessimism but hope. He bears not only vision but also conviction, will and total trust in the grace of God.

It is not too much to say that John Paul II rescued Vatican II from disaster. His total awareness of the presence of the Holy Spirit at the Council, the new Pentecost, suffused his every action as Archbishop, then Cardinal, of Krakow and later as Universal Pastor of the Church. He brought back a sense of in-carnation, concreteness, discipline and practicality, and he has been an indefatigable theoretician. No sooner did the world's Catholic universities gear up for a year of conferences on one of his important encyclicals (formal letters intended for the whole Church) than he issued another (by June 2003, 14 in all). He has given a thorough and authoritative interpretation of Vatican II. More than that, by his actions he has dramatised its key emphases worldwide and in many ways shown hesitant bishops, and bishops intimidated by the immensity of the task, how to do it.

In a nutshell, Wojtyla proposed the following principles for the development of the Council (and continues to do so as Pope): that the chief ideologies and intellectual currents of modernity are exhausted; that the world needs and seeks a new and authentic universal humanism; and that it is just this humanism that the Church was called into existence to offer.

The creator of the universe, who created human beings, created them free at the same time. He calls them to be his friends, in freedom and not in slavery. He made them so that by nature they seek and inquire – restlessly, urgently. He infused an eros of understanding into their hearts, so that they might turn away from all that falls short of or falsifies truth. This faithful pursuit of nothing but the truth guarantees their freedom. It is their shield against self-deception, illusion and slavery. Such a pursuit is a communal, not merely solitary, adventure. For we correct and inspire one another, and not only in one country but as a worldwide community.

In this way, further, the Christian mysteries of the Trinity and the Incarnation – the community of God in three Persons, and the taking on of historical flesh by One of the Three – unveil the community, freedom and *eros* of inquiry embodied in the human person. Our creator and Father wills a universal humanism, a civilization of friendship. The Church must open itself to the world, shouting the good news of this highest calling. The Church is the forerunner of human destiny. God has called humans toward his own infinite beauty (hinted at in sunsets and mountain streams, peonies, Alpine peaks, rolling white-capped waves, the eyes of a beautiful woman, the music of Mozart, and the breathtaking lines of the great national poets of all nations). He unites them in solidarity with one another and with him. Communion is the inner tendency of creation. *L'Amor*, Dante writes, *che muov' Il Sol' ed altre stelle*. The Love that moves the sun and all the stars.

So also I am glad to have come to know Karol Wojtyla, if not in 1963, then in his time as pope – John Paul the Great, as I think he will be known, the pope who rescued Vatican II and gave it urgent focus; and who taught us relentlessly to focus where he focuses: on Christ. I cannot think of the Council

47

without thinking of the pope named for the two popes of the Council, John and Paul – and without thinking of the One to Whom he points: '*Sia lodato Gesù Cristo!*' Were these not his first words as pope?

Notes

1 This is a revised and abridged version of the Introduction to Michael Novak's *The Open Church* (New Brunswick, NJ, and London: Transaction Books, 2nd edn, 2001); original version, *The Open Church: Vatican II* (New York: Macmillan, 1964).
2 'Non-historical orthodoxy', the theology of the Roman Curia prior to Vatican II, imagined theology as a set of eternal principles, outside of time, 'a building absolute and perfect, in whose possession the faithful may stand safely and securely', as one among them put it. Its practitioners did not worry overmuch about that system's historical justification, or about making it relevant to the historical present.

3

Tradition and Reaction: Historical Resources for a Contemporary Renewal

Eamon Duffy

In a tribute to John Wilkins it seems appropriate to reflect on Catholic identity, Catholic tradition, and the relation between them for the future. And I begin with two novels.

The first, published in the USA in 1959, Walter Miller's *A Canticle for Leibowitz*, is a science-fiction novel about the rebuilding of world civilisation after a new dark ages brought on by nuclear war. In the aftermath of that war the world had turned its back on technology and science, and most of the scientists had been lynched. The novel focuses on a new religious order, the Order of St Leibowitz, dedicated to the preservation and copying of the remnants of the world's learning: monks in the great desert fortress monastery (somewhere in Arizona I would guess) copy and illuminate elaborate symbolic diagrams which, we realise but they do not, are in fact electrical circuit charts and machine blueprints. As the world had collapsed in nuclear ruins, the Church survived, though Rome was liquidated and the papacy is now established somewhere in America. The monks preserve Christian civilisation in a world populated by cannibalistic desert mutants and ruled by robber barons. In due course there is a new Renaissance, and a new scientific revolution, in which the monastery's precious archive plays its part. But once more pride and sin precipitate war: as the novel closes, the monks of St Leibowitz set off for the stars in a spaceship aboard which are a group of cardinals, among them the next pope: behind them, nuclear winter descends.

Miller's book is a witty meditation on the difference between knowledge and wisdom, and on the relation of the Church to human culture, in an essentially Augustinian framework. Everything in the novel changes, except the desperate sinfulness of the human heart, and the ancient abiding certainties of the Church and her liturgy: at the end of the fictional fourth millennium the liturgy is still in Latin and the forms of the Christian life are exactly as they had been in 1959, down to the bishops' buskins. Miller's grand vision of the collapse and flux of human society through millennia betrays not the slightest premonition of the revolution which, in 1959, the year of the novel's publication, was about to transform the Church which for Miller, was the one constant in a world perpetually falling apart.

By contrast, David Lodge's *How Far Can You Go?*, published in 1980, is a painfully funny evocation of what it was like to be a young university-educated Catholic in Britain in the 1960s and 1970s. It opens with an early morning Mass set in the gaunt London church of our Lady and St Jude (hopeless causes, a nice touch!) on St Valentine's Day 1952, attended by the group of students who will form the dramatis personae of the book. Most are the products of intensely Catholic backgrounds, soaked in and acquiescent to the minutiae of Catholic teaching and sub-cultural peculiarity, and the opening pages of the novel offer a crash course in some of the more exotic features of Catholicism as then understood: transubstantiation, holidays of obligation, works of supererogation, the difference between mortal and venial sin, the rosary, plenary indulgences, purgatory, and the almost permanently tormented state of a pubescent young Catholic male's conscience.

The novel culminates a generation later with the televising of an experimental 'seventies' Easter Vigil, organised by a group called COC (Catholics for an Open Church) in which white-robed charismatic nuns dance on a college playing field as the sun rises, a Latin-American theologian in a combat jacket preaches revolution, and a voice-over by a well-meaning but slightly bewildered young priest, soon to leave the priesthood for a Ph.D. in sociology and marriage to a secretary, expresses doubts about the Resurrection. An anonymous commentator sums up the changes which the book has chronicled.

Many things have changed – attitudes to authority, sex, worship, other Christians, other religions. But perhaps the most fundamental change is one that the majority of Catholics themselves are scarcely conscious of. It's the fading away of the traditional Catholic metaphysic – that marvellously complex and ingenious synthesis of theology and cosmology and casuistry, which situated individual souls on a kind of spiritual Snakes and Ladders board, motivated them with equal doses of hope and fear, and promised them, if they persevered in the game, an eternal reward. The board was marked out very clearly, decorated with all kinds of picturesque motifs, and governed by intricate rules and provisos. Heaven, Hell, Purgatory, Limbo. Mortal, venial and original sin. Angels, devils, saints, and Our Lady Queen of Heaven. Grace, penance, relics, indulgences and all the rest of it. Millions of Catholics no doubt still believe in all that literally. But belief is gradually fading. That metaphysic is no longer taught in schools and seminaries in the more advanced countries, and Catholic children are growing up knowing little or nothing about it. Within another

51

generation or two it will have disappeared, superseded
by something less vivid but more tolerant.

Lodge's fictional analysis of the psychological, social and
intellectual upheavals which underlie the comic dilemmas of
characters caught in the flux of modernity and the dissolution
of inherited Catholic certainties is very shrewd, and still
touches a nerve. His point is that the Catholic metaphysic was
inseparable from the tight web of Catholic practice. Apparently timeless certainties had actually turned out to be part of
a package, wound into and in part dependent for credibility on
a set of cultural practices and attitudes which have now gone or
are going as irrevocably as the demise of the dinosaurs. This
Catholic culture was vivid, and often endearing – it is evoked in
the football scores of the Catholic youth clubs in South London
in the 1950s in another of Lodge's novels, *Therapy*: 'Immacu-
late Conception 2, Precious Blood 1 ... Perpetual Succour 3,
Forty Martyrs, nil', but it was part of the life of a community
whose history of disadvantage and discrimination, and whose
dominant first-, second- or third-generation Irish component gave it a distinctive and strongly defined sense of identity.
In Lodge's admittedly highly coloured portrayal, Catholicism
on the eve of the Council was not a set of opinions; it was a
community and a way of life one signed up for.

But it was a way of life which, though it seemed immemo-
rial, was actually a cultural construct, the product of a network
of specific circumstances. In the 1950s, it was a community on
the crest of a wave. The Catholic Church throughout Britain
was one of the principal beneficiaries of the Butler Education
Act of 1944. In the 25 years after the Second World War
a swelling wave of pupils from Catholic schools would flood
into the universities. The community itself was growing, the
estimated Catholic population of England and Wales moving

rapidly towards 4,000,000, baptisms topping 100,000 a year, adult conversions (many of them by people 'marrying in') touching an annual 15,000. The seminaries and religious orders were packed, and ambitious new building programmes were adopted to accommodate the boom.

Yet despite all that, the Church in Britain was intellectually ill-prepared for the Council. Its leaders were practical men, for whom theology was a bore. The Cardinal Archbishop of West-minster, John Carmel Heenan, was a gifted and charismatic pastor, but on his own admission 'had never had a serious doubt in his life'. He was temperamentally and intellectually ill-equipped to steer the community through the theological white water of the seventies.

The Council: The Decisive Break

The Council profoundly changed the orientation of Catholic theology, ecclesiology and spirituality. The whole tone of its documents, and the fundamental decision to produce no new definitions or anathemas, marked in themselves a decisive break with what one may call the tradition of the Vatican Jeremiad. This was the spirit of confrontation, the repudiation of non-ecclesial culture, which had characterised the official utterances of the Church for more than a century. The shift to the vernacular in worship reintroduced into Catholic liturgical and devotional experience a decisive element of regional vari-ety which was bound to have theological as well as pastoral implications, however carefully policed it might be. It also introduced in an acute way the question of the meaning and value of tradition – an issue I shall return to presently. Finally, the conciliar process itself, the sense of the shared labour of the whole Church and not simply the central organs of the papacy to discern and proclaim the Catholic faith which comes to us from the apostles – all this decisively and permanently shifted Catholic perception of the nature of the Church, and the role of the magisterium within it.

The Council left us with a very different sort of Church, more responsive to lay expectation, more theologically alert and diverse. Yet there were and are those who believed that this amazing and Spirit-led experience should have produced a far greater conversion of hearts, minds and structures. Lay expectation was growing. When, not very surprisingly, a heavily clerical and authoritarian institution failed to transform itself at once into a place of dialogue and partnership between laity and priesthood, sharp disillusion set in. That sense of failure – 'Whatever Happened to Vatican II?' – has persisted among Catholics of a certain age, old enough to have shared in the initial euphoria of reform in the white heat of the conciliar years themselves.

One prominent and persistent theme of the liberal critique of the present state of the Church has been its failure adequately to absorb the characteristic values and institutions of democracy – dialogue, consultation, accountability. The pressure for greater involvement of women – and maybe their eventual ordination – derives some of its force from 'democratic' rather than strictly theological arguments. Yet for many, this process of accommodation has gone disastrously too far. The Catholic Church in Britain is now far more at ease in the culture than it was on the eve of the Council: Catholics are to be found at every level of English life, and the once pervasive cultural anti-Catholicism has receded. In popular perception, the Reformation no longer seems the key stage in the creation of a British identity, but a far-off battle long ago, and, outside Scotland and Northern Ireland, the Reformers, as often as not, are perceived as Paisley-like men who broke a lot of lovely statues.

Yet there are some who view this rapprochement with the establishment with dismay. In *The Two Catholic Churches: A Study in Oppression*, a powerful and controversial book published in 1986, the (then) Dominican Antony Archer suggested that the transformations of the Church in England after Vatican II were a betrayal of the working class to whom on the eve of the Council the Catholic Church had unique and privileged access. The advent of a vernacular liturgy and forms of Christian involvement, which placed a premium on discussion and activism, had, he thought, merely taken control of the Church away from the clergy and handed it to the articulate middle classes, who had every interest in making the Catholic Church as much like the Church of England as possible – and that, with the cooperation of a newly professionalised clergy, was what Archer thought had happened. The Church had opted for power, acceptability and talk, and in the process had abandoned its proper constituency among the powerless and inarticulate.

Archer's attack on the actual outcome of the conciliar reforms in England was launched from the Left: he was not opposed to change, but disliked the form change had taken. On the Right, there were those who, quite simply, thought the faith had been betrayed, that ecumenism and doctrinal deviation were the poisoned fruits of liturgical change, and that the Council, if not the cause, was at least the occasion for a disastrous collapse of Catholic values, which had to be reversed. This point of view was less fiercely and divisively expressed in England than elsewhere, but the case drew strength from the fact that in the years since the Council the English Church's post-war boom has been steadily evaporating. The indicators of Catholic practice began a downward spiral in the early 1970s, which has continued and grown steeper, bringing the Church in this country into line with the rest of Europe.

In the immediate aftermath of the Council there was an exodus from the priesthood and (especially) the religious orders, and recruitment to the seminaries dipped. In 1968 there were almost 5,000 secular priests in England and Wales, and 2,762 ordained male religious. In 1998 statistics indicated just over 4,000 secular priests and 1,682 religious, their age-profile steadily worsening: cobwebs gather in the corridors of the seminary extensions of the early 1960s. Perhaps more significantly, Mass attendance has declined to not much more than a million each week, a quarter of the estimated Catholic population. Once-flourishing Catholic organisations like the Children of Mary have nose-dived, and the religious orders, especially the active or 'apostolic' orders founded in the eighteenth and nineteenth centuries, have been decimated.

Living with 'Decline'

These apparent symptoms of decline are of course open to a host of interpretations. Many of them are clearly aspects of wider social change which has little to do with Catholicism as such, and even the more spectacular manifestations of decline are by no means unprecedented. Monastic recruitment has always fluctuated with shifts within the culture. The religious life seemed in near-terminal decline in France and Germany in the eighteenth century. By contrast, the nineteenth century saw an unprecedented blossoming of religious orders. Many of the missionary, teaching and nursing orders founded then were patently a Christian response to particular social conditions: they recruited young men and women from backgrounds in which economic, social, educational and, it needs to be noted, sexual opportunity were rather limited. Quite apart from spiritual considerations, which I would certainly not wish to minimise, the religious life offered economic security and educational betterment for people who frequently could not have expected much in the way of economic or domestic security, and provided a culturally respected and worthwhile outlet for untapped energies and abilities. The emergence of alternative forms of opportunity for the laity in the developed world in the last few generations is almost a sufficient explanation for the collapse of at least the more recent and activist forms of the religious life.

Almost, but not quite. The shrinkage of Catholic institutions is clearly part and parcel of a much broader unsettlement within Western society. It is not merely Catholic marriages, for example, which are in decline, but, it would seem, the institution of marriage itself. The moral pattern imposed by the Church (slowly and with enormous difficulty) on European sexual behaviour and family structure from the early Middle Ages onwards seems now to be collapsing. Later than most of the rest of the Churches of the West, the Catholic Church is increasingly confronted with the need to evolve a *modus vivendi* with these apparently inexorable social trends, which can be lived by ordinary people with integrity. Marriage is above everything else a social institution, and if the Church is not to decline into being a sect for the saintly, ordinary Catholic couples cannot realistically be expected to live lives untouched by the social and sexual expectations and mores of the culture as a whole. The tragically large and growing number of Catholics in irregular unions is both an indicator of the way in which the values of society shape the lives and perceptions of Christians and also, in pastoral terms, a ticking time bomb, which by one means or another is going to have to be defused if it is not to decimate the Catholic community and, more importantly, deprive thousands of people of the sacramental support and light they need.

The Danger of Ignoring Roots

The Church of course is called to transform cultures, not merely to accommodate itself to them. A Christianity whose moral and social behaviour is not much more than a sanctified version of even the best secular morality is clearly in trouble, especially when the culture patently lacks any consensus about an agreed (much less an objective) code of morality, and in which the fundamental moral good is the market 'virtue' of *choice*. The experience of other Christian Churches in which this process of cultural accommodation is more advanced than in our own is not encouraging. That perception certainly informs the tough pastoral line adopted by the Vatican on issues of family and sexual morality, and the more general stiffening of Roman attitudes towards doctrinal and organisational diversity which has been so notable a feature of the present pontificate, as the Vatican has increasingly used the weapon of authority to attempt to halt what it sees as a process of secularisation within the Church.

This response is part of a wider conservative analysis of the plight of Christianity at the beginning of the millennium, which sees in the 'liberalisation' of Catholic doctrinal and moral attitudes since the Council a disastrous capitulation to the secular values of the Enlightenment. But the attempt to close down particular lines of thought by the simple exercise of authority has an unhappy history, and in our society has little chance of success. No Catholic in their right mind would want a rerun of the anti-modernist witch-hunts encouraged by Pope St Pius X, or the unedifying harassment of great (and holy) theologians like de Lubac and Congar which disgraced the later years of the pontificate of Pius XII.

There is a tendency to describe those who call for the strong exercise of authority, and the end of debate, as 'traditionalists',

58

and that usage should alert us to something which has gone badly wrong within the Church since the Council. Any Catholic who lived through the 1960s and 1970s will recall the orgy of destruction of the immediate past which took place in the name of the Council – the gutting ('reordering') of venerable buildings, the destruction or discarding of vestments, statues, pictures, the scattering of libraries – precisely the aspects of Catholicism which, in Miller's *Canticle for Leibowitz*, are deployed as potent symbols of the Church's stability in the midst of the flux of the *saeculum – stat crux dum volvitur orbis*. This sort of psychic evacuation is really a form of exorcism, and it is a feature of any cultural revolution. It may be that something of the sort was a necessary act of liberation for a community which had inherited a past that sat heavy upon it, inhibiting fresh development. The surest way of damning and dismissing any idea, institution or emphasis in those years was to say that it was 'pre-conciliar', as if the Council had invented the gospel, and as if the test of Christian authenticity was radical discontinuity with the Christian past. Of course, much that was then discarded was indeed worthless or tacky, and much that posed as 'traditional' was in fact the product of the quite recent past. It is now possible to see, however, how wholesale and indiscriminate this communal repudiation of the past was, and in a Church which claims to set a high theological value on tradition and continuity, this is a mystery which needs explanation.

It is a mystery, because, by and large in the past, Catholic theologians advocating change, even radical change, have been as anxious to invoke the notion of tradition as have those seeking to maintain the status quo. At the heart of the 'New Theology' of de Lubac, Congar and the other theological midwives of the Council, was a passionate call to *rediscover* the tradition. They set about freeing the Church from the narrow straitjacket of a debased neo-scholasticism by opening up the riches of the deep tradition of the Church, in the Scriptures, the liturgy, the Fathers. For them the past was not a sterile cul-de-sac to be escaped from, but an inexhaustible well of Christian experience and wisdom, which liberated theology and the Christian imagination by demonstrating how diverse, subtle, endlessly inventive the Church has been, and is called to be, in her journey through time.

Within ultramontane Catholicism, however, the notion of tradition had been in danger of narrowing to mean little more than the current Roman theology. Pio Nono's notorious 1870 aphorism '*I am* the tradition' was a telling reflection of the day-to-day reality of an increasingly powerful central authority, which strangled Catholic theology (and episcopal teaching) for a century. Most of the citations in the (rejected) draft declaration of faith drawn up on the eve of the Second Vatican Council by the Holy Office under Cardinal Ottaviani, for example, were from the writings and speeches of Pius XII and his immediate predecessors: no church document earlier than the Council of Trent was cited, and there were no quotations from Scripture. Tradition had shrunk from being a cathedral of the Spirit to a storeroom in the cellars of the Holy Office.

The conciliar reforms did a great deal to correct this sterile and authoritarian notion of tradition, to recover a sense of the variety and richness of the Christian past as a resource for the Christian present. But whatever the roots of reform, a good deal of the emphasis in liturgical, theological and catechetical work since the Second Vatican Council has been in fact without much in the way of solid grounding in theology, and represented a search for immediacy or authenticity of experience, rather than attentive encounter with the diversity, depth and wisdom of the tradition. In place of a philistine authoritarianism, cut off from the riches and complexity of the Christian past by a mindset described as 'non-historical orthodoxy', we have tended towards a non-historical liberalism which has if anything even less to offer. The effects of this are evident in any hymnbook, but they are visible even in the texts of the liturgy themselves. The Collect at Mass for Trinity Sunday, for example, resoundingly declares that, in sending into the world 'the Word of Truth and the Spirit of Sanctification', God 'has declared' (*declarasti*) his own wonderful mystery – the whole prayer is an address to God praising him for his amazing and gracious self-revelation. Characteristically, the version in our current missals switched this emphasis round, from God's self-giving, to our receiving – *declarasti* was 'translated' not as 'you have declared' but 'we come to know'.

The Need for Recovery of Tradition

The equation of tradition with external and oppressive authority, the dead hand of an unmeaning past, meant that the implementation of conciliar reform often took the form of the stripping away or abandonment of the externals of Catholicism. It was widely felt that we had fiddled around with rules and regulations too long, when what was needed was largeness of spirit, a focus on essentials. At the time, it seemed easy to tell them apart, to eliminate the inessential. It became a widely accepted axiom that no observance could be truly sincere and meaningful if it were obligatory. As a result, some of the most ancient and eloquent expressions of Christian identity were simply abandoned as so much unmeaning lumber. Though the obligation to perform some penitential act on Fridays remains in theory, for example, in reality Catholics are now without any meaningful discipline of fasting and abstinence, a break with universal Christian practice for 2,000 years, and with the practice of Israel for centuries before Christ. Christianity's most ancient and most resonant communal act of identification

with the passion, of solidarity with the hungry, and of acknowl-
ledgement of our own frailty, became a mere devotional
option, and in practice has all but disappeared.

The effective abandonment of fasting and abstinence as a
communal observance rather than a private option was just
one example of the sort of *ritual decentering* which has characterised the life of the Church in the years after the Council.
That decentering is certainly a contributory element to the
more general loosening of the Catholic community's hold on
Christian value, and its accommodation to the secular world
around it. Social anthropologists such as Professor Mary Doug-
lass sounded the alarm almost at once about the naïveté of this
retreat from symbol, and emphasised the indispensable role of
external observance in the maintenance of religious value systems, but it is a warning which has gone largely unheeded. The
Church has increasingly accommodated itself to the rhythms,
and hence the beliefs and values, of the society around it, with
such apparently benign measures as the shrinking of the ritual
calendar, the displacement of holidays of obligation to the
nearest Sunday, and the desacralisation of Sunday itself. All
these moves can be perfectly sensibly justified in terms of practicality and convenience. But their cumulative effect is the elimination of more and more of the remaining expressions of what
one may call *ritual resistance*, without which it seems impossible to maintain the larger counter-cultural values of Catholic Christianity.

Yet these symbolic points of resistance seem to me at the
outset of the third millennium to possess a prophetic value for
the Church, the importance of which can hardly be exaggerated. Our culture sets an enormous value on the quick fix: the
instant delivery of information, the packaging of everything in
bite-sized – or sound-bite-sized – parcels. Anything complex is
too complex, anything difficult is too difficult, anything which

does not yield its meaning immediately is fit only for the scrap heap. Such assumptions pervade much of our thinking about preaching, catechesis, the structure of the liturgy itself, and they are the opposite of the ruminative, meditative work of the liturgy, or the monastic practice of *lectio divina*, the slow, reflective brooding over the tradition, which lies close to the heart of a distinctively Christian critique of society. The Church has never needed so urgently the sort of deep grounding in its inherited wisdom, seen not as a straitjacket but as a resource-pack. Modern Catholicism is strong on civilisation and decency. But civilisation and decency are not enough.

The Church on the eve of the Council was narrow, and drew strength from its narrowness. That narrowness in England as elsewhere was the product of a unique blend of circumstances – Reformation history, Irish immigration, ultramontane clerical formation: it cannot be recovered or repeated, and nostalgia is a poor fuel for a march into the future. We need now to find a new source of strength which does not close down our horizons. The likely social realities of the twenty-first century – the breakdown of the traditional family structure and of monogamous marriage, the growing disempowerment and probable redundancy of more and more people in the global economy and the pressures of the market, the reshaping and rethinking of the role of women – are not forces outside the Church: many Catholics already live with these things. If the Church is to find a Christian response to these issues and energies, it needs more than decency and pragmatism. It needs a stronger sense of its own identity, it needs to re-establish its contact with its own deepest resources. We need a liturgy which preserves the gains of the Council – the vernacular, greater intelligibility, greater lay participation, deeper and deeper encounter with Scripture – yet which is not only expressed in worthier language but also transmits the

distinctive wisdom, poetry and challenge of Roman Christianity, as our current translations do not. If, as Catholics, we
are to witness to and live out gospel values, in a world
increasingly bewildered and sceptical about such values or any
values, we need an educational ideal to match that wisdom:
we have to develop a shared attentiveness and asceticism, not
as a devotional option but as part of the fabric of Christian
believing. We need to foster a common vision, and one which
can be articulated in and shared with the culture at large. We
cannot, in Lodge's sense, recreate the 'Catholic metaphysic': if
we are to survive as a community, however, and deserve to
survive, we need to be able to explain to the culture at large,
and to ourselves, just who we are and what we stand for.

The neo-conservative phenomenon, in the Church as in the
world at large, is no answer to this problem. A sense of identity cannot be supplied by the exercise of authority: in a family,
you cannot maintain unity, love and shared purpose by kicking
people into line. A common mind and heart come from the
shared exploration of a common inheritance, and the shared
pursuit of a common hope. Tradition is not orders from above,
or the status quo, a code of law, or a body of dogma. It is
a *wisdom*, embodied in a complex tissue of words, symbols,
law, teaching, prayer and action, a way of life which has to be
practised before it yields its light. The Church of course has to
engage people living, struggling, suffering, muddling along; its
tasks are above everything else practical ones. If we have
learned anything in the 40 years since the Council, however, it
is that action must grow from deep spiritual and theological
roots if it is to remain *Christian* action. Our society is impa-
tient of reflection, unwilling to wrestle with difficulty, insistent
on instant intelligibility. It wants its knowledge in sound-bites,
it wants its uplift in soothing magazine-style snippets, it sees
religion as at best a comfort and a crutch. This dumbing down

has been at work in the Church too, and has not always met with much resistance. To recall the Catholic community to the shared labour of living the tradition, attentive to its wisdom, open to its fresh possibilities, seems a good item on a Christian agenda for the twenty-first century.

Part II

The Unfinished Journey

4

On Having the Courage of One's Convictions[1]

Hans Küng

We all need courage and encouragement, not least theologians, journalists and editors. But encouragement for what? There are many different answers to this question – and that applies to the Church as well. Just think:

We live in a time when, after terrible misuse of the word, talk of 'virtues' seems inappropriate and a 'virtuous' person is often regarded more as a caricature of the free Christian.

Yet we live in a time when more than ever we need moral attitudes which are effective beyond a particular day or a particular action.

And we live in a time when these moral attitudes, too, are subject to marked change: virtues like obedience and humility have become discredited, but others have become all the more important.

I have felt that within the Church, originally a place of truth and freedom, it is necessary to emphasise truth and even more freedom, that freedom which Jesus lived out in his struggle, his suffering and death, and which the apostle Paul put forward as a programme to combat anything that might lead to its loss, 'the freedom for which Christ has set us free' (Galatians 5:1). This is the freedom of the Christian which later Martin Luther above all called for once again in opposition to the medieval Roman Church system.

Today, however, the issue is no longer just the freedom of a Christian, as it was in Luther's time. It is human freedom generally, and especially free speech and action. It is not only apostolic boldness, but quite simply having the courage of one's convictions, what in German is called 'civil courage' (*Zivilcourage*). And what does civil courage mean, I have asked myself, first of all for me? What does it mean for a theologian, a scholar or a media figure – if you like, for an 'intellectual'?

The Meaning of Courage

There are good reasons for asking this question. For 'courage' doesn't come from the 'intellect' or even from 'reason'. It is not a product of the process of 'reasoning', judgement, reflection and verification which are characteristic of scholarship and science. Perhaps it is because of this orientation to reason that one looks in vain for the word 'courage' in some dictionaries of psychology, sociology and education in which it ought to appear.

It is clear that intellectuals of a variety of disciplines and theologians of different Churches do not know what to make of 'courage'. The origin of the term is quite clear: 'courage' comes from *coeur*, 'heart'. 'Le coeur', runs Pascal's famous word-play, which is almost impossible to translate, 'le coeur a des raisons que la raison ne connaît point' – 'the heart has its reasons of which reason itself knows nothing'. If one is set only on following reason – and I emphasise the 'only' – one will seldom show courage. For know-alls, the boldest horse is the blind horse – as if a blind horse ever won a race! They say that only fools have real courage – as if clever people did not have to be bold but above all cautious, restrained and moderate!

70

Blaise Pascal, who wasn't just a clever man but a real mathematical, philosophical and literary genius, set the logic of the heart against the one-sided reasoning of science. This logic of the heart could combine 'reasoning' and 'sentiment', both of which have their limitations. For Pascal, as for Luther, who wears his heart on his sleeve, 'heart' does not mean just the irrational and emotional as opposed to the rational and logical. No, 'heart' means the spiritual centre of the person, its innermost core, from which relations with others flow. To be precise, 'heart' means the human spirit: not, however, in so far as it thinks and argues in a purely theoretical way but in so far as it is spontaneously present, has intuitions and knows existentially.

So human courage has its seat not simply in 'pure reason' – here the moralist Kant would doubtless agree, with his reference to 'practical reason' and the conscience – but in the heart.

'Civil' Courage

And what about that term used in Germany, 'civil courage'? The adjective 'civil' was taken over from the French as early as the sixteenth century and is derived from the Latin *civilis* – 'for the common good'. This is the dimension expressed in the term 'civil courage'. It is worth reflecting on.

Civil courage has to be dissociated from the proverbial soldier's courage, which is so often misused in history. For civil courage has a quite unmilitary meaning. It is the courage that one shows by speaking one's mind openly and in public, even to superiors and those in authority, without heed of any possible consequences, speaking out fearlessly. If I am right, the term 'civil courage' was coined for the first time in 1864 by Bismarck, the 'iron chancellor' – not, however, to praise his Germans but to criticise them for their lack of this virtue.

Of course a fearless Chancellor could speak like this. But no bishop of any Church would do so today; the exceptions prove the rule. Bishops are normally afraid of speaking their minds. Even Lutheran bishops rarely refer to Martin Luther, who was exemplary in this respect – at any rate when they are addressing the pope. They usually leave the protesting to Catholic reformers and leave themselves to be photographed with the pope instead.

Christian Courage

That raises the question: when there is so much talk today of having the courage of one's convictions, of 'civil courage', what about 'Christian courage'? There is the courage of the soldier who knows that only he who dares wins. There is also the courage of the worldly, who fool themselves that the world belongs to the brave. But why is there not a proverbial *Christian* courage alongside civil courage, just as there is Church law alongside civil law? Why has the term 'civil courage' been coined, but not 'Church courage' or 'Christian courage', both of which sound very strange because they are artificial?

This Christian courage must once have existed. Otherwise there could not have been people like the courageous St George, patron of so many churches, who famously killed a dragon. But the disparagement of courage by the Church must have begun at a very early stage, else we would not read in the ballad 'The Fight with the Dragon', by the classic German poet Friedrich Schiller:

> The Mameluke too courage shows,
> obedience is the Christian's jewel.

Obedience the Christian's jewel? Bishops and popes love to hear such statements. And in Schiller's ballad these words are in fact spoken by a high-ranking Churchman to a simple Christian who really does kill a dragon, but in so doing unfortunately violated the oath of obedience which forbade him to engage in any fighting.

What a long way we Christians have come from the one who always said his 'Yes, yes' and 'No, no' so clearly, who always spoke out fearlessly in public and to whom we owe the saying, 'Whoever seeks to gain his life will lose it, and whoever loses it will gain it.'

What a long way we have come from that 'apostolic boldness', the *parrhesia*, once proverbial, with which the apostles, like Jesus himself, spoke out in public, even against a hostile public. How far we have come from the boldness of the apostle Paul who, as he himself says, 'opposed to his face' Peter, Kephas, 'the rock'. Why? Because Kephas/Peter, at that time by no means yet infallible, did not 'live by the truth of the Gospel'! That is a harsh remark to make to the one whom people in Rome think was the first pope! And this narrative is not a pious legend, like that of St George, but rather a completely historical account from the second chapter of the apostle Paul's letter to the communities of Galatia. At least until the Second Vatican Council, however, the Church of Rome, not particularly interested in this kind of courage, never had this passage read out in the liturgy. Paul's courage could have infected the episcopate and indeed the Vatican.

Bravery (*fortitudo*), an attitude that has much in common with courage (which is directed more towards the moment), is one of the four great Platonic cardinal virtues. It is a virtue mid-way between two extreme vices, which is how Aristotle saw every virtue: between cowardice and audacity, between not being courageous enough and being too courageous. However, Aristotle already recognised that alongside militant bravery, which Plato associated with the warrior, there is also a civil bravery, the bravery of fearlessly standing by one's own convictions, even at the risk of coming into conflict with others, especially the powerful.

The Cardinal Question

This virtue is important enough to be classified as a cardinal virtue, yet does not seem to be a virtue of cardinals. Why is civil courage – *Christian* courage – so often lacking in the Church sphere, especially at its higher levels? This was a great trial for me at the Second Vatican Council. Why did not bishops protest about this or that? Why did not a cardinal – who after all could not rise any higher – raise his voice in a decisive session?

This 'cardinal question' bothered me so much that I put it to other knowledgeable contemporaries, three famous scholars at the University of Tübingen.

The Marxist philosopher Ernst Bloch replied: One often does not argue for a cause because it has already been espoused by someone with whom one does not want to be associated. One is afraid of approval from the wrong side.

The liberal sociologist Ralf Dahrendorf, now Lord Dahrendorf, formerly head of the London School of Economics and Warden of St Antony's College, Oxford, replied: Even those in high places do not like to make themselves unpopular. To speak out freely requires a special psychological and moral effort – even for a cardinal.

The philosopher and educationalist Otto Friedrich Bollnow, who wrote an excellent book on *The Nature and Transformation of the Virtues*, replied: Bravery in civil life seems to be even more difficult than bravery in war. It is probably connected with the human herd instinct, which means that it is easier to risk one's life in war along with others and even to allow one's bravery as a soldier to be exploited for reprehensible ends than to swim against the powerful current as an individual in civil life.

Escaping Tutelage

These are all important comments, remarks which touch on partial aspects of the problem. Of the classic philosophers, Immanuel Kant seems to me to have given the most elementary and the best answer. In his *What Is Enlightenment?* he writes:

> Laziness and cowardice are the reasons why such a large number of people, having long released nature from alien governance, nevertheless like to lead their lives in tutelage; and why others find it so easy to set themselves up as their guardians. It is so convenient to be in tutelage.

And indeed, effort, toil, risk are all bound up with having the courage of one's convictions, civil courage. Some of those who are well versed in such courage can bear witness that in a great controversy it is not easy to bear the taunts of former friends and colleagues. It is not easy to be outmanoeuvred by those who think that they possess the truth, even if they only possess power. It is not easy to be ridiculed publicly and by certain media as an idealist with illusions, as a dreamer.

Certainly one can withstand many pressures. But this resistance cannot be taken for granted. And it is even less easy to keep showing civil courage in the face of all difficulties. It is not easy for anyone to keep maintaining the courage that is constantly sapped in one way or another. As a believing Christian I would say that this courage too must be a true gift; it is a real grace.

So it is only with these reservations that I can agree with the proverb 'God helps the courageous'. That often seems as uncertain as the ancient promise *Fortes fortuna adiuvat* – 'Fortune favours the brave'. After all, who can rely on the goddess Fortuna? Indeed, what brave man, what courageous woman, does not know the lack of courage, the despondency, the weariness which sometimes comes despite all courage, and which threatens to become timidity and utter despondency? In such moments it is better instead to say, 'God, my God, give me courage to help myself.'

Of course I am well aware that today many people are sceptical about belief in God. But I am convinced that after the collapse of Communism and in the struggle for a new world order the question of religion needs to be discussed again. In our context it is worth reflecting on some words about the courage of faith by the eighteenth-century German philosopher Georg Christoph Lichtenberg, who was decried as a free thinker. His *sapere aude* ('Have the courage to use your mind') at the same time recalls his contemporary Immanuel Kant:

> One of the most difficult arts for a man is to give himself courage ... Since there is so much suffering in the world which has to be encountered with courage, and no human being can sufficiently give weak consolation, religion is admirable. It is really the art of gaining comfort and courage in suffering, and strength to work against it, without any other means, by thinking about God. I have known those whose good fortune was their God. They believed in a good fortune and faith gave them courage. Courage gave them good fortune and good fortune gave them courage. It is a great loss for a person if he has lost the conviction of a wise being who directs the world.

Happily not only in the time of the Reformation, but also in recent decades, there have been many examples of civil courage in the power of faith in God: the other Martin Luther (King) and so many others in North, Central and South America, as well as those in the Philippines, in South Africa, Poland and the former German Democratic Republic.

My article also pays homage to all those who, like John Wilkins, have ventured to speak out fearlessly and to act courageously. They know that *persistence* is more difficult than the civil courage of the moment, bold speech or courageous action. It is more difficult courageously to maintain a cause which is seen to be right over years and decades. As we read in *Der Stechlin*, a novel by the nineteenth-century German author Theodor Fontane, 'Courage is good but endurance is better. Endurance is the main thing.'

Courage to speak out undeterred, courage to persevere: that is my heartfelt wish for this editor of *The Tablet* and his successors. May they not be afraid when they have views which do not suit the powers-that-be. Even more, may they not be deterred from expressing such ideas in public. May all those who are active in the Church media have the courage to listen to people more and to the Church bureaucracy less, and to put into practice what they have recognised as the truth of the gospel.

Note

1 The editor wishes to express his gratitude to John Bowden, the former director of the Publishing House SCM Press, for translating this article. Bowden writes: 'This is my bit of homage to John whom I admire tremendously and I would like the translation to be my minor contribution to the Festschrift.'

5

Images of the Church: From 'Perfect Society' to 'God's People on Pilgrimage'

Rembert Weakland

St Paul was a perceptive catechist. He knew that images were more effective than a thousand abstract concepts. So to describe the Church he put forth several creative images. The Body of Christ, where Christ is the head and each part has its own proper function and contribution, has remained throughout history the strongest (1 Cor. 12:12–27; Rom. 12:3–8). Nor should one forget the image of a building where Christ is the capstone and each brick contributes to the structure's solidity (Eph. 2:19–22). In using such vivid images Paul was following the example of Jesus, the master himself, who offered many striking ways, especially in St Matthew's Gospel, to depict the nature of God's kingdom. And what example could surpass that of the vine and the branches to depict a life-giving relationship, one with such intimate vitality (John 15:1–7)?

For centuries these biblical images and the ways they were interpreted helped to shape how Christians conceived the Church and the active participation in it of its members. Yet, in each period of its history the Church continued to create other images to describe itself that corresponded to the times in which it lived or that were reactions to the forces it struggled against. It was only natural that the leaders and scholars of the nineteenth century, too, had their favourite image for the Church: that of the perfect society, the *societas perfecta*.

The Perfect Society

This term, most popular in the nineteenth century among popes, canonists and scholars, does not seem to have been used in the Middle Ages. But the concept, predominantly a juridical and defensive one, had its origins at that time, elaborated by canonists during the struggles for power between popes and emperors. Some civic officials, to limit the authority of the Church, postulated a division of powers into spiritual and temporal in an attempt to keep the Church out of the temporal order and limit it to the purely spiritual. Medieval canonists insisted that the Church was a complete society with all the means a society needed to pursue its own aims. No-one knows who invented the term *societas perfecta* to express this kind of independence. When they used it, the nineteenth-century canonists were declaring that the Church was, first of all, a *society*, that is, a community that could be visibly delineated, had its own reasons for existence, possessed aims and ends particular to itself, was endowed with its own governance, and not dependent on any other society even in temporal affairs. Entrance into that society came through baptism where only the Church could be the gatekeeper. Moreover, the Church had the structures of authority needed, like any *societas*, to function in the temporal order; and did not need the State in order to fulfil its mission.

This concept was especially convincing to Catholics of that century as they struggled against the disastrous effects on the Church of the French Revolution and the Enlightenment. The philosophies of the age sought to reduce religion to a private affair while the ideologies of Gallicanism, Febronianism and Josephinism wished to make the Church dependent on the State. The concept of *societas perfecta* resisted such pressure. Applied to the Church by popes and canonists in the nineteenth

79

century, it reiterated those aspects of the Church as a society that had been outlined in the Middle Ages. But it also affirmed that religion was not merely a private affair, that there was a horizontal relationship among the members of the Church, which was a true society. They wanted also to refute those reformers who denied that the Church possessed the supernatural means necessary for the salvation of its members. Finally, it meant to them that the Church possessed the authority structures needed to function adequately and to enforce its decrees.

It is understandable why the theologians who put together the schemata on the nature of the Church for the First Vatican Council used these ideas as the basis of their definition. The schemata were never discussed or voted on, but they corresponded perfectly to the sentiments of Pope Pius IX in his struggles with the newly formed Italian state and over the loss of the papal states.

The description of the Church as a perfect society was especially favoured by Pope Leo XIII, who used the term in many of his encyclicals which dealt with the Church's nature and its relationship to the State. In *Immortale Dei* of 1885 he clearly called the Church 'a perfect society in its nature and in its title' because it is a supernatural and spiritual society 'possessing all needful provisions for its maintenance and action' (#10). In the encyclical *Libertas* of 1888, he affirmed that, as a perfect society, the Church could legislate, judge and punish, and must not be restricted to just exhorting or advising, as some would have it. In *Sapientiae christianae* (1890) and in *Satis cognitum* (1896) he did not hesitate to state that God made the Church a society even more perfect and superior to any other, citing its divine origin and more spiritual nature and scope. With these statements he moved away from the juridical approach – in which the Church was said to possess the necessary means of salvation – towards implying that it was *in actu* the perfect society because it possessed the fullest degree of holiness and spiritual perfection above all other societies. The move from potential to actual perfection took place also in the minds of many of his Catholic readers.

The theology manuals used in most seminaries during the first half of the twentieth century continued to employ the phrase in this fuller sense. Canonists, in contrast, tended to hold to the older meaning. Pope Benedict XV, for example, in promulgating the Code of Canon Law of 1917, used the phrase in its more pristine form.

But it was not much of a leap for Pope Pius XII in his encyclical *Mystici corporis Christi*, in describing the relationship between Christ and the members within the Body, to state that 'Christ wills His Christian community to be a Body which is a perfect society' (#68). He made the Pauline metaphor of the body coalesce with the canonical concept of the perfect society so that 'perfect' refers to the life of Christ within the Church in the here-and-now; at least, this was the way many spiritual writers from then on interpreted the term. In this way he confirmed a trend among some Catholic writers to affirm that the Church was the model society, to be imitated by all other earthly societies, because it was the perfect society not only potentially but in reality. Theologians were usually more restrained; but at times they gave the impression that the Church had a kind of Platonic existence 'out there' somewhere, separated from the baptised who are its members with their sins and failings. Louis Bouyer described this tendency as an overly idealistic view of the Church as appropriating to itself the holiness of Christ himself.[1] One could phrase the criticism in another way by saying it was anticipating the Church of the eschaton into the here-and-now, but shorn of its human imperfections.

The Prefect of the Holy Office and guardian of the orthodoxy of the faith at the opening of Vatican II was Cardinal

Alfredo Ottaviani. In a second edition of his work on the nature of the Church (*Institutiones juris publici ecclesiastici*), published in 1958 just before the opening of the Council, he stated the theme of the perfect society in simple, terse, but unequivocal Latin terms: 'Ecclesia est societas iuridica et suprema; iamvero, societas iuridica suprema est natura sua iuridice perfecta. Sequitur ergo Ecclesiam esse societatem juridice perfectam.'[2] ('The Church is a juridical and supreme society; moreover, a supreme juridical society is by its very nature juridically perfect. It follows that the Church is a juridically perfect society.') Here the Church is not just a juridical society that is perfect but a superior one.

Images of the Church at the Beginning of Vatican II

The bishops who gathered for Vatican II were therefore faced with a medieval tradition reinterpreted by canonists, popes and spiritual writers in the nineteenth century, enlarged by Pope Pius XII in the twentieth century, and then taken up by the scholars who prepared the preliminary schemata for Vatican II. As was to be expected, this medieval tradition and these ideas dominated in the preliminary drafts presented to the bishops as they took up the document on the Church that was later to become *Lumen gentium*. The first schema took the Pauline image of the Body of Christ and, in accord with Pope Pius XII's *Mystici corporis*, interpreted it as an image of the perfect society. The bishops rejected this approach, opting to begin their document instead with the Church as mystery; and then followed it with a chapter on the image of the People of God. Giuseppe Ruggieri summed up the debate this way:

> Thus on the nature of the Church there was the conflict
> between a juridical conception of the Church as a

society, reflected in the unyielding defence of the identification of the Catholic Church and the Mystical Body, and a conception of the Church that was more sensitive to its mystery.[3]

But the image of the perfect society did not disappear. From its original and canonical meaning of the perfect or complete society there was still much to be saved: in the reference, for example, to the visible Church as having all the means of salvation necessary for its members and as possessing all the qualities appropriate for governance as in any society. But the more spiritualised definition of the perfect society as appropriating to itself all the holiness of Jesus Christ also continued in the minds of many. Hence the consternation when, later, Pope John Paul II began with some frequency to apologise for past errors of judgement on the part of Church officials, beginning with the case of Galileo. Not all the cardinals were pleased with his gesture of asking for forgiveness: some thought it placed a blemish on the record of the perfect society and involved a clear contradiction; others asserted that to apologise so often diminished the value of such apologies. The second group had a point. But the more serious criticism came from those who believed that such admission of error weakened the idea of the Church as the perfect society.

The bishops at Vatican II avoided the trend towards over-spiritualisation that tended to see a Church almost minus its sinful members. Nor did the bishops accept the opinion of some who, in reaction to an exaggerated spiritualisation, seemed to reduce the Church to only its experientially visible realities. The bishops retained the idea that the means of holiness, through the Holy Spirit, were present to the Church and its members, but that the full perfection would only come with the eschaton. For that reason the Church was always in need of reform – *semper reformanda* – but full of hope because of Christ's promise to remain with his Church till the end of time. The images they finally accepted to express all of these aspects of the Church can be summed up in two phrases: the People of God and the Church on Pilgrimage. The bishops and their *periti* found images that were biblical and at the same time vivid and appealing – good catechetical tools as in the Pauline practice.

The Council's Images

Perhaps no other phrase sums up the popular view of Vatican II as that of an assembly of the People of God. The image's attractiveness comes first from its relationship to both the Old and New Testament, in which Israel was called 'God's people', a title also used of the fledgling community of Christians (1 Pet. 2:7–10). It is true that some of these New Testament texts have the flavour of 'replacement' theologies, but most Catholics were unaware of such subtleties.[4] The advantage of using the word 'people' instead of 'society' was that it implied a certain and equal 'belongingness' on the part of all members and assumed a clear universalism, one that coincided well with Catholics' aims and ideals in the twentieth century. It is true that some interpreted this term, not in its biblical context, but in a contemporary democratic way, which could imply a non-hierarchical Church. By beginning with this image and notion, however, the bishops consciously created the impression that the Church is indeed the people – all the people, and not just the leaders. There is no avoiding that perception; it was an intended one. It also includes the ideas of the Church as a society found in previous definitions and images, because a people are by nature a social reality and communitarian.

As God's People, the Church could well see itself as having been formed by God's will and not by the desires, whims or choices of the members. Within the Church, then, we experienced a renewal of covenant theology that followed on the use of this image. The two went well together. The use of biblical language in one instance fortified its use in other circumstances. It also pointed out that the Church's formation was God's design and that God first took the initiative. Covenants also require a response: this concept gave birth to a new articulation of moral norms and their biblical roots.

These have all been positive aspects of the image of People of God. It is true that Christ and his role are not explicitly mentioned by such a title; some of the bishops in their interventions at the Council were well aware of this shortcoming. Believing that something was needed to complement the image, they spoke often of the Church as a pilgrim, as being on pilgrimage. Under this concept they were able to see the Church as not yet fulfilled, as still sinful and in progress. This concept satisfied the wishes of some of the members that the eschatological nature of the Church also be emphasised. Cardinal Karol Wojtyla was one of those who spoke in favour of the expression 'People of God' but who also felt a need for some qualifying term to make clear that the Church was indeed 'a perfect society, in the sense that it has all the means of attaining its supernatural end'.[5]

The two images – 'People of God' and 'Church on Pilgrimage' – form the framework of *Lumen gentium*, the Dogmatic Constitution on the Church. After talking about the Church as mystery in the first chapter, the bishops went on in the second to speak of its nature as God's People. In the seventh chapter, the second to the last, they elaborate on the concept of the Church as an eschatological phenomenon. Chapter 8, which ends the document, is devoted to Mary, and acts as an epilogue and an admirable summation of all that the Constitution sought to expound.

In the second chapter on the People of God the bishops took a starting point that was not common in previous Catholic treatises since it based its approach on the way all the people share in Christ's role as priest, prophet and king. Although it did not want to give the impression that all shared in the same way in these functions, it still gave preference to the idea that all were equal members of the Church and equally called to an intimate relationship with Christ in the fulfilment of their baptismal commitments. As priests, all participate in the offering of the Eucharist and the reception of the sacraments, albeit in differing ministerial functions. As prophets, all are witnesses to Christ and receive the gifts of the Spirit that correspond to their calling. By sharing in Christ's kingship, they are called to a universal, a truly Catholic, Church. Amid this diversity of roles the Holy Spirit is the binding force of unity among all the members.

The seventh chapter, truly one of the most important in the document, was added, it would seem, through the insistence of Pope John XXIII. It reminds all the members of the Church that they belong to an *Ecclesia peregrinans*: that the Church is now on pilgrimage, yearning for the consummation when all shall be reconciled in Christ. In the pastoral constitution on the Church in the modern world, *Gaudium et spes* (#45), all followers of Christ are reminded that what this Church on Pilgrimage has to offer the world in the here-and-now is 'the mystery of God's love' for all. It reminds the faithful: 'The Lord is the goal of human history, the focal point of the longings of history and civilisation, the center of the human race, the joy of every heart, and the answer to all its yearnings.' As members of the *Ecclesia peregrinans* all are reminded that they hasten to that consummation of human history.

One can see why these two images taken together, *Populi Dei* and *Ecclesia peregrinans* – 'God's People on Pilgrimage' – sum up the whole of the teaching on the Church. The other images are not slighted, but these two act as the frames to give life to the rest.

The Extraordinary Synod of 1985

When bishops from around the world gathered in 1985 in an Extraordinary Synod to study what had happened in the Church since the Council, they produced a Final Report in which they encouraged more study of the Council documents. They named all the images that had characterised the document on the nature of the Church and mentioned the 'People of God' only as one among many. The omission was due to their fear that the term had been used to create a false impression of the nature of the Church, namely, that it is a democratic body in which there would be minimal if any hierarchical structure, and, if such a structure existed, it would have to correspond to modern democratic norms, namely, be accountable to the will of the majority of the people. It is a shame that the term 'People of God', so popular among the faithful, had to be almost set aside because of this fear. If it had been used with the companion phrase of a Church on Pilgrimage with its clear eschatological end, such a fear may have been averted. Many observers noted at once the way in which 'People of God' had been downplayed in the Synod. They felt the bishops at the Synod were thus not being true to the documents of Vatican II themselves and to their own admonition that people should not engage in revisionist views of the Council.

The most important contribution of the Synod of 1985 was to add to the discussion on the Church the insight that its nature is really one of a *communio*. This term describes the nature of the Church primarily as consisting of relationships. First comes the relationship with God, then with Jesus Christ in the Holy Spirit, next among the baptised themselves, and finally with all others in a given society. This theology of communion was already a favourite in ecumenical dialogues and had great merit. But it remains a theological term; there is no adequate image to accompany it, and such an image continues to elude both theologians and catechists. For this reason, it has not gained much popularity among the faithful.

Consequences for the Church Today

Perhaps the most striking result of the use of this term 'People of God' with its Old Testament roots, coupled with its eschatological orientation in the phrase 'on pilgrimage', was that it gave bishops the freedom to talk about the sinfulness of the Church and so come to terms with some of the less pleasant aspects of its history. In this sense, Pope John Paul's proneness to ask for forgiveness was already anticipated by the Council. In fact, Pope Paul VI had already begun this trend by apologising to other Christians for offences Catholics may in the past have given them. Other bishops spoke of the need for the Church to admit its own culpability in causing the divisions that took place.

Already during the Council this acceptance of the Church as imperfect and in need of constant conversion was evident. One of the most moving interventions in this regard was presented by Bishop Stephen Laszlo of Eisenstadt, Austria. He stated that so often theologians talk of the Church as if it were one of saints, when in reality it is one of sinners. He asked how we should respond when this is pointed out to us. His words of wisdom still ring true today:

If our answer wants to convince people of our day, it must not be compounded of triumphalism and pretence, but must be realistic and completely sincere. In other words, on the earth we may not proclaim only an ecclesiology of glory; that belongs to the end of time. When we speak of the pilgrim Church, we must always begin from the ecclesiology of the Cross ... The Church cannot be understood except as the eschatological people of God, on pilgrimage through time, proclaiming the death and resurrection of the Lord until he comes ... We say the Church is on pilgrimage because in all its difficulties and miseries this people is not without fault, not without sin.[6]

He rightly adds that if people wish to use the word communion, they must talk of a communion of sinners and consequently a communion of penitents. Bishop Francis A. Quinn, retired bishop of Sacramento, California, expressed this same idea when he described the Church as 'not a museum of saints, but a hospital for sinners'.[7]

Some observers, especially the Lutherans, criticised the bishops at the Council for taking too optimistic a view of the world. Perhaps one could say they also took too optimistic a view of the Church. So much of the triumphalistic rhetoric did not ring true. Theologians have been debating how deeply wounded the Church can be while still maintaining its purpose and function. But it would seem that Yves Congar's position is the most solid. Certainly sin will be found – and frequently – among the members, he noted. This includes the hierarchy, not only in their personal lives but also in the decisions that touch their official duties and functioning. But, he concludes, the Church 'will always be faithful to the inner law of its being'.[8]

Because of its sinfulness the Church will have to be much more humble now than in the past in how it presents itself, avoiding all signs of haughtiness and superiority. The tendency to want to witness to the world as the perfect society must be guarded against. This more humble stance fits well with the attitudes expressed in *Gaudium et spes* about the way the Church should relate to the world around it, namely, more as a companion on the journey that shares in all the joys and anxieties of the others and as a source of hope and consolation, rather than an aloof or other-worldly judge. As long as it is *in via*, moreover, the Church must constantly admit its own need of reform.

Finally, the Church must be a forgiving community. All members are constantly in need of God's forgiveness and the forgiveness of one another. Not to be a forgiving community would be to betray its role as a means of salvation, an instrument through which Christ's saving love can reach all its members. Pilgrimage means walking together, sustaining one another, encouraging one another, forgiving one another. Perhaps in today's world the old adage, 'See how these Christians love one another', should be expanded to include, 'See how these Christians, as God's People on Pilgrimage, forgive one another.'

Notes

1 Louis Bouyer, *The Church of God*, trans. Charles Underhill Quinn (Chicago: Franciscan Herald Press, 1982), p. 495.
2 Vatican Press, vol. 1, p. 150.
3 G. Alberigo and J. Komonchak (eds), *History of Vatican II*, vol. II (Maryknoll: Orbis, 1997), p. 281.
4 See Daniel J. Harrington, SJ, 'Why is the Church the People of God?' in Lucien Richard, OMI, Daniel T. Harrington, SJ, and John W. O'Malley, SJ (eds), *Vatican II: The Unfinished Agenda* (Chicago: Paulist Press, 1987), p. 49.
5 *Acta Synodalia II, 3*, pp. 155–6.
6 'Sin in the Holy Church of God', in Yves Congar, OP, and Daniel J. O'Hanlon, SJ (eds), *Council Speeches of Vatican II* (New York: Paulist Press, 1964), pp. 45–6.
7 Francis A. Quinn, 'A looming crisis of faith', *America*, 188 (7 April 2003), p. 16.
8 Yves Congar, *The Mystery of the Church*, trans. A. V. Littledale (Baltimore: Helicon Press, 1960), p. 92.

6

Wanted: The Other Half of the Church
Joan Chittister

I hear the statement 'I was raised Catholic' more often than I like these days. Too often, it seems to me, it means that someone formed in the faith no longer identifies with it. Too often many of these people are women: middle-aged women; young women; women on whom the future of the transmission of the faith depends.

At one time to say 'I was raised Catholic' had the ring of the pedestrian to it: after all, so many of us were. In a Catholic immigrant population, to be raised Catholic communicated a person's cultural identity as much as it marked their convictions. It bore the stamp of national pride and political meaning, as much as it denoted a set of religious beliefs. To be raised Catholic had something to do with a person's whole identity.

But even then the words carried a particular spiritual connotation for everyone. For me, they meant that I went to Catholic schools and haunted Catholic churches like a small ghost. In those days, churches were never locked until sometime after dark, and children could do such things with impunity. I did it all the time. I hunted churches down, tugged at the great wooden doors that signalled their entrance into another world and escaped into the cool, damp dark inside. There was something there for me that touched a quiet, inner place that was touchable by nothing else on earth.

I would skate around a neighbourhood corner and run right into one after another of them: Hungarian, Polish, German, Irish parishes, all catering to their own kind, all the same and all slightly different. They existed to revere differences, to acknowledge distinct histories and cultural customs. At each place, I would take off my skates on the church steps, hide them in the bushes outside and tip-toe down one dark church aisle after another, smelling the candles, studying the windows, struggling to read the Latin inscriptions that circled the frescoes over the altars. I was a Catholic through and through. In the church I felt safe. I felt at home. Something here both catechised and completed me.

It took years before I began to realise, as have a number of other women, that the fact is that a woman is not completely 'at home' in the Church at all. In fact, her 'completeness' may be more in question here than any other place in society. Her catechesis – that God is love, that God created all of us in God's own image, that women, as well as men, are fully human – remains always problematic.

Because They Said So

The words 'I was raised Catholic' have a particular connotation for women. A woman discovers over time that there is a difference between being raised in the faith and being part of the Church. As the years go by, it becomes clear: women get the faith; men get the Church to go with it.

That's the way things are, we hear. That's all there is to it. That's the way God means it to be.

For centuries, the social parallels that developed out of that kind of theology were obvious. Women were simply expected to take the ancillary role God had decreed for them, everywhere, at all times, in all situations: in marriage, in politics, in business, in professional arenas, in the home and definitely in the Church.

But the last half of the twentieth century, devoted to the human sciences, awash in biological and genetic data, began slowly but surely to give the lie to those ideas, to suspect the rationale for those ideas, to shatter that assumption from one ambit to the next. Theologically, the notion was even more suspect. What kind of a God was it that made humanity of two types: one superior, one inferior; one godly, one not?

Around us, every other organisation in the Western World teetered on a consciousness of the fact that its composition mirrored only half the human race, listened to only half the human race, respected the insights of only half the human race, incorporated into itself the ideas and directions and agendas of only half the human race. But not the Church.

As all these other institutions and organisations restructured themselves to remedy what was clearly an aberration of the human condition, a distortion of both theology and Scripture, of biology and science, the Church alone failed to address the issue as a major theological question in its own right. Instead, women were told that the Church was a divine institution set up by Jesus himself to keep women at a distance from all things sacred. The apostles were all men, we were told repeatedly, as if the 12 apostles – symbolic Christian surrogates for the Twelve Tribes of Israel – were the only ministers in the Church. No mention of Mary who bore Jesus, or of Mary Magdalene and the women of Israel who were the first to support Jesus 'out of their own sustenance', or of the Samaritan woman to whom Jesus revealed himself as Messiah before having said a word to Peter, or of the women who laboured with Paul to build the early church. No mention at all of them, of the women disciples of Jesus, of women in their own right. Nothing.

But then, astounding things, life-changing things, began to happen. Pope John XXIII, in his encyclical *Pacem et terris*, listed the woman's issue as one of the 'signs of the times', along with poverty and nuclearism. Vatican II issued a document on the vocation of the laity, and made no distinction between lay men and lay women. New liturgical norms eliminated the altar rail and allowed women entry into the sanctuary, the Holy of Holies, alongside male lectors and male ministers of the Eucharist and male altar servers. Com-munion in the hand, with its clear implication that women as well as men were worthy to touch the consecrated host, became a commonplace.

Apostolicam actuositatem, the Document on the Laity, said it directly: 'Since in our times women have an ever more active share in the whole life of society, it is very important that they participate more widely also in the various fields of the church's apostolate' (AA, 9).

And for a while it looked as if they would. Male universities began to admit women to degrees in the sacred sciences on a par with men, in the same classes, under the same academic requirement. Lay Ecclesial Ministry Programmes began to emerge everywhere. By the year 2002, US universities had graduated over 34,000 lay ministers, two out of every three of them women, only 3 per cent of them women religious. Under their aegis lay women, too, became theologians, canonists, liturgists and parish administrators.

Clearly, even the Church was beginning to flirt with the possibility that women were an idea whose time had come.

Finally, for the first time in history, in 1985, a pope wrote an encyclical on women. It is a gracious letter and a fulsome one. Nevertheless, the encyclical, *Mulieris dignitatem*, con-tinues to imply the notion of a separate or dual anthropology: that man, the male, is one kind of human but woman is another. That biological differences have something to do with spiritual differences. That Jesus who became 'flesh' became one kind of flesh that apparently does not include the other kind. Ten years later, however, Pope John Paul II carved out another new moment in the history of women in the Church when he wrote a letter of apology to the women of the world for failures of the Church in the past to recognise the equality and value of women. He wrote: 'Such respect (for women) must first and foremost be won through an effective and intelligent campaign for the promotion of women, concentrating on all areas of women's life and beginning with a universal recognition of the dignity of women.' Accent on 'effective and intelligent campaign for the promotion of women' and 'on all areas of women's life'. Surely here was the beginning of a new world for us all. And for a while it seemed to be true.

A Step Forward

Dioceses everywhere, in response to the documents of Vatican II and encouraged by papal support, began to include women on boards, in chanceries, in parish administrative positions.

Parishes accepted women into liturgical ministries: little girls began to be altar servers alongside little boys, women read from the Scriptures at Mass, lay Eucharistic ministers, women as well as men, served homes for the aged, hospitals, and at regular liturgical celebrations.

Congregations began to take for granted that women would also serve in new kinds of parish work. Lay programmes gave degrees in Pastoral Ministry, Theology and Theological Studies, Divinity, Religious Studies, Spirituality and Pastoral Counselling. Now marriage preparation conferences were as easily staffed by women as by men. Liturgical planning, adult catechesis, parish organisational activities and decision-making positions on parish boards became common for women as well as for men.

Most significant of all, perhaps, the Church began to change the language of liturgical events to include the recognition of women as part of the assembly.

Discussions began in theological circles about the theological possibility of the restoration of the diaconate for women as it had been for men.

Women, it seemed, had finally arrived as full adult members of the Church. They were now in the language of prayer, in the offices of the diocese and on the altars of parish churches. Barely, perhaps, but there, nevertheless. Now it was only a matter of new practices becoming ordinary before women would be taken for granted as leaders in the Church and bearers of the Spirit. Both the Fatherhood and the Motherhood of God were slowly coming into consciousness, into public view.

Then, slowly but surely, the reversal began. The 'programme' the Pope called for died a rude and insidious death. Almost imperceptibly, at first, new statements began to be released, most of them with little fanfare but with far-reaching results. The doors, one at a time, began to close.

Seminarians were directed in *Pastores dabo vobis* in 1993 to have priests as their spiritual directors, despite years of being free to choose whomever suited them best: men or women. Clearly the men of the Church had nothing to learn from the women of the Church. That door closed.

Word leaked out, of course, of seminarians who asked their women directors to continue with them regardless. But the system itself stayed male, sterile, untouched by a regularised feminine dimension of the mystical, a safer place, apparently, but possibly a more barren one, as well. In fact, some researchers estimate the lifespan of a new priest to be five years, whatever the measures in place to encapsulate young priests in a male world.

Two Steps Back

Sr Carmel McEnroy was peremptorily removed from seminary teaching despite years of outstanding teacher evaluations. The charge against her was that she signed a statement asking the Church to open a discussion on the ordination of women. One by one, teaching positions in theology closed to women. In some cases the exclusion was more subtle. Women were simply relegated to elective areas of theology programmes so that traditional ideas, male ideas, could never be broadened to include the insights or questions of women on subjects of theological substance. Another door closed.

A woman religious with a certification in Clinical Pastoral Education gave years of free service in hospital ministry. When a vacancy arose, she asked the local bishop to hire her as Catholic chaplain. He refused. That door closed. In the end, she was hired by the hospital itself as 'ecumenical chaplain' – which, ironically, makes her doubly effective in her work. She meets more patients, gives more spiritual consolation, is respected by more people. But, at the same time, she remains officially unacknowledged by the Catholic community whose faith informs her ministry. In the meantime, she answers every emergency call in the deep of the night and then phones rectory after rectory in an attempt to get priests to administer the Sacrament of Healing to Catholic patients.

Altar girls have come to be more and more rare, not more and more common. Some dioceses forbid them altogether and without apology, let alone the grace to blush. Apparently the Church against whom the gates of hell cannot prevail can be brought to perdition by little 11-year-old girls carrying water

from one side of an altar to the next. With this door clos-
ing goes the commitment of many of the women of the next
generation.

In diocese after diocese, where they have served in official
capacities for years, women are being removed from every
office in the chancery except, perhaps, as vicars for religious.
And at the same time, new documents, notably the *Instruction
on Certain Questions Regarding the Collaboration of the Non-
Ordained Faithful* of 1997, remind priests that they hold the
ultimate authority in every dimension of church and parish life,
regardless of their lack of experience or professional preparation in any of them. In those cases, the doors to any kind
of official hearing of the issues or concerns of women have
closed soundly and completely.

One by one, inner-city parishes find themselves done away
with for lack of priests or served only by men too old, too tired
themselves to do more than say an occasional Mass. But
women, even those with degrees in lay ecclesial ministry programmes, who ask to be allowed to serve those parishes get no
welcome. So the parishes disappear silently where the congregations are too small, too old, or too poor to have their protests
heard. This kind of exclusion has other consequences, as well.
Many of the women, after years of trying to serve the Church
and being rebuffed, go with them, to other work, to other
Churches, or to no Church at all. And they are taking their
daughters with them.

In 1965 in the United States, 549 parishes were without a
resident priest. In 2002, there were 2,929 US parishes without
a resident priest. Around the world, those figures had risen
from 94,846 priestless parishes in 1980, the first year in which
data began to be collected on a global scale, to 105,530
parishes in the year 2000.[1]

Bishop Raymond Lucker of New Ulm, Wisconsin, now deceased, loved to tell the story of his attempt to maintain the traditional parish structures in the face of the dwindling number of priests. His solution was to assign a priest to three parishes at a time, a kind of circuit-rider eccesiology. The priest would reside in the largest of the three parishes, but preside at the weekly Sunday liturgy for the other two, as well. Women religious acted as residential parish administrators in the parishes that had no daily access to a priest. After several years of this arrangement, Lucker decided it was unfair for one parish to have continual access to a priest while the other two did not. He decreed then that the priest would move from parish to parish every three years. Suddenly, he reported, the mail started pouring in asking him not to do that. The underlying message in all of them brooked no doubt: 'We haven't had this kind of parish activity for years', the letters said. 'We don't want a priest. Just leave Sister where she is.'

But every day that kind of joint ministry fades, those doors close. Universities report that of the records they have on the ministerial positions of their graduates, most now occupy volunteer positions in catechetical programmes.

The diaconate programme, now restored for men only, has grown to over 12,000 ordained deacons since its inception. But the thought of even discussing the restoration of the diaconate programme for women, too – an institutional staple in both the Eastern and the Western Churches for over 10 centuries – has been dismissed without consideration in the document *Institutionis Diaconorum Permanentiarum* on the grounds that it could lead to the expectation of priestly ordination for women. Despite the fact that the same argument is not used in regard to married men. Nor can ordained deacons do anything that any other lay person cannot do without permission (except, of course, maintain the male character of a sacramental Church).

Finally, in what may be the most subversive move of all, new documents – notably *Liturgiam authenticam* in 2001 – completely obliterate female references from the prayers and hymns of the Church, even in Scriptures clearly addressed to the whole Christian community, let alone in references to the infinite, unknowable and totally spiritual Godhead who has been made completely captive to maleness. The door to existence for women, even in the pronouns of the Church, has been closed.

Philosophers and social psychologists alike know that what is missing in the language is missing in the mind, and that what is missing in the mind will never be embodied in the structures of a people, a culture, an organisation, a Church. Whom we do not address in a conversation does not exist for us. Language is not a trivial issue. Language is the ultimate delete.

Still Wanted: The Other Half

And the question is: why? Why all these exclusions in the face of a Council of the Church that called for equality, an encyclical on the gifting nature of women, a papal letter of apology for the past sins of the Church against women and the promise of 'programmes, etc.'? Why these sudden reversals of practice in a Church that had found new life, new energy, new witness in the world as a result of its long overdue recognition of the full humanity of women? Why the changes now in the face of the clear but new awareness of the implications for the Church of the gospel descriptions of Jesus with women? Why the new abandonment of women in the light of the theological significance of a creation story that insists on the common human identity of both Adam and Eve – 'bone of my bone; flesh of my flesh'? Somebody, Adam recognises, who is just like himself. Where, in all of this, is the 'campaign for the promotion of women, concentrating on all areas of women's life and beginning with a universal recognition of the dignity of women' promised by this Pope that will promote the advancement of women in the Church as well as in all other sectors of society?

Why do we have thousands of priestless parishes, thousands fewer seminarians and, at the same time, thousands of unemployed lay ministers – most of them women – unless it is more preferable to close parishes than to allow women to maintain the very lifeblood of a communal Church?

What can we conclude? That the papal letter to women lacks integrity? That the Council has been hijacked? That papal messages are routinely ignored by those who claim to accept them? It is a question of great ethical and ecclesiastical import. On it may well rest not only the renewal of the Church but its future as well: its future effectiveness, its future witness, its very impact and influence in years to come – as secular society, rather than the Church, leads the world to a new understanding of creation.

Note

1 Statistics on Lay Ecclesial Ministers are from Center for Applied Research in the Apostolate (CARA), Georgetown University, Washington, D.C. (Cara.Georgetown.edu).

7

Augustine, Aquinas or the Gospel *sine glossa*? Divisions over *Gaudium et spes*[1]

Joseph A. Komonchak

One of the most striking developments in the first decade after the close of Vatican II was the splintering of the coalition of theologians who helped at the first session to break the power of those who had controlled the Council's preparation. Those theologians played a major role in the deliberations which resulted in conciliar documents marked by a quite different spirit and offering a quite different message to the Church and to the world. But then they bifurcated along paths symbolised by two new theological journals. The first issue of *Concilium* appeared in 1964, while the Council was still meeting; *Communio* was founded in 1972 by several theologians who had since resigned from the editorial board of *Concilium* (and was inevitably therefore labelled an 'anti-*Concilium*'). The seeds of this schism were planted long before the Council opened, slept in the soil for the first two sessions, then broke into the light as the Council moved to its close. Anyone interested in healing the division would be well advised to trace them to their roots.

The differences began to appear, especially, in the last stages of the preparation of *Gaudium et spes* and were consistently reflected, also, in the initial commentaries on the pastoral constitution. I will consider those differences through the commentaries on the redaction of *Guadium et spes* of three theologians: Marie-Dominique Chenu, Joseph Ratzinger and Giuseppe Dossetti.

'What Now?': The Question of Schema 13

The split among the progressive majority suggests that the theological dynamic of Vatican II was more complex – as Giuseppe Alberigo, echoing Joseph Ratzinger, has observed – than the simple opposition between a 'curial tendency' and a 'progressive tendency'.[2] It is significant that both men made this comment in the course of observations on *Gaudium et spes*. For although differences among the progressives with regard both to practical tactics and to theological orientations were not lacking in earlier moments of the conciliar deliberations, they had then been largely subordinated to the common interest of opposing the ecclesiastical and theological system which was reflected in the official texts prepared for the Council's discussion and expected approval. In the midst of that struggle it appeared sufficient to analyse the conciliar tension as one between 'two tendencies in modern theology', to use the title of Mgr Gérard Philips's famous essay.[3] But once that struggle had ended a question arose, nicely stated by Joseph Ratzinger: 'The preparatory work was unsatisfactory, and the Council rejected the extant texts. But the question at this point was: What now?'[4] The question was particularly acute with regard to Schema 13.

After its initial discussion during the third session of the Council, Schema 13 was extensively rewritten, particularly during and after the long and fruitful meeting at Ariccia in January–February 1965. A useful description of the new plan and method was provided by Mgr P. Haubtmann shortly before the Council resumed its work.[5] In response to criticisms of the previous version, the redactors had constructed a Christian anthropology set out in the four chapters of the first part of the schema, which was followed by a consideration of material on some more pressing problems that previously had been treated in appendices. Addressed first to Catholics and through them to all people, the schema would take the form, not of an authoritative claim to jurisdiction over the issues discussed, but rather of a testimony, one that simply stated what the Church is, what it believes, and what it thinks about contemporary questions. This required a style and form both simple and direct; it also called for a method that would begin 'from facts and truths the most commonly acknowledged, would then illumine and judge them in the light of Revelation, and finally would centre them upon Christ himself'. The method was theologically motivated: 'for facts and human development ('*devenir*') in their own way constitute a *locus theologicus* in which the believer must seek ... the appeals and the solicitations of the Spirit'. The result was 'a *sui generis* type of schema'.

Rahner's Criticisms of Schema 13

The Ariccia text encountered serious criticism at the meeting of German bishops in Fulda at the end of August 1965. A set of observations prepared by Karl Rahner were discussed and in large part adopted by the German and Scandinavian bishops. Despite the great effort that had been expended on its revision, the schema, according to Rahner, still had many defects.

First, it lacked a sufficient 'theological gnoseology' that would explain how it had arrived at its analysis of the contemporary world – how much of it had been borrowed from contemporary analysts, how much derived from the faith – and how the authors had come to the concrete and practical conclusions it stated. Secondly, Rahner argued that the schema did not adequately address the relationship between the order of creation and the order of redemption, particularly the meaning of the human activity that was profoundly transforming the world. The inner-worldly significance of this activity was neglected in favour of its immediate religious and moral significance. The concept of the 'world' in the text also needed further clarification. Thirdly, the German Jesuit said, the schema lacked 'a real and profound theology of sin': it was content with lamenting immorality in a way that scarcely surpassed what mere experience might yield. The ineradicable depths of sin were overlooked; the ideology of a 'better world' obtainable if people only willed it had replaced the 'legitimate and necessary "pessimism" that Christians must profess before the world'. Fourthly, said Rahner, it neglected what a Christian theology of history must acknowledge: 'that the antagonism between a world under the power of the Evil One and the disciples of Christ will never be mitigated but will grow ever more bitter in the course of time'.

Finally, said Rahner, the schema lacked the needed Christian anthropology. The idea of the 'image of God' was presented too rapidly and too briefly and ignored the complexities of the notion. The reflections on human dignity were too abstract, too formal, and too oriented toward contemplation. The text lacked a 'theology of the cross' and of its implications for the history of the world and of the human race. Rahner's proposal was that the text either be remanded to a post-conciliar commission or that it be reduced in authority from a 'pastoral constitution'.

Joseph Ratzinger echoed many of Rahner's criticisms and added others of his own. The text came close to a Teilhardian identification of Christian hope with modern confidence in progress, according to Ratzinger; it seemed 'unaware of the ambivalence of all external human progress'. Its descriptions of contemporary movements were so polite and reasonable that the eventual references to Christ seemed half-embarrassed afterthoughts. Unclarified notions of the relationship between the Church and the world reflected habits formed while the Church had been retreating from the general course of modern developments into its little ecclesiastical sphere from which it was now trying to speak to the whole of humanity. After the council Ratzinger would repeat many of these criticisms in his commentaries on *Gaudium et spes*.

In order to prevent these disagreements among habitual conciliar allies from endangering the text, several French- and German-speaking bishops and theologians met on 17 September. After the former defended the schema from the critiques of the latter, the common decision was made to accept the schema as a basis but to try to improve it. Joseph Ratzinger, who attended the meeting, described the 'new fronts [that] had emerged in the face of new tasks and new problems' as reflecting 'a certain opposition between German and French theology' within the ranks of the progressives.[6]

But there was a third voice in the debate, that of Giuseppe Dossetti (1913–96). Not very well known outside Italy, Dossetti played important roles at two of the most important events in twentieth-century Italian history, as a layman at the Constituent Assembly of 1948 that produced the Constitution for the new Italian Republic, and at the Second Vatican Council, where he was the chief adviser to Cardinal Giacomo Lercaro (1891–1976), Archbishop of Bologna. In Italian politics he had belonged to the left wing of the Christian Democrat party. Frustrated at his lack of influence, he began to work for a renewal of the Church that might be able to promote a badly needed different form of politics. After a quixotic run for mayor of Bologna, he was ordained a priest in 1959. He established the well-known Institute of Religious Studies in Bologna. After Vatican II, he withdrew into the quasi-monastic community he had founded.

A very evangelical vision inspired the speeches Dossetti prepared for Lercaro and a few other bishops and the memoranda he composed during and after Vatican II. He insisted that if the Council did not embody and call for a very radical conversion to the gospel (*sine glossa*, he liked to call it – without extenuating commentary), it would fall short of the epochal intentions of Pope John. The Council, of course, did not go down that road, and Dossetti regarded its final texts as greatly compromised by Paul VI's caution and his desire for near-unanimity.

As the debate on Schema 13 was about to resume Dossetti wrote to Cardinal Lercaro of 'our position between two fires (the conservatives and the progressives)'.[7] This comment, along with the intervention Dossetti prepared for the cardinal, reveals the presence of another, more radical and evangelical, approach to the questions.

Three Theologians, Three Approaches

The three men – Chenu, Ratzinger and Dossetti – were in broad agreement in a number of areas. They agreed on the inadequacy of modern 'Catholic social doctrine' which argued on the basis of a natural law, accessible, it was thought, to right reason, and practised a method of deduction from rather abstract first principles. They were all opposed, too, to an approach – from within an ecclesiology of the *societas perfecta* – that would be content with service of a separate little Catholic world. They agreed on the need for a biblically inspired engagement of the Church and the Christian with the world of history. They all wished to overcome an anthropology which so stressed the distinction that it became a separation between nature and grace, reason and faith, world and Church. And yet, for all these agreements, their assessments of *Gaudium et spes* often differed sharply. Why is this?

Leaving aside an inevitably superficial explanation in terms of 'optimism' vs. 'pessimism', one might be tempted to be content with the differences between an incarnational and an eschatological approach. But who would wish to suggest that any one of the three theologians would consider compromising either of the great mysteries, the Incarnation or the Cross? The relative weight given to one or the other, in contrast, may be traceable to differences in basic theological or methodological stances.

M.-D. Chenu was, by religious commitment, by training, and by expertise, a Thomist. Within his comments on the pastoral constitution one can hear echoes of the theological epistemology and anthropology which he defended 25 years before the Council not only in scholarly works on Aquinas but also in works that urged a typically Thomist approach to theology for a Church that is present in and for the modern world. Then and later he saw the Thomist method as corresponding to the logic of the Incarnation and of Redemption as the recapitulation of all things in Christ, including the physical universe and the embodied spirit of man. Then and later he urged that theological anthropology had to go beyond the realm of the psychological to include the social, cultural and the historical dimensions and to see these latter, neglected, dimensions not only to be constitutive of man but also the locus of those same orientations toward and created capacities for the supernatural that Thomism had defended, for example, in categories such as that of 'obediential potency'. A sharp disjunction, such as the one that is content with the two categories of sin and grace, was inadequate on Thomist grounds because it neglected the created autonomy and intelligibility of the world of nature, man and history; and because it tended to compromise the methodological autonomy of the sciences that study it. Chenu's defence of the basic method and orientation of *Gaudium et spes* did not derive, or did not simply derive, from his congenital optimism; it had theological grounds.

In Joseph Ratzinger's assessment of the pastoral constitution one can see a theological method and vision that stands far closer to the streams of Augustinianism that during the Middle Ages and in the post-Reformation era had been very reserved towards the Thomist effort. Ratzinger seems far more at home in the world of the Scriptures, the Fathers and St Bonaventure. In his remarks on *Gaudium et spes*, as also in many other writings, he makes clear his preference for Augustinian (and even Lutheran) notions of freedom and his belief that Thomists (if not Thomas himself) had so stressed the autonomy of the world and of human reason that the first constituted a separate world capable of being understood by the second, with the result that the world disclosed by revelation and accepted by faith appeared to be a more-or-less arbitrarily imposed alternative. To a Thomist epistemology he regards as inadequate he prefers a typically Augustinian distinction between *scientia* and *sapientia*, the former, imitated today by the necessarily reductionistic modern empirical sciences, content with mere phenomena and indifferent to the ontological truth of things, which is only apparent to the latter, itself the fruit of faith. The pastoral constitution continues to reflect the myth of pure reason which leads it to a necessarily ineffective method of dialogue that neglects that faith is not demonstrable; what is needed is kerygmatic witness, the simple presentation of the gospel and an invitation to enter its world of intelligibility and rationality. The basic issue remains that of the relationship between faith and understanding.

Giuseppe Dossetti is more difficult to place. At least in his participation at the Council and in his remarks on *Gaudium et spes*, he appears more as a prophet than as a scholar, less as a professor than as the engaged Christian he had been in both society and Church. He seems closer to Ratzinger, first, in his distrust of the modern self-professedly Thomist theological tradition elaborated in the service of a *societas perfecta* that he thought had compromised the evangelical engagement that should mark the Church; second, in his preference for the engagement typical of early Christianity; and, third, in his insistence on the radical rupture in intelligibility, the redefinition of rationality, required by the Cross. For him, too, the primary presence of the Church must be one of testimony (a word used by all three men), but this is witness to an utterly supernatural vision and reality, which in the end cannot be rendered reasonable to non-believers. For that reason he quite disagreed with Chenu's assessment of the analysis that underlay *Gaudium et spes*, which he thinks scarcely surpasses the level of a common-sense sociology that is content with a banal general understanding and promotes a timid Christian engagement. At the same time, he clearly disagreed with Ratzinger on what the question of war and peace required of the Council, and so, far from being content with Ratzinger's apparently inconsistent resignation to the conciliar position on the question, he regards the latter as indicative of the radical incompleteness of the whole conciliar experience and achievement. For Dossetti the Council missed a unique opportunity. Underlying the failure, for him, is the Council's inability to escape, with the radicality required, from the institutional constraints and from the theology that served them, for the sake of a gospel *sine glossa*. It must also be said that of the three men it is Dossetti who actually attempted something like a reading of the 'signs of the times', while Ratzinger remained unconvinced of the very idea and Chenu was content with remarks of great generality.

Of the three men, clearly Dossetti was the most radical in the demands he placed on the conciliar fathers and in the criteria by which he subjected their achievements to judgement. Dossetti found the draft's analysis of the contemporary world nothing but 'common sense propositions', at the level of 'journalistic popularisation'. The text should be revised, he said, in order to give the response of the gospel to concrete problems and to do this 'in the immediacy and relevance of its most vigorous statements'. He, too, wished the Council to offer an optimistic and positive message; but, he went on, there is a great difference between 'an utterly supernatural Christian optimism' that anticipates 'a transfiguration and regeneration that is like a resurrection from the dead, solely in virtue of the blessed passion of Christ', and a naturalistic optimism that 'indulges in a phenomenology of human progress and ignores or flees the principle that everyone and everything must be "salted with fire" (Mark 9:49), by the fire of the Cross and of the Spirit of Christ'. The draft's optimism was not salted in this way, he argued; it conformed to common opinions, was uncritical and timid.

This affected most particularly, in his view, the text's treatment of war and peace. The text tried so hard to be non-judgemental, he thought, that it ignored the judgements on contemporary evils the Church is called to make in the name of Christ. On so crucial a point as war, he wanted the Council's discourse to be 'absolute, synthetic, evangelical'. Only this approach could respond to the anxiety of peoples; only this could 'banish war and make peace, not by human calculation but by the creative force of the Word of God'. This is the witness to faith in Jesus Christ that the whole Church is called to give; in this moment of supreme danger, it could give no truer response than to say to the world: 'Entrust yourself not to defence by arms and by political prudence, but only to the protection of the Lord Jesus.' When the bishops failed to follow this evangelical call, articulated at the Council by Lercaro and a few others, Dossetti thought that the value of the Council as a whole was called into question. The failure demonstrated how tight were certain institutional and theological knots that could not be loosened 'except by a sword, by the sword of the Word of God, clear and simple, beyond all other theological reflection'.

There is visible in his final assessments of Vatican II a good deal of the distinct position he urged upon Cardinal Lercaro from the first session onwards and which was reflected in the speech in which the Archbishop of Bologna pleaded that the whole conciliar agenda be reconceived in terms of the problem of poverty. Dossetti was fiercely critical both of the method, compromising from the beginning, reflected in the decision to retain as much as possible of the preparatory schemas, and of the at best only half-successful results this fatal choice permitted. Neither in the Council's doctrinal texts nor in the texts on the Church's relationship with the modern world did Vatican II achieve the breakthrough Dossetti thought could alone correspond to Pope John's vision. It was a theological, indeed a religious, commitment that underlay Dossetti's disagreement over the Council's programme and tactics – a disagreement that, as quickly became apparent, set him apart not only from the intransigent minority but within the progressive majority as well.

Aquinas vs. Augustine

The final stages of the redaction of *Gaudium et spes* also revealed the sorts of disagreements within that majority that are illustrated in the figures of Chenu and Ratzinger and that, perhaps inevitably, appeared when, with the preparatory drafts rejected, the Council faced the question: what now? It was one thing to delegitimise the theological system that had guided the preparation of the Council; it was quite another to write texts that would reflect the positive and pastoral aims Pope John had set out in his opening speech. In the course of the elaboration of the texts, it is clear that there were differences within the majority now in charge of redacting the conciliar documents, even the ones on the Church *ad intra* but especially in those on the Church *ad extra*, to use the unfortunate division commonly invoked at the time. These differences inevitably reflected the theological background, training and interests of the theologians employed in the tasks, as is clear from the comparison of Chenu and Ratzinger.

Their differences may be traceable to the differences between a typically Thomist and a typically Augustinian epistemology and anthropology. Perhaps the analysis may be extended beyond these two men. Commenting on the much-reduced presence of St Thomas Aquinas in the final conciliar texts, Yves Congar remarked that, nevertheless, 'St Thomas, the *Doctor communis*, furnished the redactors of the dogmatic texts of Vatican II with the foundations and the structure of their thought.'[8] In Congar's mind, if with *Gaudium et spes* and *Dignitatis humanae* the Council had finally broken with 'political Augustinianism', it was because it achieved something similar to what the 'Albertine-Thomist revolution' had effected in the thirteenth century.[9]

Ratzinger, however, provided a different account of the Council's inspiration. In a generally negative paper written ten years after the Council began, he asked what theological and spiritual resources the Church had with which to face the Council's disappointing aftermath. The only hope lay, he thought, 'in those forces that really had made Vatican II possible and shaped it but that shortly thereafter had been overrun by a wave of modernity'. This was:

> a theology and a piety which essentially were based on the Holy Scriptures, on the Church Fathers, and on the great liturgical heritage of the universal Church. At the Council this theology succeeded in nourishing the faith not only on the thought of the last hundred years but on the great stream of the whole tradition in order thus to make it richer and more vital and at the same time simpler and more open.

He dismissed two other options: the post-conciliar progressivism that had arisen out of J. B. Metz's transformation of Karl Rahner's transcendental Thomism into, first, a theology of hope and, second, a political theology. This stream Ratzinger thought had lost its usefulness because of its uncritical surrender to vaguely Marxist analysis. As for the scholastic philosophy and theology defended by conservatives at the Council, Ratzinger said that it no longer played any role; in fact, he observed how rapidly defenders of a pedestrian scholastic theology had laid down their arms and surrendered to a vague modernism.[10] The omission of Thomas and the dismissal of the Thomist tradition in these remarks is notable, reflecting, one suspects, not only the state of Thomism at the time but also Ratzinger's personal and theological preferences.

These differences with regard to the theological inspiration of the texts of Vatican II suggest two lines of research which it may be useful to undertake for the history of Catholic theology in the twentieth century. The first is retrospective and concerns the nature of the theological renewal that prepared for Vatican II and which is often over-simplified today, as it was then by its critics, as 'la nouvelle théologie', the singular term suggesting a single stream. If almost all the leaders of that renewal agreed on the necessity of a *ressourcement*, it is also clear that they drew their chief inspirations from various sources. Louis Bouyer, Jean Daniélou, Henri de Lubac, Joseph Ratzinger and Hans Urs von Balthasar, for example, were far more at home in the mental world of the Fathers, the monastic theologians and the medieval neo-Augustinians than they were not only in the watered down neo-scholasticism of the modern era but also in the scholastic milieu and dialectical methods of St Thomas himself. While certainly not neglecting the Scriptures or the Fathers or the liturgical renewal, in contrast, Chenu and Congar were great admirers of Aquinas and of what Congar calls the 'Albertine-Thomist revolution', and with them may be linked in this respect men such as Karl Rahner, Bernard Lonergan and Edward Schillebeeckx who attempted a reconciliation of Thomism and the modern philosophical turn to the subject. Within the ranks of the leaders of the twentieth-century renewal of theology there were not insignificant differences; which were almost bound to appear in full force once the hegemonic power of neo-scholasticism was broken at the Council.

My second suggestion is more prospective. It is striking to note that after the Council it was among those who chiefly promoted the recovery of the patristic and monastic traditions who were most critical of what was happening in the Church and in theology in the wake of the Council. One may think of the often very critical and at times even bitter post-conciliar writings of Bouyer, Daniélou, de Lubac, Ratzinger and von Balthasar. While not uncritical of post-conciliar developments, the great promoters of Aquinas, such as Chenu, Congar, Lonergan, Rahner and Schillebeeckx, displayed a greater sense of balance, offered more careful analyses of the problems and more nuanced responses to them, and took up a challenge which they often compared in extent and seriousness to the one that faced Aquinas in the thirteenth century. Appreciation of St Thomas, of course, is not by itself the predictor of these differences in attitude, as the examples of Jacques Maritain and Étienne Gilson show. (But they, of course, were philosophers, not theologians.)

This line of research may be worth pursuing despite the fact that, as Gerald McCool has written, 'The history of the modern Neo-Thomist movement, whose *magna charta* was *Aeterni patris*, reached its end at the Second Vatican Council.'[11] Its place has been taken by a very diverse plurality of theological methods, no one of which has gained anything like the hegemony enjoyed by the unitary method of neo-scholasticism. This is not the place to attempt an inventory of them all. Within their often chaotic variety, David Tracy has offered a distinction,[12] which might usefully be considered, between a correlation-theology, the contemporary equivalent of Aquinas's engagement with Aristotle, illustrated in the work of Karl Rahner and Bernard Lonergan, and an epiphanic theology, the contemporary equivalent of a more Augustinian and Bonaventuran approach, illustrated in the work of Hans Urs von Balthasar and in '*der Positivismus des Glaubens*' [a faith-positivism], as Joseph Ratzinger calls it.[13] What is called 'post-modernity', with its critique of universal reason and of foundationalism and its insistence on the incommensurability of linguistically mediated worlds, is often considered to resemble the latter approach with its abandonment of the myth of pure reason and its insistence on the unbridgeable gulf that the Cross of Christ digs with regard to the very notion of rationality. In this line, Dossetti and Ratzinger would appear, at least temporarily, to have won the victory. One suspects, however, that Chenu would question whether this approach is faithful to the achievement of Vatican II.

Notes

1 This is a fuller version of my article 'What road to joy?', *The Tablet* (30 November 2002), pp. 11–12.

2 Giuseppe Alberigo, 'La Costituzione in rapporto al magistero globale del Concilio', in Guilherme Baraúna (ed.), *La Chiesa nel mondo di oggi: Studi e commenti intorno alla Costituzione pastorale 'Gaudium et spes'* (Florence: Vallecchi, 1966), p. 184n. Alberigo cited Joseph Ratzinger, 'Der Katholizismus nach dem Konzil', *Das neue Volk Gottes: Entwürfe zur Ekklesiologie* (Düsseldorf: Patmos, 1969), pp. 302–21 (316–17).

3 Gérard Philips, 'Deux tendances dans la théologie contemporaine: En marge du IIe Concile du Vatican', *Nouvelle Revue Théologique*, 85 (1963), pp. 225–38.

4 Joseph Ratzinger, *Die letze Sitzungsperiode des Konzils* (Köln: Bachem, 1966), p. 28; ET *Theological Highlights of Vatican II* (New York: Paulist Press, 1966), p. 148.

5 P. Hauptmann, 'Le schéma de la Constitution pastorale "De Ecclesia in mundo huius temporis"', *Études et documents*, no. 10 (25 August 1965), 11pp.

6 Ratzinger, *Die letze Sitzungsperiode des Konzils*, p. 30; *Theological Highlights*, p. 151.

7 Dossetti to Lercaro, 27 September 1965, published in *Per la forza dello Spirito: Discorsi conciliari del card. Giacomo Lercaro* (Bologna: Dehoniane, 1984), p. 254n.

8 Congar, 'La théologie au Concile', Situation et taches présentes de la théologie (Paris: du Cerf), p. 53.

9 Yves Congar, 'Église et monde dans la perspective de Vatican II', in *L'Église dans le monde de ce temps*, vol. III, (Paris: du Cerf, 1967), p. 31, where he adds in a note: 'This point about correspondence is, of course, one of those that allows good commentators to regard GS as profoundly Thomist in inspiration.'

10 Joseph Ratzinger, 'Zehn Jahre nach Konzilsbeginn – wo stehen wir?' in *Dogma und Verkündigung* (München: Wewel, 1971), pp. 437–9.

11 Gerald A. McCool, *From Unity to Pluralism: The Internal Evolution of Thomism* (New York: Fordham University Press, 1989), pp. 230. See Joseph A. Komonchak, 'Thomism and the Second Vatican Council', in Anthony J. Cernera (ed.), *Continuity and Plurality in Catholic Theology: Essays in Honor of Gerald A. McCool, S.J.* (Fairfield, CT: Fairfield University Press, 1998), pp. 53–73.

12 David Tracy, 'The uneasy alliance reconceived: Catholic theological method, modernity and post-modernity', *Theological Studies*, 50 (1989), pp. 548–70; see also John McDade, 'Catholic theology in the post-conciliar period', in Adrian Hastings (ed.), *Modern Catholicism: Vatican II and After* (London: SPCK; New York: Oxford University Press, 1991), pp. 422–43.
13 Joseph Ratzinger, *Einführung in das Christentum*, p. 32; *Introduction to Christianity* (San Francisco: Ignatius Press, 1990), p. 28.

8

Power and Powerlessness in the Church: The Chance for Renewal

Timothy Radcliffe OP

The greatest crisis which the Church in the United States has ever faced is about power: its use and abuse. The terrible scandal of sexual abuse by some members of the clergy is about power. The root of the problem is neither clerical celibacy nor the high percentage of gay priests, but the sexual immaturity of those who cannot cope with equality and who therefore seek relationships in which they can dominate. In the United States, the anger at this scandal of abuse has been vastly increased by the way that some bishops have reacted, since this has also been seen as an abuse of power. The anger is against a power that gives no account of itself to the People of God, in which the only accountability is upwards.

There is no simple relationship between the abuse of power by priests who sexually exploited minors and the structures of the Church. The vast majority of bishops and priests do not exercise power in a way that is abusive, and usually there is a profound respect for the dignity and freedom of the People of God. But such institutional structures mean that priests who are sexually and emotionally immature are not necessarily challenged to grow into maturity. These structures can provide a shelter from demanding relationships of equality. The crisis is also one of powerlessness. There is a crisis of leadership: bishops seem paralysed, caught between the Vatican and the media; priests often feel powerless given the lack of leadership of the bishops; and the laity feel powerless faced with an institution that does not empower them. It is as if the structure emasculates all attempts to find solutions. So we are faced with a crisis of power and powerlessness.

The accusations against priests of sexual abuse and against some bishops for covering this up have not been confined to the US. In England we have suffered some of the same traumas but less severely, because early on Cardinal Cormac Murphy O'Connor appointed the Nolan Commission and its recommendations have been widely implemented, so the relationship of trust between the bishops and the people has been largely undamaged. But the American crisis has focused our attention on issues that must be faced by the whole Church. How today should power be exercised in the Church?

Lessons from the New Testament

We can begin to look for a way forward by glancing at what the New Testament teaches us about power.

The Church was born in a crisis of power. At the Last Supper Jesus has lost control of his life. He has been sold by Judas to his enemies; Peter is about to deny him; his disciples are on the verge of fleeing. He will be imprisoned and killed. The Church begins in this moment of utter collapse. It is also the moment in which Jesus performs that most powerful gesture upon which our Church rests. He takes bread, breaks it and shares it saying, 'This is my body, given for you.' He shares the cup of wine as the foundation of the new Covenant.

We have nothing to fear from crises. The Church was born in one and is renewed through them; they are our speciality! Every Eucharist enacts the memory of the crisis of the birth of our community. We are living through a crisis today, but it is a comparatively minor one, compared with the Last Supper and others of our history. If we do not panic, it will bring life and renewal.

At the Last Supper the power of Jesus is exercised through his words. It is the power of meaning. It is not a brute or blind power but works at the level of significance. Jesus performs the founding sacramental act, and all the sacraments are symbolically powerful. St Thomas Aquinas says sacraments are *in genere signi*.[1] They are powerful through what they signify. If the Church has always related the exercise of power to the sacraments, then it is because power for Christians is inseparable from meaning, from word and communication. God created the universe through the speaking of a word.

This is hard for us to grasp since for the last few hundred years our imagination has been captured by a mechanical understanding of power. We have harnessed new forms of power to change the world: steam, electricity and nuclear power. We have reshaped our world with dams, roads and railway lines. Power equals force. God has been thought of as a mechanic or a clockmaker. The idea of power as meaning has become either incomprehensible or at best weak, something that happens in our heads rather than the real world. In the real world it is not ideas that are strong but the imposition of our wills.

Yet our world is changing. The old world of the industrial market, founded on the production and distribution of goods, is passing away. We are now entering a world in which what are mainly exchanged are information, signs and symbols. We are becoming members of the 'semiotic society'. What zings around the World Wide Web are not so much heavy things like cars and coal but concepts and culture and above all money. We live in a world that may understand sacramental power rather better than our immediate ancestors – though as a Church we are, as usual, rather slow in getting this point.

It follows that the Christian exercise of power cannot be unaccountable. It belongs to its nature that it gives an account of itself, because it is the speaking of a word of grace. Nicholas Lash writes that all governance in the Church is an act of teaching, 'set, from start to finish, at the service of our common apprenticeship in holiness and understanding'.[2] Discipleship is initiation into learning. A blind act of power would not only be unchristian. It would also be, in the deepest sense, ineffective, which is why in this crisis the Church is felt to be abusive of power but also powerless.

So the exercise of proper authority in the Church necessarily implies the engagement of our hearts and minds. There is no teaching, and so no act of Christian power, unless there is understanding. And this implies the asking of questions, the demanding of explanations, the raising of objections, the sharing of experience, the testing of arguments. Teaching is necessarily a process in which those who learn are actively engaged. As Aquinas wrote: 'If the Master decides a question simply by using sheer authorities, the hearer will certainly be left in no doubt that such and such is the case, but he will acquire no knowledge or understanding and will go away empty.'[3]

As Master of the Dominicans I sometimes took decisions that my brethren must have found incomprehensible. But in our tradition for someone to obey without understanding is not a good example of obedience: 'Brother John is wonderful, planting all those cabbages upside down just because he was told to.' Herbert McCabe OP wrote:

> Obedience only becomes perfect when the one who commands and the one who obeys come to share one mind. The notion of blind obedience makes no more sense in our tradition than would blind learning. A totally

obedient community would be one in which no one was ever compelled to do anything.'[4]

So clearly the ordained priesthood cannot be a caste that gives no account of its acts and life. It is at the service of meaning. It is a way of life that belongs to the articulation of a Word made flesh. And the Last Supper shows us that this is a Word that gathers into communion and throws down the divisions that divide human beings, the barriers between Jews and Gentiles, saints and sinners, and ultimately between the living and the dead.

The Last Supper transforms the Old Testament idea of holiness. God's holiness is no longer in separation from all that is impure and imperfect. This is a new covenant in which God's holiness is shown in the embrace of all that is unholy, and even that most impure thing of all, death. Holiness is shown in the scandal of a dead body on a cross. All this is made explicit in the letter to the Hebrews, where the high priest is shown dying outside the camp. 'Therefore Jesus also suffered outside the city gate in order to sanctify the people by his blood. Let us therefore then go to him outside the camp and bear the abuse he endured' (Heb. 12:12f.).

How can we understand the gap between this vision of power and priesthood and what many people experience in the Church today? It is tempting to blame it on centuries of power-hungry clerics who have betrayed the original purity of the gospel, as if all that is necessary is to return to the New Testament and wipe out the intervening two millennia of failure! That is tempting, but it would be both unjust and naïve. The renewal of the Church always occurs through a return to the gospel but during those two millennia the Holy Spirit has not been absent. She did not descend at Pentecost and then disappear. If she had, then what grounds would we

123

have for believing that we might do any better? Somehow the Church as it has evolved, with all its failures and distortions, must also teach us something of the nature of Christian power.

The Nature of Christian 'Power'

Christian power should always be part of the preaching of the gospel and so of the articulation of meaning. All that is said and done should speak of grace. But this never happens in a vacuum. Christian power is exercised in the context of the powers of this world. In some ways it inevitably becomes conformed to them, inculturated. In other ways it stands over against them, and is counter-cultural. Our beloved Mother Church as we know her today, with the power structures that shape her, is the fruit of two millennia of inculturation and counter-culturation. Of course, one person's inculturation is another person's betrayal; and one person's counter-culture is for a third unrealism!

All the institutions which are now most contested evolved under the dual pressure for the Church to conform to the powers of this world and to oppose them: a centralised institution in the Vatican; the naming of bishops by Rome; and a celibate clergy. All of these have certainly expanded because of the desire for clerical power. But they have also been the fruit of the resistance to other institutions that have wished to deprive the Church of freedom. The Church has battled against Roman imperial persecution, the Christian emperors, the feudal aristocracy, the Holy Roman Empire, the rise of the absolutist monarchies, the French Revolution, the nineteenth-century empires, and against Communism and Fascism. The Church is like an old warrior that has come to look in some ways like her foes. If the papacy has become like a monarchy, then it is because for centuries it fought monarchs. If the

Vatican sometimes looks like the Kremlin, it is because Communism for decades was seen as the Church's greatest foe.

In the struggle of the Church to remain free and counter-cultural, there have been four institutions that were seen as crucial. Two are contested today, one has passed away, and the other is alarmingly weak in the West.

First, the evolution of a centralised Church bureaucracy and the naming of bishops by Rome have been contested by secular powers ever since Constantine. The balance between the cathedral chapters, secular rulers and the papacy has swung to and fro. At the beginning of the nineteenth century the rise of empires and secular states had almost entirely deprived the pope of the power to name bishops. This was a profound threat to the freedom of the Church. Of the 646 dioceses of the Church, 555 were appointed by the State. The pope, as bishop of Rome, had the right to appoint only 24 bishops: in Russia, Greece and Albania.[5] When the Code of Canon Law was published in 1917 the pope claimed to appoint all the bishops.

Second, the celibacy of the clergy was deeply linked with the Church's struggle to remain free as a counter-cultural institution, especially from the time of the Gregorian Reform in the eleventh century, when dioceses and abbeys were threatened with appropriation by the feudal aristocracies. Urban II, Gregory's successor, boasted that the Church must be 'Catholic, chaste and free'.[6] Again, the absorption of the Church by the State and the loss of its freedom often went with attempts to abolish celibacy, whether in the sixteenth or the nineteenth centuries.

Third, for most of the history of the Church the papal states seemed central to the Church's freedom. Henry Manning, the future Cardinal Archbishop of Westminster, declared that the temporal power of the pope was the sign of 'the freedom, the independence, the sovereignty of the kingdom of God upon earth'. The papal states were 'the only spot of ground on which the Vicar of Christ can set the sole of his foot in freedom'.[7] They have turned out to be unnecessary.

Fourth, religious life has been a bastion of counter-culture. For the Gregorian Reform of the eleventh century, it was the monasteries – above all Cluny – which powered the resistance to feudal and royal power. During the Counter-Reformation and the struggle against the rising centralised power of the monarchies, then the Jesuits' obedience to the pope was crucial. Today religious life has become very weak throughout most of Western Europe.

My purpose in these superficial observations is not to justify the Church as it presently exists but to help us to understand the nature of the crisis that we now face and imagine how to move beyond it. There have been and always will be power-hungry clerics, but that is not a sufficient explanation for the present state of affairs, and so merely denouncing clericalism will not lead to renewal.

The Need for Undistorted Communication

If evangelical power is part of the preaching of a word of grace, then ideally it calls for what Habermas calls 'undistorted communication', communication undeformed by injustice, domination or exclusion. The most massive exclusion within the Church is that of women. I will not dwell upon that because it is obvious and frequently discussed. Instead I wish to focus on some forces in our society that are less obvious and yet which distort communication and so may deform Church power.

The Church needs spaces of undistorted communication. We need places where our attentiveness reaches across the divisions. These are sadly lacking. Even the Synods of Bishops are not really places of deep discussion. For there to be such places of clear communion within the Church, it is not enough to reflect upon the Church's institutions. We must think about the social and political powers at work within our society that might distort communication within the Church. What are the powers at work that make our power blind and dumb? For us to resist such deformation, then, the Church needs bases of counter-cultural resistance. The Church has become as she is because for two thousand years she has constructed such bastions of alternative ways of thinking and being. What does the Church need now if she is not to be sucked into conformity with the powers of the world?

If the Church has a highly centralised power structure, this is partly because most of her life she has been fighting other centralised powers, from the Roman Empire until the Soviet Empire. What are the structures of power within which the Church must now live and against which she must sometimes speak? Have we left behind the need for such a strong, centralised government?

Yes and no. We have entered the new age of the World Wide Web. Here power operates in a different way. It is not centralised but multifocal. It works not through rigid hierarchies, but through horizontal networks. As Scott Lash and John Urry write, we have moved 'from place to flow, from space to stream, from organized hierarchies to disorganization'.[8] To be empowered is to be connected to the web. Jeremy Rifkin wrote:

> The gap between the possessed and the dispossessed is wide, but the gap between the connected and the disconnected is even wider ... The great divide, in the coming age, is between those whose lives are increasingly taken up in cyberspace and those who will never have access to this powerful new realm of human existence. It is this

basic schism that will determine much of the political struggle in the years ahead.[9]

In many ways this new world may be hospitable to the Church. It may be more receptive to our sacramental way of thinking. The link between power and meaning is more understandable than when power was the centralised control of goods and armies. Its horizontal networks are closer to an understanding of the Church as a communion of local churches. Horizontal networks are more hospitable to a Trinitarian understanding of the Church than monarchical power structures. If the structures of the Church sometimes make us feel powerless, perhaps it is because as an institution we have hardly begun to move beyond that earlier monarchical world. We are like knights in heavy armour, weighed down with the arms of the past, unable to move swiftly in a new age when speed is key. We feel powerless because power no longer flows vertically through endless chains of command but horizontally around the web.

But it would be naïve to think of the World Wide Web as an innocent space in which the Church may flourish, freed from the tyrannies of monarchs. It is a field of communication that suffers from its own distortions. We must understand these if we are to imagine the renewal of the exercise of power in the Church. There are, at the very least, three interrelated powers that rule this world: still-centralised states, the power of money and the power of the media. How can the Church maintain its freedom in the face of these?

There still are strong states that threaten the freedom of the Church as they have done since the beginning. Think of China, home to a quarter of humanity; or Vietnam, North Korea and Zimbabwe. In all of these places the local Church needs the support of the whole Universal Church. The authority of the pope to name bishops is still deeply important in many places where otherwise state power might impose bishops who were docile to the regime. The Chinese authorities understood exactly what is at stake when they established the Patriotic Church, which acknowledges no authority outside China. The Pope understands this equally well, having grown up in the Soviet Empire. The old battle is not entirely over.

There is only one empire left: the United States. There is a profound nervousness about the future evolution of the States. There are signs of a retreat from involvement in international institutions such as the United Nations and the rejection of international agreements, such as the Kyoto Protocol. There was the refusal to ratify the International Criminal Court. The war in Iraq lacked legitimacy in the eyes of most of the world. As a Church we are concerned by power within the Church that gives no account of itself. But the Church in America must operate within a power structure that increasingly gives no account of itself to the rest of the world.

American Catholics may be called upon to be increasingly counter-cultural, to stand against the tide in their own country. To endure they may need deep links with the wider Catholic Church, a universal communion that includes the poorest and most powerless. When war began to look imminent, the Dominican Leadership Conference of the United States issued bumper stickers that said, 'We have family in Iraq'. The Synod of the Americas was intended to fashion new links between the local Churches of North and South America. Not much has changed. We need to be inventive of new channels of communication, new institutions, which will keep the American Church firmly rooted in its Catholicity. This is a challenge in a country in which only 7 per cent of its citizens even have passports.

The Dangers of Riches

What principally circulates on the World Wide Web is money. From the beginning, the Church has had to resist the distortions of wealth in its use of power. The Eucharist is the archetypical Christian act of power, but already in 1 Corinthians Paul complained that the rich use it to display their wealth and humiliate the poor. For most of the history of the Church the laity have been trying to get their hands on the wealth of a rich Church; now it is rather the clergy trying to get their hands on the wealth of the laity! In the modern Church the power of benefaction is immense, especially in the United States. I have seen Stations of the Cross in which every station proclaims the recognition of a benefactor: 'Jesus falls for the third time. In memory of Henry Jones Jr III'! How far does the flow of wealth threaten to deform power in the Church today? In the 1980s the American Episcopal Conference published *Economic Justice for All*. This infuriated many wealthy conservative Catholic businessmen. How far do they mute our voices?

What nurseries of counter-culture does the Church need to resist the deformation of wealth? In the eleventh century, it was the monasteries that provided the focal points of resistance. Celibate monks were free from the networks of blood and hereditary wealth. Monks cannot found dynasties to hand on bishoprics to their children. Does celibacy still offer us this freedom? There is a real discussion to be had here. In a class-ridden society such as Britain one could argue that celibacy does dislocate us from social structures and gives us a real freedom to cross social boundaries. But I would not be completely convinced that clerical culture is always an island of resistance to the seductions of a comfortable life.

Religious life has always offered pockets of counter-culture. In the eleventh century it was principally in terms of celibacy.

In the thirteenth century, the mendicant friars embraced poverty. Faced with the absolute claims of sixteenth-century monarchs, the Church needed the absolute obedience of the Jesuits. Certainly today we need communities of religious who radically embrace poverty. Cardinal Etchegaray made a plea at the end of the Synod of Religious for a real option for poverty. The weakening of religious life in the West is undermining this traditional oasis of other ways of being.

How Can We Be Present in the Media?

The third great power in the World Wide Web is the media: the newspapers, the TV channels, the cable networks such as CNN. These are the powerful barons of today. They shape the world in which the Church speaks. The question is not whether we are in favour or against the media, but how we are to be present in them.

Since the eighteenth century the media have reflected a new form of power – public opinion.[10] The media calls all institutions to account. In many ways the present crisis would never have happened if it had not been for the media, especially the *Boston Globe*. We can hardly protest at this since it belongs to the nature of Christian power that it gives an account of itself. But who calls the media to account? The problem of unaccountability is far more radical than simply that of the Church but of governments, wealth and the media.

The media present us with the challenge of inculturation and counter-culturation. Our preaching must take form within this world, while resisting certain distortions and deformations. First of all there are only certain sorts of stories that are told in the media. Typically these stories conform to a plot that is confrontational. It is structured by the opposition of Left and Right, of tradition and progress. It reflects the origins of the media in the eighteenth-century Enlightenment, with its broadsheets and coffee houses. Catholic thought can make little sense of this dichotomy between tradition and progress. For us what has been handed down to us is the source of endless renewal and challenge. You can no more fit Catholicism into the narrow confines of Enlightenment dichotomies than you can squeeze a fat man into a thin man's suit.

The second challenge is that the world of the media is one of total disclosure. But we Christians live by a language that is haunted by silence. At its worst this is the silence of denial in the face of this crisis. At its best it is the silence that comes from living at the edge of language. How, in the world of 'The Bitch in the House' can we keep alive ways of thinking and talking which retain an acute sense of what cannot be said? As Barbara Brown Taylor wrote: 'In a time of famine typified by too many words with too much noise in them, we could use fewer words with more silence in them.'[11] The world of the media requires of us a profound creativity. We need to create new institutions that sustain other ways of being and thinking, other forms of meaning. *The Tablet* has been a fine example under John Wilkins's guidance.

The Church was born in a moment of powerlessness. In this crisis Jesus was the creative, speaking, transforming Word. The idea of an unaccountable blind and brute power makes no sense for a Christian. All exercises of power are linked to proclamation. When we look at the present crisis of power and powerlessness within the Church then, like Jesus, we need a creative response. It is necessary but not enough to look at the functioning of the institution. We need to do that but more. We must look at the world in which our words of faith must be spoken. We must see how the powers of this world form and deform communication. It includes the exciting new world of the World Wide Web, with its horizontal structures and its celebration of sign and symbol. It still means facing centralised states, the forces of wealth that operate even within the Church, and the power of the media. To face all these we need faith, hope and love, but also creativity. We need the grace of God's infinite fertility. If we may be so blessed, then the Church will be renewed by this crisis.

Notes

1 ST III 60.1
2 'Authors, authority and authorization', in Bernard Hoose (ed.), *Authority in the Roman Catholic Church: Theory and Practice*, (Aldershot: Ashgate, 2002), pp. 59–71 (68).
3 *Quaestiones Quodlibetales*, Qn 9, art. 3, quoted by Lash, 'Authors', p. 65.
4 *God Matters* (London: Chapman, 1987) p. 228.
5 Eamon Duffy. *Saints and Sinner: A History of the Popes* (New Haven and London: Yale University Press, 2001), p. 274.
6 Ibid., p. 128.
7 Ibid., pp. 290f.
8 *Economies of Signs and Space* (London: Sage, 1994), p. 323.
9 *The Age of Access: How the Shift from Ownership to Access Is Transforming Modern Life* (London: Penguin, 2000), p. 13.
10 Cf. Charles Taylor, 'Liberal Politics and the Public Sphere', *Philosophical Arguments* (Cambridge, MA: Harvard University Press), pp. 257–88.
11 *When God is Silent* (Cambridge, MA: Cowley Publications, 1998), p. 113.

9

Religious Freedom: The Limits of Progress

Michael Walsh

John Wilkins has never made any secret of the fact that he owed to Vatican II his decision to be received into the Catholic Church. Nor has he disguised his concern that some at least of the achievements of Vatican II which so attracted him to the faith have been eroded, especially during the pontificate of Pope John Paul II. As I attempted to demonstrate in a piece written for the series John commissioned to mark the fortieth anniversary of the Council's opening, that erosion is to be found in the the Pope's understanding of Religious Liberty as it is enshrined in Vatican II's Declaration on Religious Freedom, *Dignitatis humanae*.[1]

Perhaps no document produced by Vatican II occasioned so much debate, both within the Council and outside it. That *Dignitatis humanae* was accepted at all by the Council fathers was one of the main reasons why Archbishop Marcel Lefebvre eventually went into schism. The Church had finally embraced, he argued, the principles of the French revolution: *liberté, egalité* and *fraternité*. The first was endorsed by *Dignitatis humanae*; the second by *Lumen gentium*, the Dogmatic Constitution on the Church with its teaching on collegiality; and the third by its Decree on Ecumenism, *Unitatis redintegratio*.

To be fair, the dissident Archbishop had a point. There is a long tradition in papal encyclicals of freedom of conscience being roundly condemned. For Pope Gregory XVI, writing in *Mirari vos* of 1832, it was the 'false and absurd, or rather the mad principle'. It was 'one of the most contagious of errors; it smooths the way for that absolute and unbridled freedom of thought which, to the ruin of Church and State, is now spreading everywhere'. And it brought in its train, he went on, the idea of 'liberty of the press, the most dangerous liberty, an execrable liberty, which can never inspire sufficient horror'.

Gregory was responding to the situation in the papal states, recently restored to the papacy by the Congress of Vienna. His remarks went largely unnoticed, and would in any case not have been too far out of keeping with the policies of most of the European regimes of his day. It was far different when Pius IX repeated the same sentiments in his *Syllabus of Errors* of 1864 (cf. propositions 77–9). Not only were many states by that time well on the way to democracy, but the papacy itself had come to be a much more significant institution, despite – or possibly because of – the virtual disappearance of the papal states. Traditionalists and Ultramontanes welcomed the *Syllabus*: many others did not. The distinguished Bishop of Orléans, Félix Dupanloup, proposed that one should distinguish two situations. In one, the Catholic Church was de facto the only religion in a state (the thesis). In such a situation the condemnation of religious toleration stood. In most countries, however, there was a plurality of religions (the hypothesis). In these religious toleration was acceptable.

It was scarcely a very satisfactory argument: that religious toleration was acceptable but only where Catholicism was not the majority faith. But for the time being it cooled tempers. One would have thought, however, that the Vatican might have learnt from the protests which followed the *Syllabus*. It did not. In *Immortale dei* of 1885 Leo XIII recalled *Mirari vos* with obvious approval and returned to the theme three years

135

later in *Libertas praestantissima* which expressly described liberty of worship as opposed to the virtue of religion.

The Twentieth Century

And that was how matters stood for the next three-quarters of a century, reiterated in Pope Pius XII's allocution *Ci riesce*.[2] The Church was pragmatically prepared to accept religious freedom where there was no alternative. But in Catholic eyes this was an undesirable state of affairs. The ideal situation was one in which a state professed Catholicism as the religion of its people, and would not tolerate the public expression of other forms of faith. 'Public' in this context is important: there was a general acceptance that, regrettable though it might be, people could be so misguided as to follow other versions of Christianity, or profess Judaism or Islam. That was a matter for their own consciences, and in their own consciences, it was agreed, they could not be coerced. The problem only arose when Protestants or others wanted to give public witness to their faith.

The best-known concrete example of this cast of mind was Spain in the decades following the Civil War. Even when, in the aftermath of the Second World War, when General Franco felt the need to reduce the isolation of his country and produced a new quasi constitution or Charter, the *Fuero de los españoles*, article 6 still read:

> The profession and practice of the Catholic religion, which is the religion of the Spanish State, will enjoy official protection. No one will suffer any interference because of their religious *beliefs*, nor in the *private* exercise of their devotions. No *public* ceremonies or processions [*manifestaciones externas*] will be permitted except those of the Catholic religion [*my italics*].

136

Pius IX could not have put traditional Catholic teaching more clearly.

The Spanish Evangelical Church, which had feared something worse, was enthusiastic, hailing the Charter as a great opportunity. The door, said an article in one of their periodicals, was beginning to open. Their enthusiasm was misplaced. The apparent guarantee of private Protestant church services led to attacks on Protestant chapels in Madrid, Seville and elsewhere. In the Seville incident, on 4 March 1952, a party of young men wearing, according to a report in the *New York Times*, the badge of a Catholic organisation, broke into a chapel while the minister was in the middle of a service, and poured petrol over pews and hymn books, setting them alight. The Spanish clergyman tried to stop them and was injured.

In the event little damage was done, but because the property was British owned, questions were raised in the House of Commons. On 19 March the Ulster Unionist MP for County Antrim, Professor Sir Douglas Savory, asked the Foreign Secretary whether he was aware of the incident, and would he protest. He had a list of nine such attacks, said Savory, including a recent incident in Orense where a Protestant chapel was blown up by a bomb.[3] These incidents took place at the height of what came to be known as Spanish national Catholicism, though it was not until after Vatican II that the term itself was first used – by the theologian Gonzalo Ruiz in an interview he gave to the French journal *Témoignage Chrétien*.[4] What national Catholicism stood for is well described in a curious mimeographed booklet, published in Madrid in 1955 by the 'Diplomatic Information Office'. The anonymous author of the Preliminary Observation (all the several contributions are anonymous) wrote:

The fact is that Protestantism in Spain has never had enough solidity to be raised to the rank of a problem. The

137

incontestable truth is that it has never been able to take root in our soil, despite all the efforts made to introduce it.

Some may say that it has been hampered by the public authorities, civil and ecclesiastical. And that is the great truth of Spain and the ultimate reason for Spain's manner of being. For in driving it out of her orbit, the public authorities have only acted as an instrument of the general conscience. It has not been the work of a Government, but the repugnance of the whole Spanish people, manifested throughout centuries ...

The reason must be sought in the innermost nature of the Spanish manner of being. Catholicism is an immanent characteristic which goes together with Spain herself.[5]

The premise of national Catholicism, therefore, was the identification of the faith with Spanish nationalism. Although Franco had his critics among the Spanish bishops – Cardinal Pedro Segura, said that the Generalissimo's title of *caudillo* meant 'captain of thieves'[6] – others, such as the Archbishop of Madrid, Leopoldo Eijo y Garay, thought his title to govern was little short of divine right.[7] Whatever their personal feelings, most, if not all, bishops regarded him as the providential saviour of the nation, who had prepared the way for a re-evangelisation of the Spanish people. They, and especially Segura, supported the harassment of Protestants. In 1948 the committee of metropolitans, the precursor in Spain of the bishops' conference, issued a letter condemning freedom of religion as an error and rejecting criticism from abroad of their, and the State's, stance on the privileged position accorded to Catholicism.

Among these critics were many in the United States. The oppression of Protestantism in Spain in particular was a significant hindrance to efforts towards ecumenism. It produced much hostile comment, aired most effectively by Paul Blanshard in

American Freedom and Catholic Power. It was first published in 1949 and went through several editions – including one in England where it was simply called *Freedom and Catholic Power.* The First Amendment to the US Constitution stated that 'Congress shall make no law respecting an establishment of religion, or prohibiting the free exercise thereof; or abridging the freedom of speech, or of the press; or the right of the people peaceably to assemble ...' As Blanshard and many others pointed out, this was in explicit contradiction to the traditional doctrine on Church and State, and on religious freedom, which was to be found in the teachings of the popes, as these have been quoted above. Spain was the example which most clearly demonstrated that such teachings were still in force, wherever the Catholic Church was in a position to insist upon them.

Tension on these issues was heightened by John F. Kennedy's bid for nomination as the Democratic Party's candidate in the US presidential election. The Jesuit theologian John Courtney Murray (1904–67) undertook to address the issues of Church and State, and of religious liberty. He sought to reconcile traditional Catholic teaching with the US project, an enterprise which though it had the backing of some of the US bishops was vigorously opposed by others. His opponents had the backing of Cardinal Alfredo Ottaviani, Secretary of the Holy Office, once the Inquisition and now the Congregation for the Doctrine of the Faith, and their campaign effectively led to his silencing. It was during this 'silence' that Murray published *We Hold These Truths: Catholic Reflections on the American Proposition*,[8] a collection of previously published articles. In the Foreword Murray wrote:

> The American Proposition makes a particular claim upon the reflective attention of Catholics in so far as it contains a doctrine and a project in the matter of the

'pluralist society', as we seem to have agreed to call it ...
The Catholic may not, as others do, merge his religious
and his 'patriotic faith, or submerge one in the other. He
must reckon with his own tradition of thought, which is
wider and deeper than any that America has elaborated.
He must also reckon with his own history, which is
longer than the brief centuries that America has lived.
At the same time, he must recognize that a new problem
has been put to the universal Church by the American
doctrine and project in the matter of pluralism, as stated
in the First Amendment. The conceptual equipment for
dealing with the problem is by no means lacking to the
Catholic intelligence. But there is the obligation of some
nicety in its use, lest the new problems be distorted or
the ancient faith deformed.[9]

The delicacy with which Murray debated the issues did him
little good in the eyes of many in the USA and in Rome.
He was, he told his friends, 'disinvited' from attending the
opening session of Vatican II as a *peritus*, or theologian to
the Council.

Religious Liberty at the Council

When the Council was first announced, Willem Visser 't Hooft,
the General Secretary of the World Council of Churches
(WCC) from its inception in 1948,[10] expressed considerable
interest, and in particular the hope that it would lead to a
change in the Church's attitude to religious freedom. Pope
John XXIII had established within the Roman Curia a Secretariat for Promoting Christian Unity (SPCU) under the inspired
leadership of Cardinal Augustine Bea with (the future Cardinal) Johannes Willebrands as its secretary. It was created

expressly as a preparatory body for the Council and at the very first plenary meeting of the SPCU six topics of future work had been outlined, of which the fourth was 'theological questions', including religious freedom. In response to the WCC's express concern, therefore, it began work on a schema (a preparatory paper for the Council) on religious freedom. This caused considerable irritation to Cardinal Ottaviani as head of the central Theological Commission (TC), who thought that drawing up schemata was the TC's job and no-one else's.

The TC then produced its own version, *The Duties of a Catholic State with Regard to Religion*. It was all the SPCU had feared. It was, indeed, basically a text prepared in 1958 by the Holy Office and which, but for the death of Pius XII, might very well have been published as it stood. It basically reiterated the thesis/hypothesis approach put forward by Dupanloup nearly a century before. According to the TC's document it was the duty of the civil authority to support the Church, giving it complete freedom and independence and excluding anything which might inhibit it in its mission, in particular the spread of false doctrines. This duty was limited to those states which were wholly Roman Catholic: in non-Roman Catholic states complete religious freedom was expected to be the norm. When the SPCU criticised this document the Holy Office accused it of having had too much contact with non-Roman Catholics.

Religious freedom appeared first of all as chapter 9 of the draft schema on the Church.[11] Critics of religious freedom stuck to their arguments despite the fact that, as Schillebeeckx pointed out, it left the Roman Catholic Church at odds with the United Nations' Declaration of Human Rights. These critics insisted, in a time-honoured phrase, that 'error had no rights'. But rights, Schillebeeckx replied, adhere to an individual, not to an abstract concept such as truth or error. It might be correct to say that one had no right to err, but that could only apply to knowledge of absolute truth, and human beings do not have access to that. People act on truth as it is known, and about that there is plenty of room for disagreement.

It is quite possibly true to say that no document of the Second Vatican Council was more fought over. Paul VI mentioned it when he addressed the United Nations on 4 October 1965. A Spanish curial Cardinal, Arcadio Larraona, Prefect of the Congregation of Rites, wrote a harsh note to Paul VI in the name of a group of Spanish bishops trying to prevent religious freedom being voted upon. Many Latin Americans and some Italians sympathised with the Spanish contingent. They were vigorously opposed by the US hierarchy. It is often said that it was the efforts of John Courtney Murray which eventually persuaded the Council to accept *Dignitatis humanae*.

For Murray, at the insistence of Cardinal Francis Spellman, the Archbishop of New York, and despite the opposition of the Apostolic Delegate in Washington, Archbishop Egidio Vagnozzi, had after all been made a *peritus* at the beginning of April 1963. By that time a text on religious freedom had been written, though it was not yet approved as suitable to be put before the conciliar fathers. It was still part of the schema on the Church: it only became a separate Declaration a year later. In between times there had been an effort on the part of the document's opponents to have it removed entirely from the agenda of the Council, and only the efforts of the US bishops kept it there.

Fr Hermínio Rico, editor of the Portugese Jesuit journal *Brotéria*, who has made a detailed study of the conciliar debate and Murray's role in it,[12] distinguishes two opposing groups. One group argued, as did the 12 bishops who wrote to the Pope on 10 September 1964, that there was a lack of theological precision in the text; that it was confused; that it was contrary to the declarations of the Magisterium in the nineteenth century (as indeed it was) and that it was replete with notions that successive popes had warned the faithful against (as indeed they had). The other group were determined to break away from Dupanloup's thesis/hypothesis approach. But they, too, were divided. Some wanted a pastoral document, recognising the fact of religious liberty, but providing no theological justification for it. This approach was quickly rejected. There was then a division between those, many of them French, who wanted the arguments to be based on theological and scriptural grounds, and those (like Murray) who based their arguments on political philosophy and on the natural law – though, according to some critics of Murray, a rather old-fashioned notion of the natural law.[13]

This taxonomy occurs in an important article by Murray, 'The problem of religious freedom', which appeared in the American Jesuit quarterly *Theological Studies* in 1964.[14] The purpose of the article, he says, is to state the two views which were being expressed at the Council in order to institute a dialogue between them. The first view is that of the Council fathers who wish to uphold the traditional stance that the 'public powers' may never authorise the public existence of religious error. The only reason for doing so, he said, was, according to the first view, the need to maintain public peace: 'The political criterion, whereby the issue of the possibility of intolerance, or the necessity of tolerance is to be decided, is the public peace.'[15] In contrast, 'the second view rejects the opinion that public care of religion necessarily means, per se and in principle, a political and legal care for the exclusive right of truth'. The role of the public powers is simply to guarantee religious freedom.[16] 'No public official is empowered by virtue of his public office to enquire into the theological credentials of any religious body'; the State may only intervene when, and

143

if, public forms of religious expression violate public order or public morality, or the rights of other citizens.[17] Murray rejects the idea of a 'confessional State' (such as Spain) because this is to confuse society (that is, the people who do indeed have a duty of worship) with the State. This distinction between State and society, he argues, was not available to Leo XIII; moreover, talk of a *princeps*, as was commonly done to indicate the source of sovereignty, abets the confusion of Church and State, because a prince is towards his subjects as a paterfamilias towards his children – and this gives him greater power to impose religion than does authority in a constitutional state.

It was his intention, John Courtney Murray remarks at the end of his article, to present the two views fairly and objectively. He hopes he has done so but leaves it to others to judge. In truth it is not difficult to see from his careful account which of the views he favours. He was conscious that proponents of the first view had the tradition of papal teaching, right down to Pius XII, on their side. But he insists he himself stands in the tradition, so long as it is understood that the tradition is a developing one.

Though his own contribution to the final text of *Dignitatis humanae* was important, Murray afterwards insisted that Mgr Pietro Pavan played an even greater part.[18] Certainly there were remarks in the Declaration with which he could not have been wholly at ease – there is an allusion, for instance, to the confessional State, and occasional suggestions that there was an obligation to seek the truth. He did not think the latter argument satisfactory, because an obligation to seek the truth, or to follow one's conscience even if erroneous, does not, he believed, imply a concomitant duty on the State to let you do so. His position, though argued for with great care and complexity in the article in *Theological Studies*, was fundamentally a simple one: the State has no competence in religious matters. All that it can do and must do is to ensure the individual may practise his or her religion. The issue for him was one of freedom.

There is no space here to recount the debate at Vatican II. It seemed at times that the Declaration, which had originally started life as chapter 5 of the paper on ecumenism, would be lost. The Spanish bishops were opposed, and set up a special commission to examine the nascent Declaration. Also opposed were several Latin American hierarchies, especially that of Colombia. Even Paul VI seemed to be bending. The US bishops, however, kept up their pressure in the aula and in the corridors of the Vatican. The Protestant observers were on tenterhooks – one can sense the swing from hope to despair to (final) euphoria in the *Vatican Diary* of the American Congregationalist Douglas Horton.[19]

Since the Council

When the Council was over the Spanish bishops were faced with the task, not just of implementing the Church's new stance on religious liberty, but of formally breaking with the Franco regime. In the week of 13 September 1971 there was a meeting in Madrid to seal the fate of national Catholicism. One of those responsible for drawing up the document on Church–State relations commented: 'Never did I dream that a gathering of priests and bishops in Spain would pronounce so clearly on the need for the Church to be independent of the State.' The end of the integralist State, however, did not come easily. There was an attempt, orchestrated in Rome by some members of Opus Dei and at least one conservative-minded

Spanish Jesuit to undermine the conclusions of what had become known as the Asamblea Conjunta. The attempt, which ostensibly came from the Congregation for the Clergy, presided over by the American Cardinal John Wright, back-fired, and served only to strengthen the position of the Arch-bishop of Madrid, Cardinal Enrique y Tarancón.[20] It seemed as if, even in the heartland of the confessional State, the battle for religious freedom had been won.

But 40 years on, questions have arisen. In my *Tablet* article discussing Pope John Paul II's understanding of religious free-dom, referred to above, I made mention of David Schindler, the editor of the American edition of the quarterly *Communio*. To quote Joseph Komonchak, there are those in the United States who believe 'that the American political experiment is in fact incompatible with Catholic teaching because it is con-trary to the ideal of the Catholic confessional state'.[21] I do not know that Schindler would go so far, but in his *Heart of the World, Center of the Church* he argues that Murray's argu-ments for religious liberty have significantly contributed to what he sees as the growing secularism at the heart of US society.[22]

Not that Schindler would deny religious liberty. It is – as almost everyone recognises – a fundamental human right. Human rights are notoriously difficult to defend philosophi-cally – the Declaration of the Rights of Man, Jeremy Bentham famously said, was 'nonsense on stilts'. And even though, prag-matically, we are ready to concede them, it is again difficult to produce a list. Yet, as the American moral theologian Lisa Sowle Chaill has argued, it is possible to claim that religious liberty, at least as a central component of personal integrity, is the one human right which may be claimed as absolute.[23] At least on that Pope John Paul II would be happy to agree.

Notes

1 'U-turn on human rights', *The Tablet* (14 December 2002), pp. 7–9.

2 *Acta Apostolicae Sedis*, 45 (1954), pp. 788–9. 'Not to inhibit [error]', said the Pope, 'by means of public laws and coercive methods can nevertheless be justified in the interests of a higher and a greater good.' But, he insisted, error has no right to exist and certainly none to be disseminated.

3 At this point Dennis Healy intervened: 'Is the right honourable and learned gentleman [Selwyn Lloyd] aware that that is the normal condition in another country? Is he aware that a Catholic church in Willowfield, Belfast, was bombed, and that the friends of the honourable Member for Antrim [Savory] were not prosecuted?'

4 At least according to José Andrés-Gallego and Anton Pazos in their *Histoire religieuse de l'Espagne* (Paris: Du Cerf, 1998), p. 153.

5 Op. cit., p. 10.

6 Cf. William J. Callahan, *The Catholic Church in Spain, 1875–1998* (Washington, D.C.: Catholic University of America Press, 2000), p. 395. Segura was Primate of Spain from 1927 until his expulsion in 1931. He returned from exile in 1937 as Archbishop of Seville.

7 Ibid., p. 390. It was Eijo y Garay who first granted juridical status in the Church to that institutional embodiment of national Catholicism, Opus Dei.

8 New York: Sheed and Ward, 1960.

9 Ibid., pp. x–xii.

10 He retired after the Council, in 1966.

11 This account largely follows that to be found in G. Alberigo and J. Komonchak (eds), *The History of Vatican II*, vol. 3 (Louvain: Peters; Maryknoll, NY: Orbis, 2000). In his opening address to the Council, *Gaudet ecclesia*, John XXIII had sided with the modernisers on religious liberty, which he specifically mentioned: 'It pains us that we sometimes have to listen to the complaints of people who, though burning with zeal, are not endowed with an overabundance of discretion or measure. They see in modern times nothing but prevarication and ruin. They keep saying that as compared with past ages, ours is getting worse, and they behave as if they had learned nothing from history, which is

nonetheless a teacher of life, and as if in time of the preceding ecumenical councils everything presented a complete triumph for Christian ideas and Christian life and for a rightful religious liberty. But we think we must disagree with these prophets of doom, who are always forecasting disaster, as though the end of the world were imminent.'

12 *John Paul II and the Legacy of 'Dignitatis humanae'* (Washington, D.C.: Georgetown University Press, 2002).

13 Cf. David Schindler, *Heart of the World, Center of the Church* (Grand Rapids, MI: Wm B. Eerdmans; Edinburgh: T&T Clark, 1996), pp. 75–6. That Murray was a rather old-fashioned Thomist is, by all accounts, fair comment.

14 Vol. 25, pp. 503–75. Rather oddly, this is not cited, at least not directly, by Rico in the bibliography to his book.

15 Ibid., p. 509.

16 Ibid., p. 522.

17 Ibid., pp. 527 and 530.

18 Cf. Richard Regan, 'John Courtney Murray, the American Bishops, and the Declaration on Religious Liberty', in John Ford (ed.), *Religious Liberty: Paul VI and 'Dignitatis humanae'* (Brescia: Istituto Paolo VI, 1995), pp. 51–66 (53).

19 They were published in four volumes, 1964–66, by the United Church Press of Philadelphia and Boston.

20 I wrote about this at the time: 'Spain on the move', *The Month* (June 1972), pp. 163–7, 175.

21 'Interpreting the Council', in Mary Jo Weaver and R. Scott Appleby (eds), *Being Right* (Bloomington, IN: Indiana University Press, 1995), pp. 17–36 (26).

22 Schindler, *Heart of the World*, pp. 43–88.

23 'Towards a Christian theory of human rights', *Journal of Religious Ethics* (1980), pp. 277–301. I am grateful to Dr Catherine Cowley of Heythrop College for the reference.

10

Where Does Catholic Social Teaching Go from Here?

Clifford Longley

How well has the post-conciliar Catholic Church lived up to the great charter of contemporary Catholicism proclaimed in the opening of *Gaudium et spes*? The Second Vatican Council's brilliant synthesis of Catholic teaching and its application to the modern world declared:

> The joys and the hopes, the griefs and the anxieties of the people of this age, especially those who are poor or in any way afflicted, these are the joys and hopes, the griefs and anxieties of the followers of Christ. Indeed, nothing genuinely human fails to raise an echo in their hearts.

It seemed to launch a new and exciting age of Catholic humanism, and to provide a bridge to other philosophical or religious systems with which the Catholic Church previously had difficulties. *Gaudium et spes* was made possible, first, by the change in Catholicism's internal intellectual climate as a result of the pontificate of John XXIII and, secondly, by the sense of self-confidence that the fathers of Vatican II began to feel as the Council moved towards its conclusion in 1965. By the time this so-called Pastoral Constitution was taking on its final shape, the bishops of the world had risen far beyond the constraints imposed on them at the outset by the Vatican

Curia in 1962 (which by this time was fighting John XXIII tooth and nail). This was to be their most mature achievement, not least because no such document was envisaged at the outset and hence the Curia had produced no draft of one.

The immediate inspiration for *Gaudium et spes* surely belonged in Pope John's momentous encyclical *Pacem in terris* in 1963. This encyclical showed a radical confidence in reshaping the tradition in the light of the changed demands of modernity, for instance, in its bold incorporation into Catholic teaching of the hitherto suspect, not to say downright heretical, notion of human rights. If *Gaudium et spes* had illustrious parentage, it too grew to have healthy offspring of its own, in the shape of the series of papal documents, encyclicals and others, that developed the tradition of Catholic social teaching far beyond the boundaries set by the two normative works up to that point, the 1891 encyclical of Leo XXIII *Rerum novarum* and its 1931 successor *Quadragesimo anno* of Pius XI.

The children of *Gaudium et spes* therefore include *Populorum progressio* of 1967, which unequivocally put Third World development at the centre of attention; *Evangelii nuntiandi* of 1975, which reconciled work for social justice with the preaching of the gospel; and the remarkable series of discourses on social teaching from Pope John Paul II, of which the principal items were *Laborem exercens* (1981) on the dignity of work, *Sollicitudo rei socialis* (1987) which took on board some of the radical insights of liberation theology such as 'option for the poor' and 'structural sin'; and *Centesimus annus* (1991), which updated the tradition's critique of capitalism and distrust of economic liberalism.

These last three may yet prove to be John Paul II's most enduring contribution to the Church, not least because the need for a theoretical basis for limiting the demands of capitalism in the name of morality and humanity was made all the more urgent by the collapse of communism. Up to that point capitalism was challenged by an external as well as an internal Marxist enemy, and if its cruelties became unbearable the people had, or at least felt they had, some other ideology to turn to. That factor was itself a major constraint on capitalism's tendency to overdo itself in the name of profit. But without such a threat, the world seemed to belong to markets, which alone were henceforth to be sovereign. It needed another 'ism' to stand up to it, and the Church had one available.

Certainly the affinities between the Pope's updated brand of Catholic social teaching and the 'third way' theories of Tony Blair and Bill Clinton were much remarked upon. Essentially their common proposition was that it was legitimate (and often necessary) to limit free-market capitalism in the name of the common good. The obviousness of this, in the minds of many, rather obscured the fact that theoreticians of the free market often talked as if it was king, not to say God, and interference in market forces was as near as a right-wing economist could get to the concept of blasphemy. And such ideas held strong sway, inside the United States, in Britain under Margaret Thatcher, and in the world at large once they became the prevailing orthodoxy in the IMF and World Bank. The international debt relief campaign prior to the millennium (organised under the banner of Jubilee 2000) was a striking example of the idea that pure economics sometimes had to give way to the overriding demands of humanity, and it is no coincidence that the inspiration for the campaign originally came from Pope John Paul II.

The Common Good

The concept of the common good was characteristic of Catholic social teaching throughout the twentieth century, as was explicit in the statement published by the Catholic bishops of England and Wales in 1996, *The Common Good and Catholic Social Teaching*. That document follows *Pacem in terris* and all subsequent papal texts in accepting and applying a doctrine of human rights; but went slightly further than they did in assuming that democracy itself was the universally desirable, if not ultimate, form of social and political organisation. Together, human rights and democracy plug what was otherwise a nagging gap in Catholic thinking about the common good. Provided right-wing dictators like Mussolini or Franco could claim to be acting to promote the common good, their political systems seemed beyond the reach of Catholic social teaching to criticise. Certainly they would have been prepared to tame the excesses of capitalism. But they would also have been prepared to place the common good above such humanistic considerations as human rights. The suppression of freedom in the name of the common good seemed to have been made papally acceptable, and Catholic dictators in Europe and South America particularly seemed content to proclaim as a political creed something like 'The Common Good – *c'est moi.*'

Clearly modern post-conciliar Catholicism, chastened by the experience of the Second World War, could not give comfort to right-wing dictators, whatever had been its role before the war. But once democracy and human rights became canonised as fundamental values of the Catholic tradition, the door was closed on Fascist leaders and parties who had claimed the sanction of Catholicism while continuing to oppress their people. Indeed, the proper and natural home of the Catholic social teaching tradition henceforth seemed to be, as in the West, liberal democracy. The common good became part of a trilogy, alongside democracy and human rights, on which civilised societies depended. Thus in theory a government was elected by the people to pursue the common good, and if it failed to do so it would not be returned to office; one of its primary functions, implicit in upholding the common good, was the defence of human rights, which could not therefore be set aside when the common good demanded it. (That is not strictly true, as for instance in war time, but the principle was clear enough.)

Nevertheless there remain tensions between the inner dynamic of liberal democracy and the requirements of the Catholic tradition as so far developed. Democracy in particular gives weight to majority opinion above all else, even natural law. Democracy itself is morally neutral. It is a method of making decisions, not a basis for making them. Of course, constitutional democracies have tended to limit what could be achieved by the sovereign will of the people by enshrining codes of human rights, which stood both below and above the law as made and remade by legislatures.

But this merely transferred the debate to other areas, such as who was to be covered by the guarantees of human rights and who was excluded from them. Were human embryos to be regarded as possessing inalienable rights, for instance, or could states legislate to allow their destruction by abortion? Were refugees, asylum seekers or even terrorist 'prisoners of war' covered by human rights guarantees, or did they first have to achieve citizenship? The idea that some rights depended on citizenship and some were universal and inalienable seemed logically necessary; but who was to say which was which? And what happened when, as was inevitable, rights collided? Was there a hierarchy of rights, some absolute and some conditional? The Catholic Church's adoption of human rights language did not offer much insight into how to handle a conflict of rights whenever it arose. This remains an area requiring more development in human rights theory, which is not helped by the tendency for debates about human rights to be taken over by lawyers.

In his study *Catholic Social Teaching, 1891–Present*[1] the American moral theologian Charles E. Curran drew attention to the limitations of the concept of the common good as applied to nation states per se. He makes a distinction between the tradition that Pope John Paul II seems to be following, of seeing the common good as the business of the State, and the more limited scope of the role of government that appeared to be envisaged in the Second Vatican Council's Declaration on Religious Liberty. The American Jesuit philosopher John Courtney Murray is often hailed as the architect of that declaration, which was pushed for above all by the Catholic bishops of the United States (waking from what had been until that point the sleep of the theologically illiterate).

The Worlock Diary

It is intensely fascinating – and entirely within the traditions of Catholic journalism – to see a glimpse of the process at work, through the eyes of one who was at the Council. Derek Worlock, later Bishop of Portsmouth and Archbishop of Liverpool, who was present as a *peritus* at that stage, also reported regularly on the progress of Vatican II for the BBC. His radio account of the battle over the declaration of religious liberty written for public consumption, vivid though it was, was far surpassed by his private diary entry, not published until after his death.

> You remember [Worlock said in his BBC report of the matter] that it came up for discussion a year ago and there was widespread disappointment when, at the end of the second Session, the document was not put to a vote because there was no time. Last September saw it back again, though cast in rather different form, and

after the debate it went back to the Secretariat for Christian Unity, charged with its revision in the light of opinions expressed at that time.

For some time now there have been those strange Roman rumours about strange Roman happenings which always seem to add up to delay ...

Once more there seemed to be an attempt to block it. The report in his secret diary is even more dramatic than the version he gave the public:

Thursday 19th November will rank as one of the historic dates in the history of the Council both for good and for evil ... I had spent the early part of the morning at my desk at the College and didn't arrive at St Peter's until just on eleven o'clock. By then things were really boiling. It seems that before the debate started Cardinal Tisserant, acting in the name of the Commission of Presidents, announced that the Council would not after all proceed to a vote on Religious Liberty. The previous day he had said that a preliminary vote would be taken to see whether or not the Fathers wanted to deal with this matter during the Third Session. But today he announced that a sufficient number of persons had asked for more time to consider this new Declaration that the President decided to postpone further discussion on the matter until the next Session.

One recognises of course that the new Declaration did contain a certain amount of new matter but the manner in which this thing was handled was certainly sufficient to set off the furore which followed. It seems that as soon as Cardinal Tisserant had made the announcement, Cardinal Meyer got up from the table and went to Cardinal

Tisserant to dissociate himself from this announcement made on behalf of the Presidents. His objections were obvious and clearly and quickly spread into the Aula itself. Nearly all the American bishops trooped out of the benches and moved into the side aisles and they were followed by a large number of others who were gravely disturbed at what was reckoned to be a calculated attempt by possibly the Curia and some of the right-wing conservatives – the Spaniards were named, though they subsequently denied that they were responsible – to block this contentious matter once again. When I arrived it was in time to find the American *periti* setting up shop in the side aisles where they had large sheets of papers and bishops were queuing up, one behind the other, to sign a petition to the Holy Father to beg that a vote be taken on this Declaration this Session. It was an incredible sight. The story went round that in order to prepare the petition, one of the *periti* had slipped into the office and pinched Felici's typewriter. [Archbishop Felici was head of the council secretariat.]

Be that as it may, the organisation of this protest petition was remarkably efficient, even though one could regret the vehemence with which the whole matter was being tackled. It soon became clear that the majority of the bishops present were prepared to sign this petition but could anything be done about it? Meantime Bishop de Smedt had been called to the microphone in order to read the *Relatio* for the Declaration, even though it was not to be voted upon. This of course was just the opportunity that was needed for high drama. Bishop de Smedt started off by saying that it was with feeling that he introduced the Declaration – and here he changed his text from 'which is now to be voted upon' to 'which is now not to be voted upon'. As he began his impassioned plea for a matter which is thought generally to be closest to his heart, his full flights of oratory soared around the ceiling of St Peter's. He sobbed, his voice broke, and he delivered the most impassioned appeal that I have ever heard, even from a Continental. As he was drawing towards his end, those bishops who had been out in the side aisles all packed in round the President's table and the Confession of St Peter's and looked down the Aula to where this lone figure was standing in a state of high emotional tension.

To an Englishman it was all rather embarrassing but there is no doubt that the cause was served by this Continental oratory on this occasion. Archbishop Heenan told me afterwards that he squirmed as he listened to his friend but I do not think that it was a put-up performance: he really felt as he sounded. Finally he regained control of his voice as he reached the end of his text. In a complete monotone, which was the more effective in that it followed after the high oratory of the earlier parts of the *Relatio*, he quietly said that the Secretariat for Christian Unity had finished with this document and passed it to the Co-ordinating Commission some three or four weeks ago: I forget the exact date which he mentioned. It seemed that nothing had happened about it until a short time before and then it had been suggested that the Vatican Press, which has to do all the printing of the official documentation for the Council, had become absolutely jammed up with the various documents which had to be given to the Fathers. He left it quite open as to whether one accepted this story or not and he merely gave the date on which the document had reached the Fathers, earlier in the week. Then with great deliberation he said:

'Let us pray at this moment for the guidance of the Holy Spirit in an issue which is of supreme importance to the Church.'

There was thunderous applause, quite the loudest I have ever heard in St Peter's, and after a while one realised that it was going to take a long time before it died down. When eventually it showed some sign of flagging, it rose once more from the far end of the Aula and it became evident that what had started as applause for a feat of oratory had now turned into a positive attempt to pass the document by acclamation. Cardinal Meyer was standing in the side aisle with some of the other American bishops and the atmosphere was quite electric. On several occasions the Moderators tried to break in over their microphones but the applause did not cease. In fact it continued for about four and a half minutes, so far as I could time it, but when at last it did die down Cardinal Döpfner, the Moderator, called the first speaker for the debate on the remaining document of the Sacrament of Matrimony.

Once it was realised that the Presidents had carried the day, the atmosphere changed from one of exhilaration to one of acute bitterness and disappointment. Cardinal Meyer went back to the Presidents' table, clearly in two minds as to what he should do. He was beckoned once more to the side and I saw Fr Molinari, an Italian Jesuit and a very good man, advising him quite straightly that he should take the petition directly to the Holy Father. Word evidently reached Cardinal Ritter and Cardinal Léger, both of whom left their places in the Aula and came down to join Cardinal Meyer. The petitions were brought in by the *periti* from the various parts of St Peter's and Cardinal Meyer rolled them up and put them under his arm. It was reckoned that there were over 800 signatures already and later that day we were told that the number had risen to over 1,000. It was a straight request for a vote of some kind on the Declaration before the Session stopped.

As poor Cardinal Gilroy laboured away, almost without anyone seeming to listen, on the subject of Matrimony, the three cardinals with some other bishop whom I could not recognise in attendance walked slowly across behind the Confessional and away up the stairs towards the Holy Father's apartments. I could not help wondering what would have happened had the cardinals walked the whole length of St Peter's before making their way out to the doors to go to the Pope. I fancy that half the bishops would have stood up and gone with them. Perhaps it was as well that they didn't but even so it was a moment of great tension and drama: something which one is unlikely to see again ...

Rome buzzed all that day with the excitement of the morning and not without reason. Some of the *periti*, notably Mgr Osterreicher, could be seen after the morning Congregation giving a full account to the press and inevitably the thing was blown to fantastic heights in the press reports which followed the next day. (When I got back to London I found this incident described widely as a 'punch-up' which it certainly was not.) But there is no doubt that it was all very regrettable and, though one must question the policy of Cardinal Tisserant and the General Secretariat in the decision which they made, there was little evidence of approval of the bitter vehemence of the American bishops. They seem to think that they have a corner in this question of Religious Liberty but I suppose that they were so disappointed in their failure to take the document home at the end of the Second Session that this third delay was just the last straw.

After supper that evening I heard that old Cardinal Heard [semi-retired judge of the Rota, resident at the English College in Rome] wanted to see me about the Jews and I could not think what was worrying him. I had heard earlier that the Pope had summoned all the Cardinals that evening in order to discuss with them the troubles of the morning but I could not think that this had anything to do with Heard's message. When I got to see him he told me that he thought that there had been some row with the Jews in the Council that morning and what insufferable people they were! He asked me if I would let him have any documentation that I might have on the subject as apparently the Pope had asked him to give a judgement about it in the morning. I was very perplexed and I went back to my room and looked over my notes and came to the conclusion that he must be thinking of the row over Religious Liberty, which of course had nothing directly to do with the Jews.

I checked with the Archbishop [Heenan] who was of the same opinion and then went back to Heard. Gently I tried to tell him that it was not a Jewish issue which was at stake. I told him what had happened in the morning and it seems that the old man was so deaf that he had very little knowledge at all of what had gone on. What made it even more remarkable was that during the audience with the Pope, the Holy Father had apparently decided to refer the protest received from the American bishops to the Tribunal of which Heard was a member. They were to meet before the following morning's session and give judgement on the point which had arisen.

It was a most extraordinary anticlimax to all the high-level excitements of the day that I should have found myself trying to explain to the old judge just what it was all about. So far as I could I remained dispassionate but it was remarkable how, once the old man had got a picture of what had happened, the judge in him returned to the surface. He said that it was a perfectly simple issue. Had Tisserant (whom he profoundly dislikes) exceeded his powers in giving the decision which he had given? If the powers were provided for in the *Regolamento*, then so far as the Tribunal was concerned, they had merely to give judgement that the Presidents had acted within their powers.

If the Presidents had no such powers in the *Regolamento*, then they would have to go back on it the following day. It was quite clear cut in the old man's mind and I left him looking into his red-bound copy of the Rules. The question of whether or not the decision was a good one or a bad one did not enter Cardinal Heard's mind. The fact that a thousand bishops might have wanted to vote on the matter was again beside the point. It was a question of the Presidents staying within the powers. It might have been interesting had he been able to determine whether the President of the Commission of Presidents, i.e. Cardinal Tisserant, had adequately consulted the other members of his Commission. But this did not seem to have entered into the matter and I had little doubt which way the decision would go the following morning.[2]

The Declaration on Religious Liberty was indeed safely passed by the Council in its fourth and final session the following year, 1965. It was the singular – and momentous –

contribution of American Catholicism to the universal Church, with implications that have by no means been exhausted.

The Role of the State

The idea that the common good is the business of states belongs, in Murray's analysis, to the age when Church and State were usually deemed a unity – a form of political 'monism'. It is a legacy, though he does not say so, of the *ancien régime* mindset still often encountered in the Vatican in the 1960s, which resented being asked to adjust to the post-1789 world. This monist polity was usually said to be according to the teaching of Aquinas, to whom Pope John Paul II in particular was wedded. This teaching said that the State had a duty to align its laws with natural law, and so to promote the good of its citizens. In the spiritual sphere this had to mean steering them into the arms of the Catholic Church and keeping them there.

Thus a state had no duty to provide tolerance for other religions or denominations, which were likely to distract people from the claims of the One True Church. Where a state could do so, therefore, it had to enact laws which, for instance, prevented divorce, prohibited the sale of contraceptives or outlawed abortion. It had no duty to enact laws to protect freedom of worship or even freedom of speech where religion was concerned. The exception would be where the Catholic population was in a minority, when attempts to impose Catholic teaching by law in the moral sphere were ill-advised because it was impractical. Thus a Catholic 'monist' (or *intégriste*) political system had no scope for dissent or conscience: error had no rights.

The American example sat very uncomfortably with that doctrine, as Murray well knew. He therefore argued for a more restricted role for the State than this all-embracing concern for the common good, confining it instead to the preservation of public order. Promoting the common good remained the priority of society and the duty of all its members – but society and the State were no longer to be seen as coterminous. His definition of public order owed a good deal to the American experience, where 'big government' had always seemed to be some sort of public enemy in a way quite unfamiliar to Europeans. Nevertheless the notion that the common good is the duty of society rather than just the State has a distinctly modern ring to it, as nations all round the world tried on the clothes of Western-style liberal democracy without necessarily having emerged from a condition where State and society were one. It left scope for the 'unofficial' or 'voluntary' sector, for all the small and big platoons of private or public initiative that constitute the intermediate institutions of civil society. Indeed, commerce and industry too, being largely in private (that is to say non-government) hands, were also planted in that area of society which was not directly organised by the State.

This issue has a direct bearing on one of the thorniest constitutional issues of the modern age, namely how to organise the government of a secular society without making it aggressively 'secularist' and therefore anti-religious. This either–or is hard to escape – either religion rules the roost, or it is pressed to the very margins of concern. What is insufficiently developed is a theology of religious and moral pluralism, showing how religion can remain as important as its adherents can make it, but without either suppressing the rights of others or being suppressed in turn. This is the handicap, in the post-modern world, of the meta-narrative – a theory which embraces everything. The English constitutional solution to this dilemma would seem to run along the lines of 'Don't ask theoretical questions, just get on with it', but as such, that is hard to export. In any event, proposals for the disestablishment of the Church of

England or even for an English republic would still require an answer to these State–Church questions. How is a secular society to be genuinely plural and not secularist? Can the State remain officially indifferent to religion while society continues to take it seriously? Or does indifference by the State lead to indifference by society?

The American example could be cited on either side of this debate. Its apologists describe the American nation state, as a result of the 'separation of Church and State', as secular. In the late eighteenth-century sense, that it has no established Church, that is true. (It is important to remember that various member 'states' of the USA such as Massachusetts and Connecticut actually had established Churches both before and after the Revolution and even after the adoption of the 'secular' federal constitution in 1789.) But the ideology of 'Americanism' is permeated through and through with religious insights and ideas which can be traced directly back to the colonial founders, whether Puritan and republican in New England or monarchist and Episcopalian in Virginia. In that sense the American project can be described as a complete synthesis of Church and State (cleverly disguised as the opposite): America is itself a 'Church', with its own creed, its own worship, even its own initiation ceremonies. One of the flaws in Murray's depiction of the American Church–State 'separatist' solution as a model to be universalised was his failure to see that God was inextricably present in the American social and constitutional woodwork, not detached from it.

John Paul II

Curran's thesis, in his review of Murray's success at Vatican II, was that Catholic teaching under John Paul II remained in captivity to the unexamined assumption that the common good and the responsibility of the State were one and the same. He relates this in part to the fierceness of the Pope's own opposition to abortion, and his determination to insist on a complete ban on it enforced by the criminal law. (A Polish pope may even have had in mind contemporary Church–State tension in Poland over this issue.) Certainly, the notion that Catholic politicians cannot promote, and Catholic electors may not vote for, anything that relaxes the prohibition on abortion was a regular theme of the American Catholic bishops in their interventions in public debate. They had failed to follow the logic of the declaration they (or their predecessors) had so vigorously campaigned for in the Second Vatican Council. This was, in Curran's view, a consequence of regarding it as still the responsibility of the State to promote the common good and all it entails, and not just regarding public order as the outer limit of the functions of government.

To follow the latter course would reduce the vexed question of abortion to a public order issue: to what extent is it conducive to public order to prohibit or to allow abortion? That in turn presupposes that individuals in society might, if they were aggrieved by too lax or too strict an abortion law, become a threat to public order. To relieve that threat the law would be moved in the appropriate direction until it achieved a new equilibrium of maximum public tranquillity, minimum threats to the peace. But this means that to change the law all that would be necessary would be to threaten violence. That does not seem a very healthy basis for law-making in a democratic society (though insisting that the law follows exactly the requirements of Catholic moral teaching on this point is not particularly helpful either).

For some reason, possibly the fact that the current situation is set by a judgement of the Supreme Court and not by a vote in Congress, the abortion issue festers in America in a way it hardly still does in Europe and elsewhere. Perhaps this is because Murray's solution – confining the State to upholding public order, leaving the common good to be the responsibility of society (defined as larger than the State) – has already implicitly been adopted without fuss elsewhere in the West, with only Americans still worrying away at it.

But without a theoretical basis for this pragmatic adjustment, it must remain unstable and liable to give way under pressure. It is clear that non-American Western societies are pluralist in theory but deeply unhappy at some of the apparent consequences. Should Western tolerance of Muslim beliefs and customs in the name of pluralism extend to allowing Muslims to practise polygamy, for instance? Should it extend to allowing Muslims to promote female circumcision (notwithstanding that most Muslims in the West would deny it is a practice required by the faith)? Should Muslims who regard all things Western as Satanic (while living in the West all the same) be allowed to behave accordingly towards Western institutions? Should they be allowed the freedom of speech, for instance, to encourage terrorism in the name of Islam (provided, in the name of public order perhaps, that they do their terrorism elsewhere)? Or is it the job of some non-Muslim authority or other – the police, the courts, Parliament – to decide what is or what is not compatible with the Muslim faith, allowing this but prohibiting that? And how does this differ from Pope John Paul II's insistence that state law should follow Catholic teaching on abortion and other moral issues? If Muslims cannot have their way on, say, polygamy, why should Catholics have their way on abortion?

The issue is sharpened for Catholics by the fact that Muslims also see the State and society as coterminous – at least in the Muslim ideal. They have their own concept of the common good, but its basic principles are those of the Koran rather than Catholic social teaching. How is this mutual incompatibility to be resolved?

These dilemmas are not far below the surface in recent debates about the 'place of God' in the new constitution of the European Union. Formal recognition of such a place implies that religious teachings may from time to time cross over from the private sphere, where most religious activity resides most of the time, to the public sphere, where they may influence public policy. Lack of such recognition (it was feared by some) might amount to a constitutional declaration that religion must stay in the private sphere. In fact, of course, in a democracy electors may be influenced by whatever they want to be influenced by, including their own religious faith or lack of it. What some European framers wanted, it seems, was an aggressive separation of Church and State in the American theoretical mould – though without the implicit background of a national religious ideology like Americanism.

Curran, following Murray, sees the Vatican II Declaration of Religious Liberty as an important plank of social teaching, even though it is not normally regarded as belonging to that corpus at all. But as long as Catholic social teaching is treated as being concerned with all 'common good' issues rather than purely economic ones, it clearly does belong. The same should be true of Catholic teaching about, say, criminology and penal reform; and must be true about the just war tradition, where a state's responsibility to the common good looms large. But a theology of war and peace does raise a challenge to the common good tradition of a different kind, a challenge also raised by issues such as terrorism, genocide, asylum and refugees, and global environmental concerns.

The Catholic philosophy of politics that says its aim is to advance the common good begs the question: what is the limit of the community whose common good is under consideration? The tradition tends to be uncritically applied to a post late-nineteenth-century world where the political unit is the nation state, and that determines the scope of the common good. While in the process of acting on that automatic assumption, the Catholic tradition also contradicts it. The duty of solidarity, which Pope John Paul II weaves into the concept of the common good, takes its force from the dignity of common humanity, not from shared citizenship or national identity. Similarly a Catholic doctrine of human rights cannot be confused with a doctrine of local citizenship rights, for human rights pre-exist any notion of the sovereign nation state. For instance, a refugee seeking entry to such a state has the same human rights as one born into it. An Afghanistani Taliban prisoner held in indefinite detention without trial in Guantanamo Bay has the same human rights as the President of the United States, notwithstanding the tendency of American ideology and practice to treat non-Americans as almost a species of sub-humanity where human rights are concerned.

The Murray/Curran approach of regarding the envelope of Catholic social teaching as wider than purely economic issues, important though they are, is surely right. Indeed, *Gaudium et spes* seems to follow the same line. Its opening words ought to be regarded as stretching the task of Catholic social teaching to embrace all that is human – sharing, analysing and addressing 'the joys and the hopes, the griefs and the anxieties of the people of this age, especially those who are poor or in any way afflicted'. It is a big undertaking. And as a mission statement for Catholic journalism, it would be hard to beat.

Notes

1 Charles E. Curran, *Catholic Social Teaching, 1891–Present* (Washington, D.C.: Georgetown University Press, 2002).
2 Extract taken from Clifford Longley, *The Worlock Archive* (London: Geoffrey Chapman, 2000), pp. 196–201.

11

The Scientific Search for the Soul

John Cornwell

Before the Second Vatican Council there was a tendency in some Catholic traditions of spirituality to stress the dualistic nature of the human person: a distinction between body and soul. Underpinned by various notions, it was widely believed that souls and bodies were composed of two quite different kinds of stuff: mortal material stuff that could be measured and non-material immortal stuff that was spiritual. The spiritual stuff accounted for the more interesting things of which human beings were capable: free will, love, the exercise of the intellect, imagination and consciousness itself. The asocial consequences of such thinking were as inevitable as they were deleterious.

Dualism of this sort was certainly not new to the modern period, and can be found, for example, by implication, in the severe nostrums of the *Imitation of Christ*, written in the fifteenth century, but still popular in the late 1950s, which counselled: 'Whenever I go abroad and mix among men, I return home less a man.' The assumption was that an individual soul was capable of a relationship with God that could be funnelled straight 'upwards', as it were, with no reference to others, no acknowledgement of one's social being. One of the advantages of substance dualism, of course, was the simplicity of its explanation for the intermediate afterlife: what happens to us between death and the resurrection of the body; the body goes to its grave while the spiritual, separable soul, wafts off to heaven, purgatory or to hell; the infant unbaptised to limbo.

Vatican II's pastoral constitution on the modern world, *Gaudium et spes*, confirmed the error of substance dualism by emphasising early and uncompromisingly that 'though made of body and soul, man is a unity'. This is no novelty in Christian thought: the Council of Constantinople IV (870) taught that, while the soul is sometimes distinguished from the spirit, the Church teaches that this distinction does not introduce a duality into the soul. Through his very bodily condition, moreover, continues *Gaudium et spes*, 'man sums up in himself the elements of the material world'. At the same time, the social nature of personhood is stressed: 'Life in society is not something accessory to man himself: through his dealings with others, through mutual service, and through fraternal dialogue, man develops all his talents and becomes able to rise to his destiny.'

Theoretical underpinning for the unitary nature of personhood, the embodied soul, of course, has a long pedigree: back to Thomas Aquinas, and ultimately to Aristotle who saw the soul as the 'form' of the body. There are sturdy antecedents for the unitary nature of the human person, moreover, in Judaic anthropology, pervasive in Christian Scripture. It was early modern theorising, in fact, which introduced the quasi-scientific explanation for dualism associated with Descartes – a spiritual substance dwelling within a material, mechanical body, linked by a part of the brain known as the 'pineal gland' – alienating, at the dawn of the Enlightenment, the individual subject from nature and the universe, with far-reaching consequences.

We can see, as Fergus Kerr has eloquently argued in his *Theology after Wittgenstein*, the philosophical inadequacy of dualisms down the ages for Christian theology. Meanwhile, cognitive scientists, several decades later than philosophers of mind (such as 'no-ghost-in-the-machine' Gilbert Ryle) have been attempting to explain the nature of the mind–brain relationship on a non-dualist basis (with the notable exception of the late Sir John Eccles). But has science yet produced an account that would satisfy Christian philosophy? With Aquinas as a necessary yet not sufficient guide, the challenge for Christian philosophers of mind in the post-conciliar era has been to make connections with new developments in cognitive science (the combined disciplines of psychology, neurobiology, artificial intelligence, neuroscience). The urgency of the task, moreover, is recognised by the conciliar imperative (also emphasised in *Gaudium et spes*) to distinguish between the 'order of persons' and 'the order of things'. To what extent, then, does recent science provide a basis on which to confirm the embodiment of the soul, without doing violence to moral agency, imagination, and the dignity and social nature of persons? What is new brain science telling us about human identity?

Human Identity: The Lessons from Science

Amid a vast number of cognitive science research programmes the most ambitious and relevant to the above questions focus on the nature of human higher-order consciousness. What processes in the brain and the central nervous system account for the sense we have of looking out at the world from the secret theatre of the self? What accounts for your uniquely personal experience of the sight and scent of a rose? That raging toothache – agonising for you and nobody else? Seeing the point of a *New Yorker* cartoon? Or sensing a pang of angst at the contemporary condition? Moral and social behaviour, a sense of worthy and unworthy actions, artistic expression, aesthetic appreciation, imagination – all involve an account of personhood that crucially includes conscious awareness, conscious autonomy, both in oneself and in others. The importance of discovering the link between our physical brain states and consciousness needs no special pleading, for consciousness lies at the very heart of what it means to be human. In the Western tradition consciousness is the very eye of the human soul.

Scientists' neglect of consciousness through much of the twentieth century seems at first sight strange. The neuroscientist Eric Kandel wrote somewhat ineptly in the preface to his 1985 edition of *Principles of Neuroscience* that 'one of the last frontiers of science, perhaps its ultimate challenge, is to understand the biological basis of mentation'. But why, at that time of writing, had neuroscientists been so laggard in a century marked by the huge strides in most other scientific explorations of nature?

In the first place it was the very vulnerability and vast complexity of the brain that kept researchers at bay. They did not have the tools or techniques to enter the living cortex without devastating what they explored. This had not daunted the hubris of those cognitive scientists who believe that real brains are as dispensable to the study of thinking as feathers are to aerodynamics (widely known as 'functionalism'); hence some researchers in the field of artificial intelligence were optimistic about replicating human 'mentation' with silicon and circuitry. Some even believed that the day would come when humans would download their minds into suitable software and so initiate an immortal existence. Such schemes, widely publicised in the early 1980s, have proved disappointing to date.

By the late 1980s, however, the prospects for cognitive science were transformed by advances in neuroscience and neurobiology. Just as the invention of the telescope and the discovery of mathematical physics gave rise to new ways of understanding the Universe, so rapid advances in non-invasive brain imaging and techniques of measuring at a micro level the activity of individual neurons, receptor sites and neurotransmitters revolutionised the exploration of the brain and the central nervous system.

At the same time, the increased power of computers enabled researchers to test their theories with ever more sophisticated models. After a century in the doldrums, neuroscience was, in its own estimation, on a voyage to the final frontiers of science.

But the idea that the 1990s would be special to brain research was due not solely to the inspiration of academic science. A crucial economic and social impulse came from the pharmaceutical industries which announced a new age of rationally designed brain drugs with cure-alls for everything from depression to Parkinson's disease. On 1 January 1990, the lobbyists were rewarded with a joint resolution of the House and Senate of the United States to designate the 1990s the 'Decade of the Brain'. A principal stated reason behind the initiative was the official estimate that some $350 billion was being lost to the US economy each year through brain-related ills, including depression, Alzheimer's and the consequences of aggressive behaviour (which alone attracted grants of $500 million for neurogenetic research in 1994).

The promise of major social and medical advances was driving the momentum and direction of investment and funding in cognitive science. But even as the discipline was being fêted in anticipation of a host of social and medical benefits, there were growing expectations, evident in proliferating symposia and published academic papers, that neuroscience had a significant role to play in the Holy Grail of Kandel's 'basis of mentation'.

Through the 1990s there appeared a new genre of 'mind–brain' or 'soul' books to explain the rapid advances and new theories to a non-scientific reading public. To mention just a few: Daniel Dennett's *Consciousness Explained* (1991), John

Searle's *The Rediscovery of the Mind* (1992), Gerald Edelman's *Bright Air, Brilliant Fire* (1992), Francis Crick's *The Astonishing Hypothesis: The Scientific Search for the Soul* (1994), Ian Hacking's *Rewriting the Soul* (1995), Paul Churchland's *The Engine of the Soul* (1995). It soon became obvious, as these works filled the bookshops, that scientists and philosophers of mind, despite agreeing at many points on the elucidations of neurobiology, were not about to agree on anything like a single theory or account of personhood.

The Problem of Consciousness

There were profound disagreements, to begin with, over the definition of consciousness itself, leading to fundamental clashes over prospects for a consensus on other crucial issues. The British philosopher Colin McGinn, for example, argued in his *The Problem of Consciousness* that consciousness was resistant to explanation in principle and for all time; while the American philosopher of mind Daniel Dennett countered that a complete explanation not only lay ready to hand but also would soon be exemplified by the construction of a conscious machine called COG at MIT (COG, to date, has not yet erupted into consciousness). Consciousness, the self, in Dennett's view was a delusion. Borrowing a notion popularised in literary theory, he likened human identity to a series of 'multiple drafts'.

The nub of the divide, however, was the issue of methodology itself, which brings us to the second difficulty that faced scientists keen to explore the mind–brain problem: the prospects for solving consciousness by means of reductionist science. Could reductionism, by which scientists come to understand phenomena by examining their most reducible physical aspects and processes, solve anything so elusively holistic and phenomenological as the mind–brain, soul–brain relationship?

Students of consciousness inclined to sympathise with this scruple began to talk about the 'hard problem' and the 'easy problem' in order to highlight a central paradox. While acknowledging that reductionist science would make progress in solving the so-called 'easy' problems – accounts, for example, of the mechanics of the neurophysiology of vision – the 'hard problem' of consciousness, the phenomenological problem, what it feels like to be a subject, would persist. The Australian philosopher of mind, David Chalmers, author of *The Conscious Mind: In Search of a Fundamental Theory*, puts the 'hard problem' like this:

> Often work [on consciousness] addresses what might be called the easy problem of: How does the brain process environmental stimulation? How does it integrate information? How do we produce reports on internal states? These are important questions, but to answer them is not to solve the hard problem: Why is all this processing accompanied by an experienced inner life?[1]

There was nothing particularly new, in the mid-1990s, about this separation of the 'hard' and the 'easy' problems of consciousness; philosophers like Thomas Nagel and John Searle had done much to popularise the conundrum in the 1970s, warning against easy solutions, or definitions, that fail to get to grips with the central riddle: which, put bluntly, is how does one explain subjectivity by means of purely objective descriptions? What seemed new by the late 1990s, however, was the vehemence of the confrontation between those who recognised the authenticity of the 'hard' problem, and those who seemed to think that it was illusory, destined to somehow simply fade and vanish in the cold light of reductionist knowledge of the processes of the brain and central nervous system. Also new

were indications that dualism was making a fitful come-
back under the banner of difficult physics. First there was the
Oxford mathematician Roger Penrose, who contended that
consciousness might be explained by quantum physics in the
brain (the action of myriad 'microtubules' in cytoskeletal
structures of neurons). Then David Chalmers gave notice of
what he called a psychophysical solution, a non-reductive
theory of consciousness that would stem from basic laws of
nature as yet unknown. For many philosophers of mind, reared
on the influence of Gilbert Ryle, the positing of quantum
physics, or a new kind of physics, as an explanation for the
'hard problem' looked like a surrogate ghost in the machine.

Closed vs. Open Theories

But amid the assorted warring theories, accompanied by
private-language insults – 'silly reductionist', 'surrogate mys-
tic', 'spooky-stuff dualist' – it became clear that there were
basically two approaches emerging, which can be described as
the 'closed theories' versus the 'open theories'. Identifying these
separate approaches may be of some help to Christian philosophers in deciding how science might come to the aid of a
unitary description of body and soul.

Two Nobel prize-winning scientists who have invested
heavily in neuroscience as a means of understanding the mind–
body relationship are Francis Crick and Gerald Edelman.
Contrasting and comparing their methods and conclusions is
instructive. In his *Astonishing Hypothesis: The Scientific
Search for the Soul*, Francis Crick has declared, unexception-
ably, that if we are to make headway in our understanding of
consciousness, we have to start somewhere: best, therefore, to
begin with something physically observable and definite rather
than get lost in foggy abstractions. Hence Crick focuses on the

fact that when higher animals appear to be aware of an object their neurons oscillate in unison at the rate of 40 cycles per second. The finding fits with his conviction that the brain is just a very complicated computational machine or device.

Crick's leap from this modest proposal to his published hypothesis is, indeed, astonishing. 'You, your joys and your sorrows,' he writes, 'your memories and your ambitions, your sense of personal identity and free will, are in fact no more than the behaviour of a vast assembly of nerve cells and their associated molecules.' That phrase – 'no more than' – is key. In the vulgarised shorthand that finds its way into general mass media acceptance, it translates into: the mystery of human consciousness is no more than 40 hertz oscillations!

Crick's reasonable protestation that his strategy is confined to empirical data, merely as a secure starting point, is hardly corroborated by a subtext that rumbles through his book like bottled thunder. For Crick's astonishing hypothesis is as much a sustained attack on religion as it is about oscillating neurons. To understand Crick's motives for bolstering a scientific argument with campaigning atheism, we need to turn briefly to the views of one of his closest philosophical allies, Patricia Churchland, author of an influential work on the philosophy of mind entitled *Neurophilosophy*. Churchland urges a view of human identity, based on computational neuroscience, that will be more 'adequate', she says, than 'that rough-hewn set of concepts, generalisations, and rules of thumb we all standardly use in explaining and predicting human behaviour'. In other words, the inadequate 'folk psychology' of history, literature, 'armchair' philosophy, common sense and, yes, religion, which are, she opines, but 'the homey generalisations of belief and desire'.

Central to Churchland's strategy (wholly endorsed by Crick) is the elimination of mind–body dualism, which, she believes, is sustained and perversely perpetuated by religion. Against this background, Crick appeals for the abandonment of religious faith in order to eradicate dualism and to make way for the Nueroscientific Enlightenment. 'If revealed religions have proved anything,' Crick declares, 'it is that they are usually wrong. Only scientific certainty (with all its limitations) can in the long run rid us of the superstitions of our ancestors.'

By identifying the error of substance dualism as 'religious', Crick gives the impression that his hypothesis offers a wholly new start; that he and those who agree with him hold the key to the human personhood by a conclusive, reductionist, computational explanation of the mind–brain relationship.

In contrast to Crick's 'closed' approach we have the thesis of Gerard Edelman. Edelman won his Nobel prize in 1978 for work on immunology, but he has toiled some 30 years on research programmes aimed at producing a neuroscientifically informed theory of the mind–brain problem. Edelman believes that the way the brain works has more in common with a vast jungle or ecological habitat than a computational system. He calls his hypothesis the Theory of Neuronal Group Selection, which argues that the brain develops, before and after birth, by a process not unlike natural selection in evolution. As a model, or a metaphor, nothing could be further from the Crick–Churchland brand of computational neuroscience which sees the mind as a machine and the world as a piece of computer tape. Edelman stresses the dynamism, the ceaseless novelty, the ceaseless creativity of mental processes (each act of memory, he declares, is a new act of creation, rather than a mechanical replication) and draws constant contrasts between the machines of our own devising and the brain's predicament as an evolved living (and dying) organism. He concludes that while evolutionary theory can elucidate the problem of consciousness, no ultimate scientific explanation of a human individual is possible. Yet, he is emphatically not a dualist, nor is he an anti-reductionist in terms of scientific method.

Importantly, Edelman argues for a clear distinction between reductionist method and reductionist philosophy. 'To reduce a theory of human behaviour to a theory of molecular interactions is simply silly,' he writes, 'made clear when one considers how many different levels of physical, biological and social interactions must be put into place before higher-order consciousness emerges.' Quoting Diderot, he likes to remind his readers that 'to be human is to go beyond physics'.

As with Crick, Edelman's theory has attracted some distinguished supporters from neighbouring disciplines, including the writer-neurologist Oliver Sacks, who believes that Neuronal Group Selection is ideally suited to his holistic approach to clinical neurology. Edelman has also caught the attention of many outside science and clinical medicine, for example, the Catholic theologian Nicholas Lash, who has publicly welcomed 'Edelman's attempts to put the mind back into nature'. If Crick is right, we must acknowledge that our minds have been finally circumscribed by reductionist neuroscience. If Edelman is right, we are invited (in the light of neuroscience, rather than despite it) to launch our imaginations with renewed confidence into the never-ending journey in every culture and civilisation, without arrival, of exploring what it means to be human.

Edelman's recourse to the open nature of theory in relation to the human mind, and hence our ability to reach final solutions, accords with a perspective that has been debated by philosophers of science for more than a century. In 1900 the distinguished German mathematician David Hilbert set mathematicians a list of problems to be solved in the new century. One of the most crucial of these problems was how to demonstrate that mathematics is a self-proving, complete system.

It took another 30 years for the Austrian mathematician Kurt Gödel to come up with his famous proof, which demonstrates that no non-trivial axiomatic system can be both complete and consistent. What this means in terms of physics is that no final theory of everything is possible: that it will always be, in the final analysis, either incomplete or inconsistent.

One of the most famous and hubristic statements in popular science in recent years was the claim of Stephen Hawking, the Cambridge cosmologist, that in a short period of time physicists would indeed produce that theory of everything. This would be the ultimate triumph of science, he recorded in his book *A Short History of Time*, 'for then we would know the mind of God'. The importance and seminal influence of Gödel's proof, published in 1931, was amply demonstrated in April 2003 when Hawking, having reconsidered the implications of Gödel, told an audience in Davis, California: 'Maybe it is not possible to formulate the theory of the Universe in a finite number of statements.' Discussing physical theories of the Universe, Hawking told his audience, 'We and our models are both part of the Universe we are describing. We are not angels who view the Universe from outside.' As a result physical theories are, like Gödel's proof, either inconsistent or incomplete.

Christian philosophers should not turn their backs on what science attempts to tell us about our nature. But we should be vigilant for facile attempts at theoretical closure, attempts to define human identity as scientististic, final, limited and necessary givens. In a gentle riposte to John Searle's 'Rediscovering the Mind',[2] Nicholas Lash reminded the audience of a symposium on consciousness in 1997:

Hydrogen does not decide what being hydrogen will be. In contrast, determining what a human being will be is part of what it means to be a human being. It follows, as

181

the Indian theologian Felix Wilfred remarked recently, that 'Defining the human is not and cannot be the pre-rogative of one civilization or one people'.

There lies the danger, and the challenge for Christian philosophy today. At the heart of the current controversies over consciousness is the bid by a vociferous group of thinkers, highly popular within the genre of public understanding of science, to reduce and distort the nature of consciousness, self-hood, freedom, in order to make a fit with closed, reductionist, computational explanations. For the reductionisms would urge what Christian philosophy would deny: that traditional notions of human identity are illusory figments of 'folk psy-chology'. And if believing in moral agency, as Galen Strawson has pointed out, is a condition of being a free agent, it seems plausible to say that in our era, backed by the power of mass media, the reductionist factions could shape, determine and finalise our understanding of the nature and scope of human identity, the soul. Reflecting on the social and unitary nature of the soul, in both the light of the Second Vatican Council and current researches into cognitive science, thus bestows a fateful responsibility on us all.

Notes

1 David J. Chalmers, *The Conscious Mind: In Search of a Funda-mental Theory* (Oxford: Oxford University Press, 1996), pp. xi–xii.
2 Nicholas Lash, 'Recovering contingency', in John Cornwell (ed.) *Consciousness and Human Identity* (Oxford: Oxford University Press, 1998), pp. 197–209.

12

The Place of Philosophy in the Life of the Church: A Time for Renewal

John Haldane

The second Vatican Council was conceived in part out of a concern to open the Church to the wider world in order that the former might better dispose itself for the benefit of the latter. Ideally, nothing good would be lost from the Church, and the process of development might be advanced so as to bring forth abundant and appealing blossoms followed by further wholesome fruit.

Notwithstanding the strident complaints from different quarters that the Council failed in its aims, either by leaving the Church an inward-looking and defensive bastion of anti-modernism, or by fostering doctrinal dissent, moral relativism and liturgical barbarism, the fact is that at this distance, and amid the other changes of the second half of the twentieth century, it remains hard to judge the general effect of the Council. It may also be a mistake to suppose that even positive development in the life of the Church can be a process of gain without loss. Aquinas writes of how the coming-to-be of one thing necessarily involves the ceasing-to-be of another, and also of how what exists ('has being') is to that extent good. It follows that change involves the loss of some goods and not merely *per accidens*.

One might reply that this kind of loss will not matter if the net result is gain, that is, more good; but apart from the risk of sliding into theological consequentialism there is also the possibility, emphasised in secular terms by philosophers in both the British analytical and Austrian phenomenological schools, that any field of values is comprised of a plurality of genuine but incommensurable goods, such that the pursuit of any one may of necessity be at the expense of another. Socialists and libertarians have often sought to define liberty and equality in ways that eliminate the appearance of tensions between these values. Thus egalitarians have often held that the redistribution of resources is liberty-promoting; while libertarians have maintained that economic freedom expresses the equal right of all to the ownership of their labour and its fruits. We are now unlikely to regard these claims as anything but self-serving sophistries, for we can see that the state redistribution of wealth involves non-voluntary transfers, and freedom can easily be at the cost of distributive justice. The implication is not that if we choose to pursue one policy the other turns out not to have value, but rather that, whichever we choose, to some extent at least, we lose something genuinely worth having.

Similarly, whatever the real value of the following policies, a greater emphasis on transparency and intelligibility in liturgy is liable to be at the cost of the sense of transcendence and profundity; the promotion of pastoral study and of social justice ethics is likely to diminish understanding of fundamental moral theology and to dilute the sense of personal sin; the cultivation of the notion of a 'pilgrim Church' travelling toward a destination it has not reached – and which may remain far off – makes problematic the idea of the ark of salvation furnished with the deposit of faith. I am not concerned to debate what in these cases counts as gain and what loss, but only to point out what change involves and to suggest that it is in no-one's interest to pretend otherwise. Whether, overall, the post-Vatican II Church is better or worse than that which preceded it is a question that should be felt to be difficult to answer, and even problematic to contemplate, for it is, after all, one and the same Church as was founded by Christ and as will persist until his return.

This said, one can certainly look at particular ways in which the Church and Catholic life and culture more generally differ now from the pre-conciliar period and consider what gains and losses the changes have involved. I wish to do something of this with regard to philosophy, relating the history of the practice within Catholic circles to that in the English-speaking world more generally. The restriction to the English-speaking world is for reasons of space and circumstance, as well as of competence; but it is worth adding that given the extent and influence of British and American philosophy this is hardly a parochial restriction. As well as describing the past and characterising the present I aim to say something about the future as it might be and, as I believe, it should be.

Jerusalem and Athens

Anyone raised in or otherwise familiar with the Roman Catholic tradition will recognise at least something of the extent to which it has long drawn upon philosophy to shape and defend its teachings. Yet even if it was inevitable that this should happen, it was certainly not obvious to members of the early church that Jerusalem had much to do with Athens. In anticipation of his journey to the heart of the empire St Paul appealed to rational reflection, maintaining that:

> What can be known about God is perfectly plain for men to see, for God has shown it to them: ever since the creation of the world, the invisible existence of God and his everlasting power have been clearly seen by the mind's understanding of created things.[1]

Given that his intended readership was probably largely one of educated Gentile Romans it is perhaps unsurprising to find him writing in terms reminscent of Cicero's observation in the widely read philosophical work *On the Nature of the Gods* that 'nothing can be so obvious and clear, as we gaze up at the sky and observe the heavenly bodies, as that there is some divine power of surpassing intelligence by which they are ordered'. Yet the unhappiness of Paul's own direct engagement with the sages of Athens must have been fresh in his mind: the Acts of the Apostles tells us that when he spoke to the philosophers, 'at his mention of rising from the dead, some of them burst out laughing';[2] and around the same time he quoted with approval from Isaiah where it is written that the wisdom of the wise is doomed,[3] adding on his own account that 'God chose those who by human standards are fools to shame the wise ... What I spoke and proclaimed was not meant to convince by philosophical argument but to demonstrate the convincing power of the Spirit'.[4]

If there is a tension here it is easy enough to see how it might be resolved. According to Paul, reason is able to discern general truths about the existence of a deity and his governance of the world – hence there is no excuse for ungodliness; but it is foolish to think that human wisdom is adequate to discern the nature of God or that the unaided will is sufficient to bring men to salvation – hence the need of revelation and of grace. This combination is a coherent one and it later took the form of a distinction between the preambles to faith and the dogmatic content of the faith itself, *depositum fidei*. Viewed from the perspective of rational enquiry it is reasonable to read Paul's passage in his letter to the Romans as an instance, be it a limited one, of natural theology, and hence as an implicit endorsement of philosophy of religion so conceived. What it remains silent on, however, is the validity and value of the practice that has come to be known as philosophical theology. The latter makes no distinction between the sources of the concepts and propositions it investigates (natural or revealed), but is concerned to evaluate them in terms of their coherence, intelligibility and possible truth.

It is not difficult to construct a Pauline case against philosophical theology on the grounds that if the concepts investigated are other than those delivered by natural theology or by Christian revelation then it is at best idle and at worst blasphemous; and if they are of the latter sorts then the gospel tells one all one needs to know. Yet apart from the fact that there might be some intellectual value in investigating ideas to which one is not antecedently committed, the fact is that there is a real question of how to understand gospel teachings. Moreover, as the Church developed so its theology broadened and deepened, and ideas were generated of which Paul could have had little understanding, even where they derived from things he himself had introduced such as that Christ's resurrection instituted a new creation (1 Corinthians), that believers are one body in Christ (Romans) and that righteousness is to be associated with faith not works (Galatians). Accordingly, rational reflection upon Christian ideas seems not merely legitimate but required.

That conclusion was reached long ago, implicitly at least by the time of the First Council of Nicea (325) at which the *homoousion* ('of one substance') formulation was received as orthodox in preference to *homoiousion* ('of like substance'). By the Middle Ages theologians moved with ease between general reasoning about the existence and nature of God and specific argumentation concerning the Trinity, the Incarnation, the Communion of Saints and the varieties and operations of grace. Modern readers of Aquinas are liable to be impressed by his range, which is indeed astonishing, but they would do well to attend to the fact that this crosses all sorts of regions between

187

which later writers, particularly in the Protestant tradition, such as Kierkegaard and Barth, attempted to erect barriers. Since for Barth reason is unable to achieve knowledge of God, which is available only through the divine revelation in Jesus Christ, it follows that natural theology is an impossibility – as is substantive dialogue with non-Christians.

While the medievals of the Latin Church did not exactly practise interfaith dialogue they were certainly willing to learn from Jewish and Muslim philosopher-theologians such as Maimonides (Moses ben Maimon) and Avicenna (Ibn-Sina), referring to them with respect. And although the Reformation put Catholicism on the defensive it did not curb the practice of interweaving philosophy and theology. It is true that scholasticism declined in the seventeenth and eighteenth centuries, but that was owing to the general Western rejection of Aristotelianism upon which medieval Christian/philosophical syntheses had drawn. Aquinas was named a Doctor of the Church in 1568, 5 years after the close of the Council of Trent and 7 after the birth of Francis Bacon. The next 40 years would see the births of Hobbes and Descartes, and within a century Aristotelianism had been widely rejected in favour of empiricist and rationalist philosophies that regarded Catholic theology as being either insufficiently warranted by history and experience or else too closely tied to them.

The fate of scholasticism reflected the general circumstance of the Church in the modern period: battered from without and subject to conflict within. The intellectual and social disruptions of the eighteenth and nineteenth centuries unsettled Catholic education and scholarship and resulted in a confused plurality of opinions and approaches. In part because of this some Church leaders saw a need to re-establish a coherent position. In 1846 the newly elected Pius IX reaffirmed the compatibility of faith and reason and in so doing encouraged a return to scholasticism. Explicit papal endorsement of the medieval style of synthesis, and more precisely of that provided by Aquinas, came in 1879 with the encyclical *Aeterni patris* published by Leo XIII in the year following his own election as successor to Pius. The Thomist revival quickly took root in Continental Europe, initially among religious but later among lay intellectuals, and from there it was exported to Britain and more importantly to the United States.

Since Vatican II

Angelo Giuseppe Roncalli was born two years after the publication of *Aeterni patris*. Within a year of becoming Pope John XXIII in 1958 he too had an announcement to make to the universal Church: that he wished to convene an ecumenical council for the purpose of renewing its religious life and re-expressing the substance of its faith. At that time most Catholics engaged in philosophy were Thomists. Much of what they thought, talked and wrote about was internal to the scholastic tradition, being concerned with the interpretation of Aquinas's texts and doctrines, and with debating the merits of later interpretations and developments. While a few looked outward in order to engage with other traditions, the vast majority regarded modern non-scholastic philosophy as a series of errors to be avoided or refuted. Pius XII's 1950 encyclical *Humani generis* condemned a range of positions that were gaining ground in post-war theology (including some dissent from seminary scholasticism). An adaptation of the phrase used as the English title of the encyclical could as well serve to characterise the view of empiricism, rationalism and idealism held by most mid-twentieth-century Thomists – as 'false trends in modern thought'.

It is hard to say exactly when the change came, but it began in Europe and North America with a series of studies of post-Kantian continental philosophers: Hegel, Marx, Kierkegaard, Husserl, Heidegger and Sartre, and progressed towards appropriation and not just description of their views. By the close of Vatican II in 1965 the pre-eminence of Thomism was seriously threatened and by the end of the following decade it was but one strand of Catholic philosophical thought and a diminishing one at that. Significantly, however, intellectual *aggiornamento* tended not to draw upon the form of philosophy dominant within the English-speaking world, namely, conceptual analysis. There are two main reasons for this. First, the very idea of clarifying the content of terms can seem a trivialisation of philosophical enquiry and not at all suited to the presentation of transcendental subject matter – it was common, even within Britain, to complain that this style of philosophy was just concerned with 'words'. Second, it was generally assumed that the sort of philosophy that was practised in Oxford and Cambridge and in Harvard and Berkeley was essentially 'logical positivism' which was famously associated with the claim of A. J. Ayer and others that religious, moral and aesthetic statements are meaningless. This second consideration also encouraged the turn to 'continental' thought among Catholics disenchanted or just bored with Thomism. It was well known that most continental and analytic thinkers had mutual disdain for one another's philosophies; and since analytic thought was presumed to be hostile to religion many Catholics inferred that an enemy of that approach must be a friend.

My own view is that overall these trends have been unfortunate for, while there is no doubt that the seminary scholasticism of the 1950s was often a dull and degenerate form of what in its medieval heyday was a glorious tradition, it was a serious mistake to abandon Thomism, given its claim to be the most effective general synthesis of Catholic doctrine and philosophical truth thus far achieved. In addition, it is a mistake to suppose that analytical philosophy – the philosophy of Russell, G. E. Moore, the early and later Wittgenstein, Elizabeth Anscombe, Peter Geach, Donald Davidson, Michael Dummett, Bernard Williams, Hilary Putnam, Saul Kripke and many others – is simply concerned with clarifying concepts or that it is the continuation of logical positivism by other means. Of the philosophers listed half are theists and three are Roman Catholics: Anscombe (deceased), Geach and Dummett. All of those named have contributed significantly to the pursuit of deep and important issues concerning the nature of reality and the character of human thought and action; and the Catholics have all addressed topics of enduring religious interest such as proofs of the existence of God and the nature of God's operations in the world. Furthermore, the turn to continental thought, particularly in its recent post-modernist variants, far from bolstering the claims of the faith has tended to produce in many who have taken that route a kind of ironic agnosticism, and even a convoluted and unspoken atheism.

More to the point, however, is the fact that philosophers in the English-speaking world are now increasingly open to different styles of enquiry and to the full history of the subject to a far greater extent than has ever been the case. In this respect at least the present is a rich and promising age. Where British, American and Australasian thinkers stand in greatest need of development is in respect of what John Paul II describes in *Fides et ratio* as the 'sapiential dimension' of philosophy. There he writes of a crisis of meaning arising from a fragmentation of knowledge consequent upon scientific development, and from an aura of scepticism produced by the proliferation of philosophical and related theories of the world and human life (section 81). It is well worth quoting in full what John Paul has to say on the matter of how philosophy might now proceed:

> To be consonant with the Word of God, philosophy needs first of all to recover its sapiential dimension as a search for the ultimate and overlapping meaning of life. This first requirement is in fact most helpful in stimulating philosophy to conform to its proper nature. In doing so, it will be not only the decisive factor which determines the foundations and limits of the different fields of scientific learning, but will also take its place as the ultimate framework of the unity of human knowledge and action, leading them to converge towards a final goal and meaning. This sapiential dimension is all the more necessary today, because the immense expansion of humanity's technical capability demands a renewed and sharpened sense of ultimate values.[5]

The Task of Philosophy Now

John XXIII attributed his calling of Vatican II to the inspiration of the Holy Spirit. Whatever its source, the intention of opening the Church to the wider world in order that that which was established by Christ might more effectively serve all humanity was a noble one. It is superficially ironic that in the period since the Council the influence of the Church in the world appears to have declined. Some, of course, argue that the former was the cause of the latter, but anyone familiar with the general trend of Western culture over the last three centuries will know that the decline began long before the Council, so that the critics are not even in the position of having committed the fallacy *post hoc ergo propter hoc*. The current position of religion in Europe is in part a consequence of the philosophically sceptical temper of modernity and in part a result of a rampant combination of individualism, materialism and hedonism. These causes have given rise to a variety of worrying trends: to the substitution of technology for learning, to the growth of relativism, to the commodification of relationships, to the decline of marriage and the family, and to the instrumentalisation of life itself. In the world of politics we have become familiar with the management of effects, but what science and philosophy both teach is that conditions are cured not by treating the symptoms but by tackling the causes.

Philosophy is sometimes castigated for its practical irrelevance. Yet nothing could be more relevant than a means of changing minds, for while natural forces may reconfigure the face of the earth it is minds – and only minds – that can change the world in accord with a plan and a set of values. John XXIII saw the necessity for the Church to re-express the substance of the faith in terms intelligible to the contemporary world, and John Paul II has seen the need to have a clear and effective understanding of the nature of philosophy in order to use it to think about matters of substance.

Neither perception diminishes the achievements of the past but both require Catholic philosophers to think hard about how best to carry the subject forward so as to be true to its vocation as the love of wisdom and to be effective in engaging the problems that confront us. There are those who will say that all would have been well if we had held fast to the Thomism that prevailed in Catholic circles in the first half of the twentieth century; and there are those who would consign that tradition to the wasteland of failed metaphysical approaches. Neither judgement is sound and both exhibit the tendency to think that all change must either be deterioration or improvement. As I remarked in the opening section, change necessarily occasions loss, but just as one should not regard this as implying a worsening simpliciter, nor should one think that if something good comes to be that this shows that overall change is for the best.

The primary task facing philosophers today is that of giving substance and general purpose to their enquiries. In so far as philosophy is an intellectual discipline it needs to be rigorous and precise (to the extent that any particular subject matter allows). Analytical philosophy has made virtues of rigour and precision, and since its rediscovery of metaphysics some 40 years ago it is more likely to put these virtues to significant use. At the same time it tends not to have a reflective sense of its own nature as an activity directed towards comprehensive truth. By contrast, continental European philosophy in the styles best known to the layperson, speaks grandly of the totality while failing to deliver much in the way of rigorous and precise argumentation. Readers of the *Summa Theologiae*, of Aquinas's 'disputed questions' and his commentaries on works of Aristotle, will know that he manages to maintain a sense of the structure and importance of the wood, while also identifying the distinguishing features of, and navigating between, the trees. That provides an excellent model, but if the substance of Aquinas's Catholic/Aristotelian synthesis is to be communicated and win converts it must first be cast in a form intelligible to the best and most rigorous non-Catholic thinkers of the day. To achieve this, it would be wise to consider the forms deployed by those very thinkers, not in the spirit of uncritical emulation but in that of further synthesis. Happily this has been happening for some while and there is evidence, confirmed by the increasing use of the expression 'analytical Thomism', that the efforts at constructive engagement are bearing fruit.

Yet the task of philosophical *aggiornamento* is not complete, and in the nature of the case it never can be, short of the end of the world and the final coming of the kingdom. That may well be some way off; alternatively it is an old and good practice to prepare for it as if it may happen at any time. Philosophers who took the latter possibility seriously might well attach priority to developing the sapiential dimension of the subject, which is perhaps one reason why John Paul II recommends attention to it.

G. K. Chesterton once observed that philosophy is just thought that has been thought out. More strictly, one might say that it is thought-out thought about the highest things as these admit of rational contemplation. That kind of thinking has to have a central place within the life of the Church and of the world; otherwise human beings will have failed to realise their nature as rational creatures made in the image of God for the purpose of knowing, loving and serving him. There really is no merit in looking back to a supposed golden age of pre-Vatican II Catholicism, for even if some things were better then than now, others were worse, and in any case the Catholic should live facing forward – the direction of life itself.

Notes

1 Rom. 1:19–20, 57–8.
2 Acts 17:32.
3 Isa. 29:14.
4 1 Cor. 1:27; 2:4.
5 *Faith and Reason* (London: Catholic Truth Society, 1998), pp. 119–20.

13

Captivated Ambivalence:
How the Church Copes with the Media

Lavinia Byrne

I want to throw open the windows of the Church so that
we can see out and the people can see in.
                                    Pope John XXIII (1962)

John XXIII's proposal looked so innocent. Through opened
windows, as he saw it, the great spiritual riches of the Catholic tradition would become accessible to the outside world.
Through the medium of the Second Vatican Council, the
Church would be able to shed the trappings that had kept
these treasures powerful – magical, even – but also the possession of an elite. The project was a grand one: the Council
would offer a means of renewal for all the faithful, as well as
initiating a mission to the world. Both those within and those
without would benefit because, significantly, the traffic would
be in two directions. The people of God were to look out and
the Church would be visible to all.

What a boost for modern media! Radio, television and
newsprint would ensure that the images from these opened
windows could be propelled around the world. The television
crews rolled into Rome; news correspondents set themselves up
in a variety of delightful venues. The media were welcomed in
because their technology could work the appropriate miracles.
'More' suddenly became 'better'. We saw pictures which

before we had never dreamed of seeing; we sat in front of our televisions enjoying the sights and sounds of Rome and processions of bishops and cardinals. Above all we loved the slightly rotund figure of John XXIII himself, because he, too, seemed to be enjoying himself. We began to search out transmissions from Vatican Radio on the frail buttons of our transistors.

The Initial Enthusiasm

The Church had embraced radio from the early days when Guglielmo Marconi would walk with the Pope around the gardens of the Vatican and discuss the potential of this amazing new medium. In 1933 he installed a microwave link between the Vatican and the summer home of Pius XI, so that the Pope could transmit broadcasts from Vatican Radio directly. In *Sertum laetitiae,* the Encyclical celebrating the one hundred and fiftieth anniversary of the establishment of the hierarchy in the United States, promulgated in 1939 by Pius XII, this enthusiasm found full expression:

> We have learned with not little joy that your press is a sturdy champion of Catholic principles, that the Marconi Radio, whose voice is heard in an instant round the world – marvellous invention and eloquent image of the Apostolic Faith that embraces all mankind – is frequently and advantageously put to use in order to ensure the widest possible promulgation of all that concerns the Church, and We commend the good accomplished.

When Vatican II was called, there was more in this vein. Not only had the Church apparently nothing to hide, but the Council Fathers realised that their theological reflections and teaching should encompass the 'means of social communication', as they called the mass media. They sounded upbeat:

'The reporting, description, or representation of moral evil by the media can lead to a deeper knowledge and exploration of humanity', they noted, 'and by employing suitable dramatic effects, to a portrayal of the true and the good in all their splendour.' Their document on social communications, *Inter mirifica*, was promulgated in 1963.

The assumption was that the whole drama of human experience would be played out on the silver screen, on radio or on television, and that 'the true and the good' would somehow prevail. These were heady days for the media, and for the faithful too, carried away by the movies we enjoyed: *Mrs Miniver*, *Monsieur Vincent*, *The Bells of St Mary's*, *The Nun's Story*. Our stars were Bing Crosby and Grace Kelly. Good Catholics could be media stars without compromising their eternal destiny. We loved seeing the Pope on telly. After *Mrs Dales' Diary* we began listening to *New Every Morning* – and even learned some Protestant hymns.

We had yet to see violence on screen. For most people, that moment came when Jackie Kennedy cradled her wounded husband's body in the back of a car in Dallas. Subsequent images from Vietnam unravelled the myth yet further. Pictures of anarchy from Algeria or Northern Ireland became a regular feature of our evening viewing.

Even as we watched, pop culture became increasingly secular. Pop music in particular reflected an irreligious world where people sought their spiritual highs in sex, drugs and rock and roll. Yet because the images were so compelling, we developed a repertoire of icons, of new saints for the secular age, people whom we admired and imitated. We bought new clothes and with them new lifestyles as image suddenly became overwhelmingly important and the TV acted as a mirror, feeding our illusions back to us. A naïve fascination with the media needed to give way to something more discerning.

Wanted: A Theology of Media

In 1971, in response to a request from Vatican II, a more complete document on social communications was issued: *Communio et progressio*. Article 11 suggested that, 'Communication is more than the expression of ideas and the indication of emotion. At its most profound level, it is the giving of self in love. Christ's communication was, in fact, spirit and life.' *Communio et progressio* too offered an exalted theology of the media and its potential for good:

> [These means of communication] ... serve to build new relationships, and to fashion a new language which permit men [and women] to know themselves better and to understand one another more easily. By this, [all men and women] are led to a mutual understanding and shared ambition. And this, in turn, inclines them to justice and peace, to good will and active charity, to mutual help, to love and, in the end, to communion. The means of communication, then, provide some of the most effective methods of cultivating that charity among [us] which is at once the cause and the expression of fellowship.

The promise was of community and shared values. The promise was of a world in which good would prevail through the transmission of 'mutual understanding and shared ambition'. The popular Canadian communications guru, Marshall McLuhan, wrote with the same kind of optimism in *The Medium is the Message,* published five years earlier:

> Electric circuitry has overthrown the regime of 'time' and 'space' and pours upon us instantly and continuously the

concerns of all other men. It has reconstituted dialogue on a global scale. In an electronic information environment, minority groups can no longer be contained-ignored. Too many people know too much about each other. Our new environment compels commitment and participation. Ours is a brand-new world of allatonceness. 'Time' has ceased, 'space' has vanished.

We now live in a global village – a simultaneous happening. In the event, human reality turned out to be much more dense and complicated than these prophetic voices could realise. Instead of a global village, what do we have? A fragmented world in which people actively protest against globalisation, and a post-modern world which shuns in horror the very idea of a shared narrative of meaning. In 2003, our experience is that, far from encouraging one world, global communication systems have instead fostered rather the kind of competitive pluralism that we are surrounded by today. Ours is such a different world from that of the 1970s that an upbeat spiritual or theological reflection on the media – which now include the Internet – would seem to be out of place. In particular there are many who are now convinced that the mass media are the enemy of religion, be it Christianity, Judaism or Islam. As religious believers, they perceive religion to be a cohesive force, because it deals with eternal verities rather than transient ones. It follows that they consider that the media are inherently bad because TV, the radio and the newspaper appear to dance to a different tune.

This judgement is severe. It claims to be based in the sense that the media deal with illusion. Media people are seen as alchemists who try to distort the truth by weaving spells with pictures and words. They create casualties because they ruin reputations. They are not honest brokers of truth: they spin it and contort its meaning. Not only is this true of words, but doubly so with pictures. In some deep-down way that we do not ordinarily bother to articulate, we know that the media manipulate – or so the logic goes. Yet we cannot deny that we are captivated. We connive, for we turn on our radios first thing in the morning; we await the thud of the newspapers on our doormats; we enjoy crashing out in front of the telly. With access to the Internet come endless possibilities: on-line banking, instant holidays and endless information about things we never knew we wanted to know. We are hooked, whether we like it or not. Human beings love stories and here come stories in abundance, packaged for our interest and entertainment.

More than that, we inhabit a media-saturated world. Inescapably, we are captured on close-circuit televisions; our transactions at the supermarket are monitored, even as we receive fidelity points for shopping there; we are tracked on giant satellite maps because our mobile telephones log our position on the planet. We are watched and we watch. We listen and are listened to. Billboards jump out at us from street corners. Junk mail clutters our mailboxes. We are material people in a material world, media people in a media world.

The Church and the Media: Ambivalent Partners

Not surprisingly this ambivalence is played out on an even more toxic scale when the Catholic Church and the media meet. Put candidly, the media's job is to disclose, to reveal, to deal in bad news as well as good. The Church's job is to deal in good news, to proclaim an everlasting and ever-living message freshly for every generation. Iniquity, sin, human frailty are not ignored, but safe liturgical boundaries contain them. The proper place for sin to go to is the confessional, where silence and secrecy rule. Daily transgressions are dealt with at the beginning of the Mass when we receive immediate absolution. In a word, we are to seek forgiveness for our sins because we need to, not because we are afraid of them appearing in the newspapers or the press.

In that sense, the Church has always been in the sin game. It knows about good and evil. It is good at sin. From the Seven Deadlies all the way through to minor transgressions, sins have been itemised as lovingly as goods on our supermarket shelves. They do not have sell-by dates because their effects go beyond the constraints of time. But there is hope. For deep within the Catholic imagination lies the certainty that sin, contrition, confession and a firm purpose of amendment go hand in hand and that they secure eternal life for us. The media intervene, though, when someone in public life sins. The media do not have the same handle on the sense that sin can lead to forgiveness and redemption. No life is more public than that of a cleric, a supposedly good man. So when he transgresses, in the eyes of the press and TV and radio, the consequences are dire.

The media close in and the story gets told. The Catholic Church has been profoundly damaged by the catalogue of bad news stories that have been released over the past ten years. Child abuse sends a shudder through the public imagination; now our priests are implicated. They have lost the aura that protected them from public scrutiny.

So, too, have transgressions against the discipline of celibacy. When homosexual or heterosexual priests get 'caught at it' the media are unforgiving, because they are not in the forgiveness game. When they investigate, they are in it for a 'kill' – a good story. Story is all. Yet the obverse is true as well. There is such a vocation as that of the religious journalist. The title is not an oxymoron. Put simply, top-quality investigative journalism may do more to renew the Church and the priesthood than we presently understand. Top-quality investigative journalists are not afraid of the power of the hierarchy because they speak from a different place. If anything, they have everything to gain from exposing the dysfunctionality of the Church, as of any other great institution of public life.

So to present the media as the enemy of religion is to miss the point. For it is appropriate to ask questions about celibacy, for instance, or about the ordination of women; about what happens to Church money and about the consequences of clericalism. It is appropriate to explore the ordinary everyday expectations of people who believe that the Church is an ark of salvation and that it exists to serve rather than to subdue the people of God. A secular or – in the case of religious journalism – a lay-owned press can present both sides of any argument without being answerable to the Church for doing so. That is where their strength lies and why the Church needs them, like it or not.

But there is a further issue: jealousy. Christians believe that they have good news to proclaim. Surely this means that the media should welcome their contribution and have, as it were, the right to proclaim such good news? So they profess to love the media. The trouble is in the subtext: we love the media when it is 'on side', when the television cameras crowd around and make us feel important. In our curiously media-saturated world, to be on telly is somehow to *exist*. When the stories are good, or when the Church looks visually sublime – captured, say, at a good liturgical moment – we revel in the affirmation that TV gives.

And we love the unseen masses of people the media reach. As a Catholic woman, I cannot preach in church. Yet six million people know my 'Thought for the Day' on the flagship BBC news programme *Today*. When I have broadcast the *Daily Service* on BBC Radio 4 Long Wave, I have taken the Word of

God into untold homes, hospitals, cars, nursing homes. Which
is seductive stuff – if one did not realise that the wireless is the
most ephemeral of media: it does not – cannot – create super-
stars, and will not tolerate for long people who take themselves
too seriously.

Like Pius XII and Marconi, I love the technology itself, in its
own right. So did Hilda Matherson, whose little book *Broadcasting* was published in 1934. Miss Matherson, who worked
closely with Lord Reith, the first Director General of the BBC,
invented the *Shipping Forecast* – that indomitable friend of
insomniacs at either end of the day or night. She saw the development of the media as a human adventure on a grand scale:

> Broadcasting is not strictly another machine; it makes use
> of apparatus (although the tendency is moving rapidly
> towards simplification); but fundamentally it is a harnes-
> sing of elemental forces, a capturing of sounds and voices
> all over the world to which we have hitherto been deaf.
> It is a means of enlarging the frontiers of human interest
> and consciousness, of widening personal experience, of
> shrinking the earth's surface. It is only possible to see it in
> its right perspective by seeing it in the scale already
> suggested – a milestone in the development of communi-
> cations as momentous as its forerunners, and, like them,
> accompanying and assisting a new stage in civilization.
> Broadcasting as we know it, moreover, is in its infancy; it
> is comparable to the rudest scratchings on the cave-man's
> dark walls, to the gutteral sounds which served the first
> *homo sapiens* for speech. It is not possible to pass final
> judgment upon its full significance; this is still wrapped in
> shadows ... Broadcasting, and its allies, telegraphy and
> telephony, are only stages in the long process that began

with man's existence some three hundred thousand years ago, and may end in some form of thought transference of which we now have no conception.

Hilda Matheson sensed that broadcasting was better than the narrowcasting that went before, the endless 'dialogue of the tribe' as T. S. Eliot called it. When John XXIII wanted to throw open those windows on the world, this is the risk he took: 'we can see out and the people can see in'. It was a metaphor perfectly suited to the television age.

The Church in the Digital Era

How can the Church engage with the media in its present-day manifestations – radio, TV, video, DVD, Internet? One answer is to see these media as a set of tools for us to use, as kit to enable the Church to enjoy a higher profile in a media-saturated world.

So we go out and buy the technology. We set up offices to teach people how to use it. We train specialists who do great work training other specialists and so it goes on.

At best, this strategy works. After all, people can be trained to be microphone- or camera-literate. But the temptation becomes to try to train them to sound sincere. And there is a huge niggle here. If they are sincere already and – as religious people, one would hope that they are – then surely the training is redundant? Cardinal Hume in an interview with the *Today* programme once referred to it as 'your show'. Had he been trained to take the programme's iconic status a bit more seriously, I doubt if he would have felt free to make such a revelatory remark. The media liked him precisely because he was sincere.

Another response is all about size. The Church missed the first print revolution, the argument runs, and is in danger now of missing the digital one. Bigger is better; massive is best of all. So wheel out the Catholic or Christian TV and radio channels; swamp the opposition; get the technology on side to deliver the goods on a global scale.

But these arguments re-run the global village fantasy of the late 1970s. The more serious question, it seems to me, goes something like this: how can the best of religious voices engage with the questions that genuinely exercise people, not of right, but because they have something to say? How can religious believers, whatever their faith community, embrace the values of openness and debate represented by the media and thereby contribute in the public domain? In the case of the Catholic community, there is a further question: for the images of light and luminosity generated by television in particular are deeply familiar to the Catholic imagination. We should not be afraid of them. If that light falls in such a way that it reveals our darkness – as has happened – do we experience the shame of seeing our sins on screen as an intrusion or as a call to live in the light?

Radio, too, is a medium with spiritual resonances for Catholics, for we believe our world to be populated by angels as well as ourselves. There is always more going on than we can presently see. Radio rejoices in the sound of human speech and human music. We should not fear them either, for we have a song to sing, along with the gospel to proclaim. And the wireless loves a good debate.

As for the Internet, it opens a dynamic world of interactive communication where genuine information will be greeted in a million homes and hearts, and where propaganda will be revealed as just that. The challenge is there. Who is going to evangelise the Internet – 'so that the people can see in'?

What is promised by the media is not so much a global village, not some idealistic community of shared values and ambitions, but a context in which discussion can flourish and in which debate can draw in and support the casualties of our post-modern world. The Christian journalist, like the informed *Tablet* reader, has a vocation as well as a task. We are called to intelligent faith, profound hope and endless charity. None of these, as the Church must realise, precludes engaging with contemporary discussion and debate.

14

The Church and the Media:
Beyond *Inter mirifica*

Alain Woodrow

Religion is of its essence communication. The word comes from the Latin *religare*, to bind or to link. The three mono-theistic religions claim to be 'revelations': God speaking to human beings. For Christians, the gospel is the good news that must be spread abroad: in other words, *broadcast*. On a theo-logical level, the central doctrine of Christianity, the Trinity, teaches that the One God exists in three Persons, who 'com-municate' eternally: the Father 'generates' the Son and the Holy Ghost 'proceeds' from the Father and the Son. St Augustine, in his *De Trinitate,* compares this double procession of the Divine Life, the Word (the Son) and the Spirit (the Holy Ghost) to the analogical process of human self-knowledge and self-love.

Religion and the mass media (or 'Instruments of Social Com-munication' as the conciliar decree of 1963, *Inter mirifica*, describes them) should logically therefore go hand in hand. Unlike iconoclastic theological traditions in Islam and early Protestantism, Catholicism has its long tradition of sacred art, with its emphasis on the tangible and the physical (relics, holy pictures, sacramentals, incense) and Ignatian appeal to the five senses. The Church regards the media, and television above all, as the ideal instrument to relay the pageantry and splendour of the Roman rite. One need only compare the successful exploi-tation of the media by the charismatic John Paul II, in his worldwide evangelisation of the masses, with the much lower profile kept by the mainstream Protestant Churches to understand their antithetical approaches.

The Catholic Church was quick to grasp the way it could utilise the media for its own ends, but much less willing to accept the legitimate demands made upon it by those same media. This uneasy attitude is shown clearly in the disastrous handling by the Second Vatican Council of its decree on the media. *Inter mirifica* is, in fact, the least satisfactory of all the conciliar documents. The Secretariat for the Instruments of Social Communication, created in 1960, was one of the ten commissions and two secretariats set up to prepare the Council. Its brief was complex and ambitious: to formulate the Church's doctrine on the media, to train the Christian conscience with regard to the right use of these media, and to make propositions for bringing the cinema, radio and television into line with faith and morals, and for making use of them to spread the gospel.

The Weakness of *Inter mirifica*

The Secretariat worked in three sections: one for the press, one for the cinema and one for radio and television. A draft schema was drawn up which comprised an introduction, four sections and a final exhortation. The first section dealt with the Church's doctrine on the media (the teaching of the Church, the objective moral order, the duties of citizens and of civil authority); Section II dealt with the apostolate (spreading truth and Christian doctrine, the means of achieving this); Section III was devoted to discipline and order (Church discipline, the organs of Church authority); and Section IV offered some observations on certain media (the press, the cinema, radio and television, other forms of communication).

It was unexpectedly announced that the schema would be presented to the bishops during the first session of the Council, in November 1962. The decision to bring the discussion forward (although the schema came last but one in the printed volume of draft texts) was to give the Fathers an 'easier' schema to discuss after their lengthy examination of the liturgy and controversial, not to say acrimonious, discussion of the 'Sources of Revelation'. It was even suggested that, since the subject of this schema was not a theological one, the bishops should accept the draft without a great deal of argument.

But this was not to reckon with the criticism levelled at the text. Archbishop Stourm of Sens drew attention to the crucial role played by the media in today's world and its prodigious power, through information and entertainment, over the public. Some (Archbishop D'Souza of Nagpur and Cardinal Léger of Montreal) pointed out that the rights of the Church were unduly stressed, while others (Bishop Enrique y Tarancón of Solsona and Bishop Ménager of Meaux) objected that the role of laypeople – who had more qualifications and experience than the clergy in this field – was not adequately acknowledged. Opinions were divided. Some welcomed the optimistic tone of the document; others wanted to denounce the misuse of the media and 'image worship' in modern civilisation. Cardinal Suenens recommended the establishment of professional ethics for journalists, Cardinal Bea suggested merging the world's Catholic news agencies and Bishop Höffner (Münster) praised the cooperation between German Catholics and Protestants in this domain.

After barely two and a half days of debate in St Peter's, it was proposed that the schema be approved in substance but drastically pruned, a decision welcomed with relief by a massive majority of the Fathers. In the interval between the first and second sessions the commission reduced the schema to its bare bones (cutting its 40 pages down to 9), while attempting to address the more important criticisms that had been raised.

It became clear during the second session that none of the major schemas, apart from the Constitution on the Sacred Liturgy, would be ready for promulgation, so that the Council would have only one finished document to present to the public at the end of two whole sessions. This explains why the Decree on the Instruments of Social Communication was hurried through, in order to provide a second finished document, mainly to appease those who accused the Council of being all talk and no action.

The new shortened text pursued two main aims: first, to set forth the Church's teaching on the supremacy of the moral law, the right to be informed, public opinion and the forming of conscience; second, to stress the importance of the media for the Church's pastoral work, namely, the preaching of the gospel to all men of goodwill and establishing the kingdom of God throughout the world. The document again came under sustained criticism, from two very different quarters. One salvo was fired from outside the Council by a group of American journalists who were in Rome to report on the event, the other came from within the assembly itself, delivered by a group of its members.

Two documents were produced: a statement by the journalists and a petition by the Fathers. The first was signed by John Cogley of *Commonweal*, Robert Blair Kaiser of *Time* and *Life* and Michael Novak of the *New Republic*. This document – which received the approval of three leading *periti* (theological experts), the American Jesuit John Courtney Murray, the French Jesuit Jean Daniélou and the Argentinian Jorge Mejía – stated that the schema, far from achieving an *aggiornamento*, was a retrograde step since it reflected a hopelessly abstract view of the media, unrecognisable to journalists working for the 'real press'.

Their objections were fivefold.

1. The moralistic approach of the schema contradicted the intrinsic value of a work of art and denied the integrity of the Christian artist.
2. The 'right to be informed' only concerned the moral obligation of those who pass on information (the journalists), not of those who are the source of the information (the hierarchy); thus the real problem of authoritarian secrecy, and its victims, was conveniently ignored.
3. The Catholic press was presented as though it possessed some quasi-infallible doctrinal authority lacking in the secular press, implying that the latter contributed nothing to the formation of public opinion in the Church.
4. The schema appeared to interpose an ecclesiastical authority between the journalist and his employer, compromising the integrity of the laymen working for the media.
5. Two important passages granted governments control over the media; such control not only threatened the freedom of the press but was expressly forbidden by the constitutions of a number of countries, among them the United States.

In contrast, the petition was signed by 90 Fathers, including Cardinals Frings, Gerlier and Alfrink. This second document also gave five reasons why the schema fell short of the standards expected of a conciliar decree.

1. Although the text claimed inalienable rights for the Church, it disregarded the fact that all communication

springs from a search for the truth and the desire to express it.

2. The media were described *technically,* as a means of addressing people, rather than as a means of true communication, a genuinely human dialogue.

3. No mention was made of true Christian and human education, which is not a matter of remote, abstract knowledge and judgement but implies a sympathetic concern for the fate of others.

4. It was most regrettable that Catholic laypeople were not given their due but kept under clerical tutelage even where they were more competent than the clergy.

5. Many problems concerning the media were not to be addressed by the Council but by national or regional bishops' conferences.

Both documents called for a radical revision of the schema or, failing this, its removal from the agenda since, in its present state, it could only 'astonish those competent in the field' and 'bring discredit on the Council'. But it was too late: the schema, with its amendments, was approved by an overwhelming majority. The protests continued, and some bishops even attempted to have the text removed for re-examination before the final vote, but the moderators, who were afraid to set a precedent which might affect weightier theological issues in subsequent votes, announced that a schema could not be withrawn once it had been accepted in a valid vote. The final vote was taken on 4 December 1963, at the last public assembly of the second session, with 1,960 Fathers in favour, 164 against and 27 abstentions. The decree, together with the Constitution on the Sacred Liturgy, was solemnly promulgated by the Pope.

According to the German theologian Karlheinz Schmidthüs, *Inter mirifica*

> was treated as a stop-gap between deliberations which seemed a good deal more vital to the Fathers. It represents a compromise between two irreconcilable attitudes: one which would have little time wasted over this matter, and another which would not neglect a subject of such importance from the pastoral point of view. Small wonder if the result was hardly worthy of that pastoral importance and really left everyone dissatisfied. The main weaknesses of the Decree are, first, that having been discussed and disposed of so early in the day it does not take account of the insights into the nature of the Church and her relationship with the world which the Council subsequently reached, and can therefore well be called a 'pre-conciliar' document; and, second, that it looks shabby when one considers the present state of discussion among intellectuals. In short, it is worthy neither of the Council nor of the learned world.[1]

The Persistent Problem of Centralism

Unfortunately, the pre-conciliar attitude responsible for this decree remained largely untouched by John XXIII's *aggiornamento*. Even today, 40 years after Vatican II, the Catholic hierarchy and the media are still uncomfortable bedfellows. Why did the Council fail to change clerical mentalities on this question? One reason is the failure of the Council as a whole to follow through its daring programme of reform. Another is the very nature of the modern media, based on complete autonomy and freedom of speech, which constantly challenges the Church's claim to possess the 'absolute' truth.

According to the French Dominican theologian Christian Duquoc, 'the conciliar revolution is more of a myth than a reality'. Those who lived through the heady times of Vatican II hoped for the 'second Spring' predicted by Newman, expecting that the Catholic Church would open its doors to the modern world, to other Christian Churches and to other religions, ushering in a new age of theological pluralism, spiritual liberty and renewal. They soon had to face the hard reality of the Church as institution; and witnessed, with the election of John Paul II, a return to centralised, authoritarian government. Revolutions are invariably followed by Restorations.

The problem, suggests Duquoc, is that while Vatican II presented a daring new vision of the Church as 'People of God', thus standing the hierarchical pyramid of the old power structure on its head, it failed to provide the means to turn this vision into reality or transform the institution. 'The Council simply poured its new wine into old wineskins', adds Duquoc wryly, 'and we have seen the result.'[2]

There is nothing new in this. Throughout history, authoritarian and liberal popes have succeeded each other. And the excesses unleashed by the Council (priests and religious abandoning their ministry, Marxism being preached under the guise of 'liberation theology', Catholics adopting a 'self-service' attitude to the Church's teaching) were bound to provoke a backlash in Rome. But the election of a pope both charismatic and authoritarian, socially progressive and theologically conservative, popular and intellectually powerful, has singularly compounded the problem.

Roman centralism, an ever-present temptation, has been accelerated by the ubiquity of this pope (thanks to television), his self-appointed (and widely accepted) role as universal leader, his sole right to appoint bishops, the multiplication of Roman documents, often bearing his personal stamp (one forgets that papal encyclicals only date from the sixteenth century), and the excessive role assigned to Cardinal Ratzinger, prefect of the Congregation for the Doctrine of the Faith. The main obstacle to free speech in the Church – particularly free theological expression – stems from the bureaucratic functioning of Roman authority, whose principal aim is the self-perpetuation of the system. 'Bishops come and go', as the Roman tag has it, 'but the Curia goes on for ever!'

The growing conflict between Rome and the local Churches is exacerbated by the prevailing liberal culture in Western democracies, which regards absolute authority as an obstacle to free speech and freedom of conscience as the ultimate good to be protected by a state. The laws of Western democracies are defined to preserve individual liberty (my liberty stops where yours begins); while the State – unlike totalitarian systems – refuses to provide an ultimate 'meaning' to life. The Western democracies do not answer existential or metaphysical questions (Who am I? What should I believe?), but offer a climate of tolerance – for them the supreme virtue – for the free exercise of the private beliefs of their citizens.

The Council's ambitious task remains incomplete because it would not – or could not – tackle the thorny question of papal supremacy. The present imbalance in Church authority is not only between pope and bishops but between the three 'voices of the Church' defined by Cardinal Newman: that of government (tradition), that of theology (reason) and that of pastoral experience (the laity). The Canadian Dominican theologian Daniel Cadrin, assistant to Fr Timothy Radcliffe when he was Master of the Dominicans in Rome, describes the current relationship of the 'three voices'. There is, he says,

> a verbal inflation of the first voice, that of the Curia, which has assumed an usurped authority. The second

voice, that of the theologians, is too often stifled, whereas they should be allowed freedom of research and doctrinal pluralism. As for the third voice, that of the laity, they have no recognised forum in which to express their opinion. The promises of Vatican II have not been fulfilled.[3]

What about the voice of public opinion in the Church? Pius XII himself spoke of public opinion as legitimate and necessary. And Yves Congar firmly believed in the *sensus fidelium*, the necesssary reception of the teaching of the magisterium by the whole community of believers, not as a simple echo of official teaching but as an original contribution. The French Dominican liked to quote Newman when he spoke of a 'conspiracy' of priests and faithful, that is, an active cooperation resulting in something richer and wider. The Church authorities continue to mistrust public opinion, however, especially when it is voiced by the media and reported by journalists. The 'forum' for the laity, whose absence is regretted by Fr Cadrin, is in fact the media, Catholic or otherwise, where they can make their voice heard, directly or through the mediation of the journalist.

Public opinion is nourished by two different modes of contemporary thought: a scientific language (the earth revolves around the sun) which is rigorous and admits no contradiction; and a free, subjective language where everything – philosophy, politics, the economy, morality, even religion – is open to question. In the second, everything is probable but uncertain, and therefore open to discussion. Belief itself has become an opinion among others. This situation is unacceptable for the Church which bears witness to a word spoken by Another, by Jesus who said, 'I am the Way, the Truth and the Life'. The Church forbids its members to define their own beliefs according to a democratic debate which is open ended.

217

The Trouble with Journalists

The trouble with journalists is that they are not accountable to the Church, even when they happen to be Christian. Their legitimacy comes from below. Journalists should never be part of the establishment, whether political or religious. They are the emanation of the public opinion they are supposed to represent and their 'mandate', delegated to them, stems simply from the freedom of speech enshrined in the universal Declaration of the Rights of Man. Their sole justification is the confidence placed in them by the public which buys their work. They are the spokesmen not of some higher authority but of the public.

Obviously a distinction should be made between the religious and secular press. Journalists working for the Catholic media cannot flout the teachings of the Church without being in flagrant contradiction with themselves and could rightly be accused of living a lie. But a large pluralism of opinions exists (or should exist) in the Church, and even Catholic journalists are bound to follow their conscience. Christian journalists working in the secular media have greater latitude, but their work is precious to the Church and should be encouraged insofar as they are useful mediators between the ecclesiastical authority, with its arcane language, and the often theologically illiterate public at large.

Moreover, the line between the religious and secular media is often tenuous, and freedom of speech is essential to both. There is obviously a difference between official Church organs such as *L'Osservatore Romano* and 'Catholic-inspired' magazines such as *La Vie* or *Témoignage Chrétien* in France. The American papers *Commonweal* and the *National Catholic Reporter*; the French periodicals *Les Études* and *l'Actualité religieuse dans le monde*; and in Britain *The Tablet* and, until recently, *The Month*, have all done much to further the cause of religious freedom in general and freedom of speech in the Church in particular by their high journalistic standards, tolerant pluralism, responsible reporting and fundamental loyalty to the Church.

I have worked both for the Catholic and for the secular press. The difficulties in the former are greater since the Church as an institution wishes to communicate its message 'undiluted' in such a way as to convey its own image of itself; and it expects the loyal Catholic journalist to relay the information obediently and passively, asking no awkward questions and resisting any temptation to investigate the reality behind the official line. To complicate matters, Church authorities claim a privileged relation to 'the Truth' and often speak in the name of God, or Christ, which makes them hard to contradict.

But there are other difficulties in the secular press. The greater freedom (with regard to the hierarchy) enjoyed by the journalist working for the secular press is counterbalanced by his need to defend his pitch (religion) in a newspaper which often regards the subject as unimportant, trivial or in the same category as horoscopes, black magic or the weirder cults. The religious affairs correspondent is torn between his loyalty to the Church, which he tries to portray truthfully, and his loyalty to his newspaper, which he tries to serve professionally. Caught between the devil and the deep blue sea, he is often reviled by both.

A Religious Journalist's Decalogue

After spending twenty years on the religious affairs desk of the French daily *Le Monde,* I submit the following 'Ten Commandments for the religious journalist':

1. *Independence.* Religious journalists in the secular media do not speak for the ecclesiastical institution; still less are they 'apostles of truth'. The Church has its own publications for that. They are not even neutral intermediaries between the religions and their public. They are independent, professional journalists with minds of their own.

2. *Competence.* They are judged not by their militancy or missionary zeal, but by their ability in their chosen field, just as are political or scientific correspondents in theirs. According to some churchmen, a religious journalist must be a member of the Church in order to understand it from within. But by the same token one should be a Communist to write about the Communist Party, or a Moonie to write about the Unification Church. At the other extreme, some church leaders prefer 'theologically illiterate' journalists who will simply relay the message without intervening. What annoys the hierarchy most is an informed, articulate journalist (often an ex-seminarian or priest) who knows his subject. One needs to be competent in order to translate ecclesiastical jargon and the abstruse language of many Roman texts into words understood by the average reader.

3. *Openness.* Like all non-democratic institutions the Catholic Church loves secrecy. Preaching virtue and claiming to be a 'perfect society', it does not like admitting its mistakes. It has only recently published its financial accounts (hence the enduring myth about the wealth of the Vatican) and still draws a veil over the workings of the Curia (the appointment of bishops, the secret trials of theologians). The journalist has a duty to break down these taboos in the interest of the Church itself, as *The Boston Globe* did in the United States when it revealed that bishops had failed to act against clerical sex abusers. In France, a long battle

to persuade the bishops to open more of their annual sessions to the press has failed: they have reverted to their former practice of holding all their meetings in private.

4. *Truthfulness.* The argument put forward to justify secrecy is that the Church should not wash its dirty linen in public. But this often means that the linen does not get washed at all. The duty of the press is to publish the truth about an institution that claims to be 'an expert in humanity'. Journalists are often reproached for insisting on the negative aspects of the Church instead of singing its praises. But by their nature the media deal with the extra-ordinary: bridges that collapse, not those that stand firm; priests who marry, not those who remain faithful to their vows; bishops who are in favour of contraception or the ordination of women, not those who toe the party line. When journalists single out a controversial phrase from a sermon, they are accused of 'distorting the truth'; but a newspaper, which has a limited amount of space, natu-rally reports the remark that stands out from a text of pious platitudes.

5. *Freedom.* The 'freedom of speech' claimed by the journal-ist – both with regard to the ecclesiastical institution and his editor or television boss – is not a personal privilege, but a necessary tool for doing the job of revealing the truth, however unpalatable, in the face of any pressure group, whether political, financial or religious. The media con-stitute the 'fourth estate', indispensable in any democracy to counter the abuses of the other three (executive, legis-lative and judiciary). Nothing would have been known of the shady financial dealings of Bishop Marcinkus, or of the secret power of Opus Dei in the Vatican, without the tenacity of the investigative media.

6. *Respect for the media.* Certain Church leaders, such as John Paul II, Cardinal Lustiger or Jacques Gaillot, have learnt to handle mass communications to their own best advantage, but most representatives of the Church have no inkling of the demands and constraints which the media impose. It should be obvious that television is a magnifying (and distorting) glass, that a news bulletin can only give a few seconds to a given subject. This may be deplored but it is one of the rules of the game. Yet bishops still produce long, detailed written statements that are of no use on television. This is why Church leaders would do well to learn how to master the media, and why the religious correspondent is a necessary mediator between the Church and public opinion.

7. *Honesty.* A journalist is necessarily conditioned by age, sex, upbringing, background, and political and religious opinions. These biases must be taken into account, and corrected. Honesty implies verifying a fact, placing an event in its historical and geopolitical context, questioning as many witnesses as possible. In presenting a papal document, for example, one should separate fact from commentary. The document should be summarised honestly and factually, and the journalist's analysis presented separately. 'Facts are sacred, comment is free' was an axiom often quoted by the founder of *Le Monde*, Hubert Beuve-Méry.

8. *Fairness.* One should take care to give space to all the Christian Churches and to other religions. In France, after the Catholic Church which dominates the scene, the second largest religion is Islam, with its five million adepts. Religious reporting should include all manifestations, from the new cults to the New Age, and should not forget the increasing role of religion in many of today's ethnic conflicts.

9. *Equal-handedness*. The fairness to all religions should also be shown to those marginalised and rejected by the Church. An independent paper should be a mouthpiece for the powerless and mute members of society. It should find space for the minority groups in the Church, the protest movements, the silenced theologian, the deposed bishop. The more the Catholic Church seeks to impose a single voice, the more the press should encourage free debate.

10. *Humility*. Leading national newspapers such as *Le Monde* – and, to a lesser exent, magazines such as *The Tablet* – wield real power in society, and are capable of making and breaking people and their reputations. There is a great temptation to use this power indiscriminately and to become self-important. Religious journalists do not exercise a rival teaching authority to that of the Church, which is why one should know when to bow out gracefully.

There will be nothing strange in this decalogue to John Wilkins. He has been a demanding, scrupulous – if sometimes infuriating – editor, who has shown the courage of his convictions while remaining critically loyal to the Church. He has always respected the freedom of his contributors, submitting any corrections to them, proved an excellent copy reader and, last but not least important, introduced a healthy dose of humour (text and drawings) into a basically serious magazine. Like many other responsible Christian journalists, John Wilkins has done much to live up to such a code. I wish him *Bon vent*! and a fruitful retirement.

Meanwhile, *Inter mirifica* remains an unsatisfactory document: it is abstract and theoretical, ignoring the practical aspects of journalism. If the Church wishes to speak with any relevance to today's media it will have to adopt a different tone – less sermonising and more empathising – and, above all, acquaint itself with the real problems faced by journalists daily: the need to meet deadlines (how to combine accuracy with speed), the temptation of sensationalism (how to square lively reporting with the truth), and the fight against financial or political pressure groups (conscience against censorship). The high ideals preached by the Church (truth, integrity, charity) need to be translated, for the media, into a clear and simple professional code of ethics.

Note

1 In the Herbert Vorgrimler (ed.) *Commentary on the Documents of Vatican II*, conceived by Karl Rahner (London: Burns & Oates; New York: Herder and Herder, 1967).
2 The remarks were made at a conference held at the Dominican monastery of Sainte Marie de la Tourette in l'Arbresle, near Lyons, in 1995. See Alain Woodrow, 'Free speech in the Church', *The Tablet* (26 August 1995), pp. 1093–5.
3 Ibid.

Part III

Signposts from Afar

15

A Lead from Asia

Thomas C. Fox

As I look into the early years of the twenty-first century I see a hopeful vision of Church coming out of Asia. It is a vision being forged by the Asian bishops and theologians. As a journalist and professional Church observer now for nearly a quarter of a century, I can say that this Asian vision of Church is both fresh and imaginative. The Asians are so excited by their vision and its radical nature that they call it 'A new way of being Church'.

How our Church views its mission in the decades ahead is of enormous consequence to the entire human family. Within the Church today, there are considerable differences of opinion as to how the Church's mission is to be shaped in the twenty-first century.

This Asian vision has been taking shape now quietly for some 30 years, largely off-stage and out of sight. We have heard relatively little about it. But during these past three decades this vision of Church has already become deeply etched into the pastoral practices of Asian Catholics. It is shaping the Asian Catholic consciousness. It is shaping the Asian Catholic approach to their continent and to the broader world.

It is a vision that places the Church in solidarity with the poor. It places the Church in dialogue with other religions. It places the Church in dialogue with local cultures, borrowing from them as it seeks its own spiritual paths.

This vision of Church first appeared on the Catholic world stage during the Asian Synod in the spring of 1998. Since then it has come to receive more attention within the Church, but not without attracting controversy. Some feel that the Asians are giving away the baby with the bathwater; and they are not pleased. They feel the Asians have become too accommodating and risk losing their Catholic identity.

The Asians responded, in essence, by saying all they really risk losing is their European identity.

In the 1970s and 1980s, many of these same critics were very critical of the initiatives of the Latin-American bishops and the influence that liberation theology was having on them. Today these advocates of the status quo have shifted their concerns. You don't hear from them talk about the threats of liberation theology. What you do hear from them today is the threat of religious pluralism. No doubt, you will be hearing more of this so-called threat in the years ahead.

In truth, certain critical theological and pastoral issues are in need of greater clarification as our Church comes to the end of one pontificate and prepares to enter another. How these questions get resolved will shape the direction of Catholicism for decades to come.

It is therefore very important that we know the issues at hand and become participants in the discussions. In these matters, I believe we have much to learn from the Asian bishops and theologians.

Questions That Must Be Faced

Consider, for example, some seemingly abstract questions that, as they are answered, will have large impacts on how we live our lives as Catholics.

How, for example, will our Church come to see the place of the Holy Spirit in the wider world? How will our Church see the hand of God operating in the other religions? How are we Catholics to view the teachings and the prophets of other religious traditions? Have these teachings been inspired by God? How are we Catholics, in turn, to evangelise the faith? Is it primarily by word of mouth? Is it by proclaiming that Jesus is the saviour to all humankind? Or is evangelisation primarily a matter of witnessing to the Gospels?

And how will we define the mission of the Church in the twenty-first century? Is the purpose to grow in numbers? Does this mean seeking converts from other religious traditions?

Or is the purpose of all religions to work together for a larger mission? Is the purpose of all religions at this time in history to be working together to build a more just and peaceful world? Is it to feed people's spiritual and physical hunger? Jacques Dupuis, one of the leading Jesuit theologians, characterises the purpose of all religions today as promoting the values of freedom, peace, justice and love in all human relations. This is what it means, he and others argue, to follow the teachings of Jesus and to build the reign of God on Earth.[1] But what is the unique role of Christianity in this environment, we are entitled to ask? Is Jesus the path of redemption and salvation for all peoples? Is Jesus the unique saviour of the world? The Asian Catholic response would be something like this: 'yes and no'.

Yes, Jesus is unique. Jesus represents the peak of God's self-manifestation to humankind. But, no, Mohammed and Buddha were inspired as well. They, too, are manifestations of God on Earth. The Asian mind often has less difficulty embracing seemingly contradictory ideas. It does not operate out of an Aristotelian logic of exclusion.

More typically it instinctively tries to find patterns of inclusiveness. Opposites are resolved in a larger arena. Opposites find resolution in a yin-yang pattern of complementarity. Within the Asian mind, there seems to be more room for ambiguity and paradox.

These critical Church issues will have to be resolved and there is no clear indication how this will happen. But this much is clear: how the issues are resolved will shape the course of Catholicism at a very critical time in our Church's evolving history.

During his pontificate, Pope John Paul II has taken significant steps to advance inter-religious dialogue. But much more needs to be done. If the world's religions learn to cooperate for the common good of humanity, the twenty-first century could become an important and liberating watershed in the human journey. If they do not – if suspicion, fear and hatred have their way – the future is gloomy indeed.

At key moments in our Church's history, believers have been called upon to reimagine the scope of the Church and to make it a more inclusive community. This first happened during the early years of Christianity when, at the First Jerusalem conference, the early Jewish followers of Jesus decided to open their communities to Gentiles without first forcing them to become circumcised or to follow Mosaic law.

I believe our Church today is reaching a similar new moment. It is again being challenged to become a more inclusive community, opening itself this time to non-Western cultures. We call ourselves a universal Church, but only now, after some 20 centuries, is our Church truly becoming Catholic – that is to say, universal.

Allow me to use an analogy. Back in the 1970s, many Western women began to say to us men: 'You don't get it.'

What they meant by this was that while we men thought we had the whole picture of Western history we were, in fact, getting only half of it. We had not begun to see and hear the story through women's eyes. It was as if for centuries we had been walking on one leg without knowing it. In much the same fashion, the Asians are saying to us today: 'You don't get it. What you think to be the universal Church resembles to us a basically Western template of Church. Until you really open yourselves to Asia and Asian ways of thinking, you are not seeing the full picture.' Our Eastern Catholic brothers and sisters are telling us we have only grasped the Yang, and still wait to meet the Yin.

The question is: 'Do we get it?' Are we willing to open ourselves to new ways at looking at our Church? And are we willing to take necessary risks to become more inclusive, more open, and more sensitive to other cultures and religions? Are we willing to allow these cultures to influence our own approaches to faith and religious practices? Are we really willing to believe that evangelisation is a two-way process, that as the Church evangelises people, cultures evangelise the Church?

We hear it again and again: we are living in an era of rapid change. But can we grasp the deeper dimensions of this change? Take simple demographics. The human family is changing shape – and rapidly. At the beginning of the twentieth century, there were roughly 2.6 billion people on the planet. At the end of the century, those two digits had reversed: there were 6.2 billion on the planet. If the world's population were shrunk to a village of 100 persons, Asia would be a very prominent villager. There would be 58 Asians and 33 Christians, of whom 17 Catholics. At the beginning of the twentieth century, 80 per cent of Catholics lived in the northern and western hemispheres: in Europe, North and South America. By the year 2020, this, too, will have been reversed. By then, 80 per cent of all Catholics will live in the eastern and southern hemispheres. Already, 70 per cent of all Catholics live outside Europe and North America.

These figures beg further exploration. Like it or not, we are becoming a Church of the poor. For some 17 centuries our Church has lived in an environment of relative privilege; increasingly this is no longer so. As the number of Catholics has grown, so, too, have the ranks of the marginalised, the hungry and the poor. Some 60 per cent of the human family, remember, lives on only one or two dollars a day. And as this essay was being written the Church officially announced that its membership now tops the one billion mark.

The Asian Catholic Story

To understand better what the Asian Catholics are saying we need to go back in time by at least one generation. The latest phase of the Asian pastoral story began shortly after the Second Vatican Council in the late 1960s. It was an exciting time for the Church worldwide and Asia was no exception. In Asia at that time the bishops and theologians could still remember first-hand the painful experiences of Western colonialism. They, too, were spirited by a greater sense of national pride and cultural identity in the post-colonial period.

It was in 1964 that Pope Paul VI, responding to some of this new fervour, travelled to Bombay for a Eucharistic Congress. During that trip he made several stops in India. He became so moved by its poverty that he gave the limousine in which he travelled to Mother Teresa. She, in turn, raffled the car and raised $100,000 for her work.

Pope Paul later noted that that trip helped inspire his 1967 papal encyclical, *Populorum progressio*, 'On the Development of Peoples'. For Asians, that encyclical was the defining point of his pontificate. For a host of reasons, *Humanae vitae* never had a major impact in Asia.

It was in 1970 that the then 73-year-old Pope Paul VI returned to Asia. The highlight of that trip was a three-day stopover in Manila where 180 Asian bishops from 15 Asian nations had gathered to receive him.

By all accounts the Manila meeting, which focused on *Populorum progressio* and the theme of development, was a major success. As the bishops approached the end of that meeting, feeling empowered and resolute, they issued a series of statements helping to define themselves and their mission. Notably at the top of their list their number 1 resolution was their desire to express themselves as a Church of the poor. After all, nine out of ten Asians live in poverty.

This was really more remarkable than at first glance one might think. For up until that time Asian Catholics were often cut off from other Asians. They often lived in Catholic ghettoes. The local Asian Churches had benefited from the colonisers. And they had become alienated from other Asians. Furthermore, these Asian Catholic Churches were cut off from each other. But when their leaders finally came together, they realised they shared many common experiences, concerns and hopes. It was during those heady days in Manila that several bishops, led by Cardinal Stephen Kim of Seoul, Korea, hatched the idea to keep the spirit of Manila alive by forming a new Asian bishops' umbrella organization. Eventually it came to be known as the Federation of Asian Bishops' Conferences (FABC). Despite deep suspicion on the part of some Vatican officials, the federation came to life – with Pope Paul's personal endorsement – in 1972.

In the last three decades the FABC has sponsored countless seminars, study groups and pan-Asian conferences. It has met in plenary session, to work out priorities and vision, every five to seven years.

At first, Rome feared the formation of the FABC. They were afraid it would become a counterweight in dealing with matters of faith and morals. Rome insisted from the beginning that the proposed FABC have no canonical 'binding authority'. This suited the Asians. They replied that they were not interested in tackling faith and morals as much as they were interested in setting pastoral directions. Ironically, as Cardinal Kim later told me in an interview, by not having this official Church authority, the FABC felt much freer to discuss Church matters and hammer out pastoral initiatives. Taking themselves less seriously, as it were, allowed them to get more work done – and to become bolder in their visions.

At the time that the FABC was coming to life so too were many Asian pastoral centres and book publishing houses. It was atime of much energy. It was also a time of great pride: pride in being Asian, pride in being Vietnamese, Malay, Japanese and Filipino. What was developing was a clear focus on local identity. This, in turn, led to a focus on local Church and local religious experiences: local language, local theology and local rituals.

Dialogue and renewal

The early 1970s was also a period in which Asian bishops and theologians were hammering out what were to become the essential components of their pastoral vision of Church. They worked through a consensus process: not by majority votes, but rather by trying to bring everyone aboard. It needs to be noted that some of the progressive–conservative divisions that we experience in our Western Churches do not exist in Asia. This is because the Asian Churches are relatively young and there is less of a pre-Vatican II model to go back to. Furthermore, the Asian bishops have placed a great emphasis on maintaining harmony – a key Asian value.

At the core of the Asian pastoral vision is what the Asians call the 'triple dialogue' – dialogues with the poor, with local cultures, and with the other religions of Asia. Dialogue, the Asians say, is both the process and the substance of evangelisation. The Asians very much see evangelisation as a two-way street. Within dialogue there is recognition that everyone has something to offer everyone else and everyone also has something to learn. No-one has full truth. Dialogue, then, takes place within the Church as well as within the wider world setting.

First, dialogue with the poor means the Church lives in solidarity with and learns from the poor. Second, dialogue with cultures means the local Church witnesses to and takes from local cultures all that is good and sacred, and puts the challenge of inculturation at the top of the Asian pastoral mission. Third, dialogue with other religions means Asian Catholics see grace at work particularly in the religious experiences of all men and women.

When the Asian Catholics first began to consider their own identities and their own places in the universal Church, they confronted some basic questions about their own heritages. It quickly became clear that it would be an insult to think that God first came to Asia with the colonisers. At the first plenary gathering of the FABC in Taipei in 1974 the Asian bishops declared in an emphatic tone: 'How can we not recognise in the religious traditions of our peoples the way in which God has sought them through their history?'

So when did God arrive in Asia? God came to Asia with life itself and with the first humans and as part of their first religious experiences. Therefore God's plan is, by nature, pluralistic. Creation itself confirms this, the bishops have stated.

235

They further reasoned that the hand of God operates in all religions. Other religions are not simply to be tolerated. They are to be studied and supported and celebrated.

At the 1998 Synod on Asia held in Rome, for example, some Asian bishops proposed having religious texts from other religious traditions integrated into Eucharistic ceremonies. Rome would have nothing to do with it.

Inter-religious dialogue is a good thing. And not just to convert, but to understand the mysterious and unfolding work of God in the world. Furthermore, inter-religious dialogue for the Asians is not simply a heady matter that takes place among theologians; openness to other religions means sharing in the work of building community. It is concrete. It means figuring out who's going to pick up the garbage on Tuesdays and Saturdays.

The Asian vision is about Church renewal. It is my opinion that Catholic Asia is today at the cutting edge of Church renewal. Should this surprise us? Should it surprise us that renewal is coming from what we – at the alleged centre of the Church – view as the periphery? Should it surprise us that renewal is coming from Catholic communities that represent small fractions of the populace in their own countries?

Most often the Asian Churches represent not more than 2 per cent of any one nation. In this regard, they are prone to be more humble Churches. Curiously, they are more like the early Christian communities of the first, second and third centuries.

In the West we have seen, especially in recent years, a fair amount of hostility – or at least suspicion – between bishops and theologians. In the East, the Asian bishops are more prone to respect and look up to their theologians. This is because Asians place high value on education. Academics are 'masters'. In fact, in virtually every Asian language the word for theologian is the equivalent of 'master'.

Can you imagine the way working relationships would change in our own Church if our bishops referred to their theologians as 'masters'? In Asia, the bishops and theologians work closely with each other and most often in greater harmony.

A More Collegial Church

The Asian Catholic vision believes that the local Church is the primary Church. Theirs is a decentralised model of Church. The universal Church, in turn, is a network of local Churches. These ideas are not popular in Rome today. Because of their vision, the Asian bishops, as a group, have become the foremost advocates for a return to a more collegial Church.

If the local Church is primary, it follows that theology is primarily local. Local theology grows out of the experiences of local Christians as they reflect on their relationships with each other and with God. In this regard, Asian Catholic theology borrows heavily from Latin-American liberation theology. But in addition to Latin-American liberation theology, which relies on the social sciences, Asian theology adds a specifically spiritual dimension.

During the 1970s and 1980s, when Vatican officials had their sights set on limiting the influence of liberation theology in Latin America, Asia's own version of liberation theology went generally unnoticed in Rome. It was only in 1989, after the fall of the Berlin Wall, when liberation theology no longer raised the spectre of socialism through the back door, that Roman prelates began to look suspiciously at Asia. But by then it was too late. The horses were already well out of the stable.

The Asian Synod, one of several called by the Pope to prepare the Church for the new millennium, opened on 19 April 1998. It was the first time the Asian bishops had the opportunity to present their vision of Church outside of Asia. In the month that followed, observers witnessed a struggle between two distinctly different views of evangelisation. It was all very polite and all very remarkable. Vatican prelates said evangelisation was all about proclaiming Jesus as the saviour to the world.

The Asian bishops, in contrast, virtually to the last person, stressed that evangelisation was all about witnessing to the gospel. In many nations, some bishops noted, to proclaim Jesus would be a capital crime. The Asians came to the Synod with many suggestions as to how to run the Church. By the time it ended, the Vatican had thrown virtually every one of them out. One Asian bishop seemed to characterise the feelings of many others when he said: 'They didn't pay any attention to our ideas here and we won't have to pay attention to theirs after we return home.'

The Lead from Asia

What emerged at the Synod was a model of Church that places at its centre the vision of building the reign of God on earth. It is not a vision of Church focused on gaining more conversions. It is a vision of Church based on working for the building of a more just and peaceful world.

I see this model of Church in dialogue with the world, giving and taking, serving and learning, gaining grounds in many parts of the Church. The Spirit is alive in the world. She will lead us if we are open to discernment and to taking risks. She will lead us if we remain imaginative and committed Catholics and faithful to the Gospels. She will lead us if we remain followers of Christ.

My sense is that we need to continue to dream and to encourage each other. We need to support each other. We need to challenge each other. We need to place our Church at the service of a very hurting and very fractionalised human family. We can do this. We must do this. And above all we must never stop being hope-filled people.

Note

1 Jacques Dupuis, SJ, 'Christianity and Other Religions: From Confrontation to Encounter', series of three articles, *The Tablet* (20 October 2001, pp. 1484–5; 27 October 2001, pp. 1520–1; and 3 November 2001, pp. 1560–1).

16

How Base Communities Started: Paraguay's Christian Agrarian Leagues

Margaret Hebblethwaite

Of all the continents, none more than Latin America seized the Vatican II torch of inspiration and carried it forward. The Council had understood the Church as 'the People of God'. In Latin America, the people are poor, so the Church became seen as the Church of the Poor, and the gospel as good news to the Poor. It was simple, but revolutionary.

The bishops' conference that decisively drew together the threads from the Latin-American countries and wove them into a new garment was the meeting of the bishops' conferences in Medellín, Colombia, which took place in that year of universal world upheaval, 1968. This was Latin America's Vatican II, which turned the Church upside down, so that it became bottom-up instead of top-down. In particular Medellín promoted what it called 'the Christian base community' as 'the first and fundamental nucleus of the Church' and 'currently the prime factor in human promotion and development'.[1]

All this is familiar and well-worn ground. What is not familiar, and never published in English – and barely accessible even in Spanish – is how this extraordinary ferment began in one of the earliest and most daring ventures of Christian base communities – the Christian Agrarian Leagues (*Ligas Agrarias Cristianas*, or LAC) of Paraguay. When historians trace the origins of Christian base communities, they customarily look

240

towards Paraguay's big neighbour, Brazil: either to the cat-echists in Volta Redonda, near Rio de Janeiro, in the late 1950s, or to the *Movimento de Educação de Base,* with its radio schools, in Rio Grande do Norte in the early 1960s. The Brazil-ian military coup of 1964 gave added motivation to work in base communities – because a vehicle of resistance was needed. The Bishops' Joint Pastoral Plan of 1965–70 (which began in the year Vatican II ended) explicitly said: 'Our present parishes will or should be composed of various local communities and basic communities.' Then came Medellín.

The part of this story that has not been told is how, at the same time as Brazil was making its first moves towards Chris-tian base communities in the late 1950s and early 1960s, Para-guay was too. The memory has been lost, partly because Paraguay, unlike its powerful neighbour Brazil, is a small, over-looked country with poor communications, and partly because the Paraguayan versions were totally eliminated in 1976. For a number of years the communities in both countries flourished under persecution, growing in religious credibility and sanctity, but in the end the Paraguayan Leagues were bloodily wiped out – and almost wiped out of memory.

Rediscovering these early communities – the forerunners of the huge network of Christian base communities that we have today – involves studying a few surviving examples of badly duplicated, typed pages on yellowing, crumbling paper, often written in Guaraní. There are six such papers, preserved by Jesuit priest Vicente Barreto (himself a torture survivor from the persecution, and today parish priest of Santa María in Misiones, Paraguay). They are only fragments of a history, but they provide half a dozen snapshots of a story familiar all over Latin America in the wake of Vatican II. Nowhere was the early story of the base communities more poignant than in Paraguay, and nowhere was it more intense.

The Birth of the Leagues

The Leagues began in Jesuit parishes in the rural area of Misiones. Like so many of the first Christian base communities, they developed under the influence of Catholic Action, with its methodology of 'see, judge, act' that brought Christian commitment right into the heart of everyday life. In 1960 the first Leagues began in Santa Rosa. Two years later, a Regional Federation was formed (*Federación Regional de las Ligas Agrarias Cristianas*, FERELAC), taking in the four neighbouring municipalities of Santa Rosa, Santa María, San Ignacio and San Patricio. The first three had been Jesuit Reductions in the seventeenth and eighteenth centuries – another Jesuit-initiated movement for organising the poor (at that date, the indigenous) which was forcibly suppressed in 1768. History repeats itself.

Were the Leagues, in fact, some of the earliest Christian base communities – possibly even the first ones? That is a matter of definition. They did not belong to the Church structure in the way of the 'ecclesial base communities' defined by the Latin American bishops' general conference of Puebla in 1979 – by which time the Leagues had been suppressed. They had more lay independence than in that definition, but it is abundantly clear from reading the typed documents that this vibrant, biblically based movement for transforming society belongs to the same family as the Christian base communities (the term used at Medellín), whether or not it is formally identified with them.

The first yellowing, typed document is a 25-page booklet called *La Iglesia Ko'agägüa Ñe'ë* ('The Word from the Church Today'), duplicated in October 1970. The type changes half-way through from capital letters to a conventional type. The leaflet simply translates into the local language of Guaraní some brief selections from four official church documents: the encyclical *Populorum progressio*, Vatican II, Medellín and a Paraguayan bishops' joint pastoral on education. There are five themes – the plan of God, justice, peace, politics and education.

Next, written on the same capital-letter machine, comes a 32-page report from a 'National Seminar of the Christian Agrarian Leagues (23–29 April 1970)', in which 80 participants from 22 Leagues tried to hammer out exactly what kind of organisation they were – what a theologian would call 'the ecclesiology of the Leagues'. There are eight questions submitted for discussion, and the answers express many ideas typical of the Vatican II–Medellín ferment, such as the dignity and independence of the laity, the essential interlinking of this-worldly and other-worldly salvation, and the importance of collaboration with non-Catholics seeking the same goals.

'Are the Leagues an economic organisation?' Answer: No. 'The economic dimension alone will not liberate people from their exploitation. The spiritual and moral formation of the *campesinos* must accompany the economic.'

'Are they a trade-union organisation?' No. 'The Leagues seek the integral liberation of all people, whatever their class.'

'Are they a political organisation?' Yes, in the sense that they 'seek the common good'. But 'we have no interest in party political polkas or colours, nor in anything else that divides *campesinos*'.

'Are they a confessional organisation?' No-one could agree on this. Yes, in that they are 'inspired by the Gospel', and 'based on Christian social doctrine'. But they are not closed to those who are not Catholics.

'Are they a Christian organisation?' Yes. 'Christianity to-day is really revolutionary', they declare. 'The documents of the Council and of Medellín are really revolutionary, but the

Gospel continues to be the most revolutionary of all.' They continue, 'This is not a parish or a diocesan organisation. It is run by its own authorities, without depending on any priest or bishop.' There is a reason for this, for 'very often the priests themselves fall into a paternalism which prevents the Leagues' growth, and this happens all the more because the *campesino*s accept so easily any idea that comes from the priests'. So 'the priest can help, but not manage, the Leagues'.

'Are the Leagues an independent and autonomous organisation?' Yes. They are 'made up of *campesinos* and directed by them'.

'Are they a unitary organisation?' All agreed on the need to unify the two Federations, the 1964-founded FENELAC (*Federación Nacional de Ligas Agrarias Cristianas*) and the 1965-founded FCC (*Federación Campesina Cristiana*), which operated in different regions. The unity actually came the following year (1971), under a new network called KOGA (*Kokueguára Okaraygua Guaraní Aty* or 'National Coordination of Christian *Campesino* Bases').

'Are they a democratic organisation?' Yes, and 'when a small group of leaders makes decisions without the participation of the *campesino*s it is an affront to their dignity'.

After these eight questions comes discussion on how change can be brought about, with many ideas typical of liberation theology, such as 'We want to make the human person the true subject of change'; 'Change is necessary if we are to work to live, not work to die'; 'If we do not change, a few will have all the wealth and the rest nothing, and this does not correspond to God's plan.' The term so much associated with Brazilian educator Paulo Freire, *conscientisation* ('awareness-raising'), makes an appearance – Freire's team had in fact visited Paraguay – as does that great Latin-American word *lucha*, or 'struggle'.

Conscientisation is important because it motivates *campesino*s to commit themselves to struggle for a just structure ... The capitalist structure is like a house that we all live in. Its pillars are rotten and need shoring up to prevent the building collapsing, and we *campesino*s are the ones who are removing the props. If we do not dismantle the house we will not be able to breathe the fresh air that we need.

In retrospect we might point out the danger of using such language in a political context where criticism of capitalism was taken as evidence of communism, and where to be a communist was to be deemed worthy of death. Talk of the gospel as revolutionary no doubt was also liable to misinterpretation.

The Activities of the Leagues

The Seminar leaflet goes on to mention the activities of the Leagues, which are typical of the services of solidarity found in many Christian base communities, but here conceived with a Paraguayan flavour. There are economic services such as the community agricultural work of *minga*, the administration of food through bulk buying, the mutual help to those in need called *jopoi*, and the *campesino* schools.

A fuller description of these services is given in a book published in 1982, during General Alfredo Stroessner's 35-year dictatorship and for safety written anonymously and published in Colombia.[2] The *minga* was an ancient indigenous custom, by which several men would work in turns in each one's field, to make the work lighter and quicker and to strengthen friendship. They could also work a field owned in common. The women would more typically keep a common henhouse, raise pigs in common or cook something to sell.

The money earned by the *minga* would be used to buy food in common, which by bulk buying could be secured at a 40 per cent discount. The Leagues would run their own shops, staffed by volunteers on a rota, so that the cheaper prices could benefit more people, not just League members but anyone who was needy, if they paid a symbolic quota. This annoyed the shopkeepers, who found they were losing trade and charged the Leagues with 'communism'. But, say the authors,

> These community shops are a prophetic cry of protest against the fact that a few, precisely because they have more money than the others, can exploit the majority precisely because they don't have money. In this way the rich get richer and the poor get poorer.[3]

The *jopoi* was another ancient Guaraní concept, which again became incorporated in the Leagues. A traditional expression of it would be that when one family kills a pig, it shares it with the neighbouring families, and they in turn do the same when they have an animal to eat. The idea of helping neighbours became incorporated in the Leagues, and often Saturday would be set aside for the *jopoi*, much of which was to repair houses.

The *campesino* schools are the subject of a separate small document of three typed and stapled pages. They began in 1971 as a response to the needs of children whose families could not afford the cost of books, shoes and uniforms, or who had been labelled as 'problem kids' because they were children of League members and put awkward questions to the teachers. So the Leagues began training teachers themselves: 28 schools were opened, serving 628 pupils. The Leagues believed strongly that the schools should be run 'from the bottom upwards', and that the teachers should be '*campesino*-born, truly Christian, exemplary, pacific, and with a deep knowledge of the principles of the Leagues'. As for teachers who were not from the *campesino* base, 'we need their collaboration, but they should accept our revolutionary cause'.

The importance of the *campesino* schools is well expressed in another anonymously written book shortly after the end of the dictatorship, which mostly consists of interviews with torture survivors:

> They had the audacity to create the explosive *campesino* schools, because they were discovering and simultaneously putting into practice a previously unknown weapon: education. This was no longer domesticating education. It was not education for domination, humiliation and fear, for quietism and for state control. The education they discovered had a capital E: it was the education confirmed by the second meeting of Latin-American bishops in Medellín as true education. Education that is liberating, that sets the whole person – individually and socially, spiritually and materially – on the road to development and liberation.[4]

The fourth crumbling document is a stapled hymnbook called *Oñopehengueixa* ('As Brothers'). It is the only one with a picture on the front – a simple black silhouette of a man in a sombrero sitting on a stool and playing a guitar, while a young man and a woman with a babe in arms stand behind him to sing, all of them underneath a little thatched roof. Theologically, this is the most interesting document of all, as its Guaraní hymns (with Spanish translations) capture a theology that is so biblically based that the hymns run in chronological order from Genesis to the Epistles – a systematic rendering of the Bible into song that I have never seen before in a hymnbook.

247

Putting the Bible into the hands of the people – and the language of the people – was one of the most important advances of Vatican II. In Latin America that meant discovering the insights of the poor, for whom more than anyone the message is good news. It has been a long-term process, for the first complete Guaraní translation of the Bible was only published in 1996, nearly 30 years after Medellín and 20 years after the Leagues were suppressed.

The crucial act of putting the Bible in the hands of *campesinos* has been well expressed by Ignacio Telesca (an Argentinian ex-Jesuit historian who has been working in Paraguay for many years):

It was only after the Council that the Bible began to be used by the *campesinos*, and by the people in general. Up to that moment the Bible seemed to be a sort of secret book that only a few people had the right to use. Not so any longer. The Bible became the key book for innumerable *campesinos*.

It is not easy for us, who were not alive at the time, to imagine the change that would be implied by being able to read the Bible, the power to take part in Masses that were now being said in Spanish. But above all, to discover that the history of the people of God, the history of Jesus himself, had so much in common with the history of so many men and women of the campo.

Imagine the situation: a group of *campesinos* hold a meeting in a circle, in the house of one member of the community or in their small chapel, and in the middle of them is the coordinator. All have their Bible in their hand and opening the very first pages they discover that God created us *to live as brothers and sisters.*

It is no longer that the priest is saying this in his homily, or that some leader come down from Asunción is giving a talk on brotherhood. It is in the Bible itself that they find the dream of God for humanity, a dream that all should be brothers and sisters. This is the fundamental starting point. Every course begins here, with the full conviction that what the Leagues wanted to achieve was precisely what God wanted for all human beings.[5]

In *Oñopehengueixa* the hymns do indeed begin with precisely that theme. The message of creation is that 'We were created brothers and sisters', while the theme of original sin is 'Broken brotherhood'. Moses' story is interpreted as 'The struggle for liberation', and the prophets bring a message that 'God does not listen to the exploiters'. In the New Testament, a hymn about Jesus is called 'Christ the Liberator':

Christ came among the poor because he knew his doctrine would bear fruit there:
From the poor and with the poor, the whole world can move forward.

Then there is 'Levelling out the inequalities' (the message of John the Baptist), 'The Liberator of the oppressed' (Luke 4, in the Nazareth synagogue), 'God trusts in the poor' (the calling of the Twelve) and 'Conditions for the Reign of brotherhood' (the Beatitudes):

Blessed are those who seek the reign of justice,
With a clean heart, so as to be pleasing to God,
Without politicking, without double intentions,
Without misleading the people, without abusing them.

Jesus' words, 'On the foundations of Moses and the Prophets', illustrate how central the Exodus theme is in liberation theology:

> What Moses and the Prophets said in bygone times
> Will be for ever a firm foundation of the brotherhood
> which is on the march.
> We live today as in Egypt, in oppression and in fear,
> And there will only be Christian love when the slavery is
> brought to an end.

'The blood of the New Covenant' teaches:

> With his redeeming blood he calls everyone on an
> equal basis
> To form a new People where Brotherhood reigns.
> We renew this pact in the Mass, which is love,
> It is the union of brothers and sisters, to give yourself
> for others.

Moving on to Acts, 'The First Communities' evokes the text so often used by Christian base communities:

> Land, work and harvest, the new people of brothers and
> sisters held everything in common,
> No one would suffer misery, everything was done
> together. [Acts 2:42–7]

The theology of the Agrarian Leagues is clear from these hymns: God made us brothers and sisters, but the experience of our poor is on the contrary one of exploitation and oppression.

Repression of the Leagues

The fifth yellowing document comprises four typewritten pages and is headed 'Persecution of the Church in the Misiones region'. This is an early record, running for only three years, February 1969 to May 1972, while the climax of the violence which wiped out the Leagues came in 1976. But it shows how the Leagues were persecuted from early on for their alternative lifestyle and economy. Here are a few extracts to give a flavour, beginning with a reference to Stroessner's huge network of informers:

1969, March: General threat of the authorities against the *campesino* organisations: LAC, JAC (*Ligas Agrarias Cristianas, Juventud Agraria Cristiana*). There are reports that the Army, through the Ministry of Defence (two generals and various colonels and officials), has developed systematic and efficient channels for getting hold of information on all the Misiones region ...

1970, October 26: San Patricio: The Government Delegate, Dr Juan Crisóstomo Gaona, in a talk to the teaching staff of the High School, gives the order to report members of the Colorado party who spend a long time talking with priests or *campesino* leaders. He forbids the teachers to go to Mass and listen to the priests ...

1971, May 17: Isidro Argüello, Corcino Coronel. Arrested and held incommunicado in the Delegation of Government. Submitted to hard labour, with systematically interrupted rest. With psychological torture that they will all suffer consequences for their health. Freed on 27 May ...

1972, February 22–23: detention and expulsion from the country of Fr Vicente Barreto, who was working in San Ignacio with the *campesinos* ... [This is the same priest whose papers we are reading.]

1972, March 26: San Juan Bautista: Photographer summoned before the Government Delegate, requiring him to hand over the photographic reel of the work he had just been doing at the Palm Sunday ceremonies ...

1972, April 18–23: San Solano (Santa Rosa), Marriage course. Esteban González (householder), captured and disappeared. The next day three *campesino*s received summonses and were seized: González (brother of the disappeared man), Garay and Medina. Transferred to San Juan Bautista and then sent to the Technical Department for the Repression of Communism (Asunción). Interrogated. Put in narrow cells and on permanent fast. They were in prison one month and 20 days. They were freed, declaring that they had been taken innocently.

There are some impressive stories of solidarity among the *campesino*s as they faced arrest. In 1970 in Quindy, when a summons was issued for a *campesino* leader, 150 *campesino*s turned up at the police station. 'Which one of you is so-and-so?' asked the officer, and they all replied they were, with one voice. Then a spokesman explained that what concerned one concerned them all, because they were brothers, and they were all willing to be arrested. Then they sat down in the street and sang at the top of their voices. There were special songs written for such times of arrest, of which the most popular went:

Let us lift our hands, let us embrace,
for we are brothers and we did not know it!
Our journey has been a long one and it has been
very hard
To discover this beautiful idea, so long hidden.[6]

The sixth and final document picks up the story later, after a gap of a few years, and is simply four pages of narrow typescript, in two columns, headed 'List of those arrested from the Agrarian Leagues 1977–1979'. There are 392 names, and they include three men personally known to me today as among the most devout and reliable Catholics of Santa María.

Those years of 1977–79 marked a different stage: no longer were the Leagues harassed, but totally suppressed.

What had happened was this. In 1976 an underground organisation, the OPM, was discovered, and a few of the members – not many – were also members of the Leagues. OPM stood for *Organización Primero de Marzo* (1 March was the date of death of Paraguay's nineteenth-century hero, Mariscal López) and it was dedicated to working for the overthrow of the dictatorship. But the more militant also began to call it the *Organización Politico-Militar*. The work of the OPM was dangerous; whenever possible, members were prevented from knowing the identity of their colleagues in case they revealed the information under torture. They would sit, for example, in church pews, one behind the other, and talk without seeing the other's face. Despite the precautions, OPM papers were found by the police, one discovery led to another, some members were killed directly, others died under torture, and others again were forced to betray their colleagues. One of these was Diego Abente, recently a presidential candidate, but nicknamed 'the golden beak' or 'the singing cockerel' for what he revealed when his pregnant wife was tortured beside him.

Because a link with some members of the Leagues had been discovered, the *campesino* movement was completely wiped out. The series of arrests was known as the *Pascua Dolorosa*, the Sorrowful Easter, because it all happened in Holy Week 1976. Some *campesino*s were killed; others were imprisoned for years in awful conditions; all were tortured; and their wives, left at home, frequently had miscarriages with the shock and the worry. Which is worse: to suffer yourself, or to imagine the unseen sufferings of a loved one? The Leagues were never refounded, though *campesino* Christian Communities (*Comunidas Cristianas*) were, in the late 1980s, with a more church-centred orientation.

The Jesuits involved with the Leagues, being mainly Spaniards, were simply expelled. The exception was the Paraguayan Jesuit, Vicente Barreto, who was both tortured *and* expelled. All the expelled Jesuits went on to do valuable work elsewhere, but they did not lose their commitment to Paraguay, and when the dictatorship ended they nearly all came back.

The Sign of the Leagues

How prophetic were these words of the 1970 Seminar booklet, to be fulfilled just six years later:

> Christ himself, who came into the world to free people from everything that enslaved them, was not understood, and was persecuted to the point of being killed. Christ had true love. Those who accepted and followed his example were persecuted, imprisoned and slaughtered. Today we call them saints. In this sense, if we take the work of the Leagues seriously and with Christian responsibility, it is very possible that saints will also appear among ourselves.

The words contain a challenge for the future, for where there are saints there must be an inspiration for future generations – what Rome calls, in its conditions for canonisation, a 'cult'. There must be a memory of the past. And all over Latin America today, as people gain confidence that the age of dictatorships is over and they will no longer be imprisoned for speaking the truth, there is talk of 'recovering memory'. One phrase that is often repeated is *nunca más* – 'never again' –

which was used as the title for dossiers documenting disappearances in Guatemala and Argentina compiled by human rights organisations. *Nunca más* means that only by recalling the abuses of the past, and condemning them, can a society have any confidence that those days will not recur.

The memory of the Leagues is weak. Even though there are survivors – in many cases with permanent health problems from their torture – they live side by side with the people who were informers or policemen. The society has to heal, as people live together a new life without rancour, but at the same time the temptation must be avoided to suppress the past. The balance is a tricky one, as Chile in the post-Pinochet era has shown. Many of the younger generation in Misiones today have not even heard of the Agrarian Leagues, even when they come from families directly involved in the organisation. Fear has wiped out the transmission of the memory: often it is the historians from Asunción who know more about the Leagues than the younger *campesinos*. Outside the country, the story is virtually unknown, and the recovery of memory is an international task that faces us all. When *campesinos* find their story valued by those who come from far away, they are helped to value it themselves.

Shortly before this book went to press, a tiny but beautiful initiative to recover the memory of the Agrarian Leagues began in a craft workshop of Santa María. In response to an order placed by Ignacio Telesca, the older women began to make banners to commemorate the life they had known in the Agrarian Leagues, with appliqué and embroidery. There is a series of six, showing the *minga* and the *jopoi*, the biblical reflection groups and the *campesino* schools, the arrests and the tortures, all set in the Paraguayan landscape of bright sun, scruffy palm trees and gently rolling hills.

'A beautiful way to remember', is how the German liberation theologian, Margot Bremer, who lives in Asunción, describes the initiative:

> No one could live with photographs of torture on their walls, but by converting these experiences into works of art, the story can be lived with on a daily basis. This is the way to hand the story on to our children.

Notes

1 'Pastoral de conjunto', *Documentos finales de Medellín* (Medellín: Segunda Conferencia General del Espiscopado Latinoamericano, Septiembre de 1968). Author's translation.
2 *En busca de 'la Tierra sin Mal': movimientos campesinos en el Paraguay 1960–1980* (Bogotá: Indo-American Press Service, 1982), with a prologue by the Brazilian Bishop Pedro Casáldaliga.
3 Ibid. p. 45.
4 *Comisión Nacional de Rescate y Difusión de la Historia Campesina, Kokueguara Rembiasa* (Asunción: CEPAG , 1992). The four volumes consist of interviews with torture survivors.
5 Extract from the book he is writing on the history of the Agrarian Leagues, not yet completed. I acknowledge with gratitude his help in preparing this chapter.
6 *En busca de 'la Tierra sin Mal'*, p. 49.

17

Truth beyond Division:
Eastern Meditation and Western Christianity

Shirley du Boulay

Since the Second Vatican Council's declaration on non-Christian religions, *Nostra aetate,* two tides seem to be running in opposite directions. On the one hand interreligious dialogue flourishes and countless individuals practise meditations based on Eastern traditions; on the other, the Church's generosity to other religions seems to have ebbed, its new attitude one of suspicion rather than the joy of discovery. This has been apparent notably in its attitude towards Christians practising Eastern meditation.

I first came across Eastern meditation in the early 1960s. After just a few weeks, for the first time after years of rather desultory Anglicanism, I began to glimpse the meaning of the Fourth Gospel; I thrilled to a new understanding of what the Psalmist meant when he said, 'Darkness and light to Thee are both alike'; I read *The Cloud of Unknowing,* moved to the core by lines such as 'A naked intention directed to God, and himself alone, is wholly sufficient.' Twenty-five years later, after hours of Eastern meditation, much reading of Eastern texts and Christian mystics, in particular Meister Eckhart, I became a Roman Catholic. The East, far from taking me away from Christianity, had drawn me to its heart in a new way.

Ten years earlier, a devout Catholic layman had made a similar journey, one that was to have far-reaching results. John

Main was working in Malaysia when he met a Hindu Swami, who ran an interfaith centre in Kuala Lumpur. The Swami introduced John Main to a method of Eastern meditation, telling him it would deepen his experience of Christianity. It did; and on returning to England he became a Benedictine monk of Ealing Abbey in west London, where he was advised by his novicemaster to give up his practice of silent meditation.

But this was far from the end of the story. While studying the early Christian tradition and the Fathers of the Church, he found a method of meditation mentioned in the *Conferences*, conversations with the great leaders of Eastern monasticism collected at the beginning of the fifth century by John Cassian. It was essentially the same method he had been taught by the Hindu Swami and been advised against practising by his monastery. In 1975 he began to teach this method to a few people at Ealing. The group grew steadily; and now, 20 years after John Main's death and under the leadership of Laurence Freeman, also a Benedictine monk (of Cockfosters in north London), it is known as the World Community for Christian Meditation. It is impossible to estimate the numbers who now practise, but there are some 2,000 groups spread through 60 countries, meeting in churches, homes, prisons and hospitals. Its quarterly newsletter goes to 25,000 people and its website receives hundreds of thousands of visitors. This 'monastery without walls' has saved countless Christians from giving up their faith, for they find in it not only a simple method of meditation, but also one that is acceptable to their Church.

The Pull of the East

Why are so many people drawn to Eastern meditation? What do they find in it that they cannot find in the prayer and liturgy of their parish churches, and why does it make the Vatican nervous?

In the sixties the thought of spending half an hour in silence was thought odd rather than sinful; I remember being told I was 'much too cheerful to need to meditate'. Once I suggested that a weekend conference on prayer should start with silent meditation in a circle and was told first that it wasn't possible, because there would be people there of different denominations, and then, horror of horrors, that 'people might SEE each other'. Again, as I looked for Christian parallels with what I was finding in the East, I lit on the eighteenth-century Jesuit, Jean Pierre de Caussade, who did much to rehabilitate mysticism, and was warned off him.

Yet despite resistance from some quarters, many Westerners have explored the Eastern traditions and in bringing back this wisdom have helped Christians to discover meditation in their own tradition. During the latter half of the twentieth century these include the American monks Thomas Merton and Thomas Keating, and the Jesuits Anthony de Mello and William Johnston. Two European Benedictines who between them spent over 60 years in India and wrote about their experience at length were the Englishman Bede Griffiths and the Frenchman Henri Le Saux, who took the name of Abhishiktananda. Bede Griffiths said he went to India to find the other half of his soul:

> I had begun to find that there was something lacking not only in the Western world but in the Western Church. We were living from one half of our soul, from the conscious, rational level and we needed to discover the other half, the unconscious, intuitive dimension. I wanted to experience in my life the marriage of these two dimensions of human existence, the rational and intuitive, the

conscious and unconscious, the masculine and feminine. I wanted to find the way to the marriage of East
and West.[1]

Abhishiktananda, who was led to India by a blind urge he hardly
understood himself, was, like Bede, devoted to the Catholic Church but painfully aware that it was in crisis. He was
convinced that the salvation of both the Church and the world
lay in the 'simple deepening of the sense of the intimate
presence of God'.[2] His longing for it burst out in a letter to a
priest friend: 'If only the Church were *spiritually radiant*.'[3]
Later he admitted that it was in his deep dissatisfaction that his
desire to go to India was born.

The pull to the East is part of the wider trend towards
globalisation, but there can be no denying that there was –
and still is – a large element of dissatisfaction with the institutional Churches. Every institution faces this danger. The
structure that longs to preserve the original spirit risks becoming frozen in the letter – hence the famous remark of the
Swiss psychologist C. G. Jung: 'I am so glad I am Jung and not a
Jungian.' Human institutions tend to become more human, less
divine, as they get further from their source; which is perhaps
why the mystical dimension of Christianity is little in evidence
to most churchgoers, who often express sadness that the Christ
they worship is presented under the trappings of a legalistic
Church. It is that mystical dimension to which so many people
are drawn today. The diversity of modern living has strengthened our need for unity; the flight from God to science and
technology has led to our realisation that we are nothing if we
do not make the journey inwards.

Abhishiktananda maintained that interiority is the special
grace of India, and that, despite the mystical depths experienced and formulated by Christians such as Ruysbroeck, Tauler

and Meister Eckhart, Western rationalism has always defied and feared the mystery of the beyond; above all it has feared interiority.[4] Yet there is today a thirst for mysticism, for interiority, a longing for experience, a total experience of head and heart over a preoccupation with doctrine and dogma – even over liturgical beauty. Though in the West this yearning tends to be overshadowed by theological formulations, it is there, for instance, in the seventeenth-century English poet and divine, Thomas Traherne:

> You never enjoy the world aright, till the Sea itself floweth in your veins, till you are clothed with the heavens, and crowned with the stars: and perceive yourself to be the sole heir to the whole world, and more so, because those are in it who are every one sole heirs as well as you. Till you can sing and rejoice and delight in God, as misers do in gold and Kings in sceptres, you never enjoy the world.[5]

So, as people searching for the vibrant spiritual life they found lacking in their Churches looked to the East, a two-way traffic began. Some physically travelled to India; many more stayed at home, read Eastern scriptures and took to Eastern practices. The traffic came the other way, too: there was an influx of Easterners, particularly Indians, bearing the message of the East to the West. There were wastrels and idlers among those going East, and the travelling gurus included charlatans and bearers of instant enlightenment. But in among the dross was gold, the gift that is the goal of every true seeker.

The Church's Response: Three Documents

The Catholic Church responded to the growing impact of Eastern religion in three documents. The first, proclaimed during the Second Vatican Council in 1965, was *Nostra aetate*, a gentle, conciliatory document which encourages dialogue and collaboration with the followers of other religions, rejects any sort of discrimination or harassment against those of other faiths and urges that past differences be forgotten. The document esteems Islam, Buddhism and Hinduism, and makes clear that 'The Catholic Church rejects nothing that is true and holy in these religions', acknowledging that they 'often reflect a ray of that Truth which enlightens all men' – a passage which Bede Griffiths in particular saw as a green light in his work towards the marriage of East and West. Four years later Archbishop Pegnedoli, Secretary of the Congregation for the Evangelisation of Peoples, in his inaugural address to the All India Seminar of 1969, described India as 'a land intoxicated by God' which 'appears today as a hope and a light of history and for the future of humanity'.[6] The doors were opening; Christians were encouraged to believe that the exploration of Eastern mysticism, far from being forbidden territory, was approved.

However, 25 years later the Congregation of the Doctrine of the Faith felt it necessary to respond to what it described as the 'urgent need' for sure criteria of a doctrinal and pastoral character on the subject of Eastern meditation. The CDF's 'Letter to the Bishops of the Catholic Church on some aspects of Christian meditation' of 15 October 1989 warns, in a section provocatively called 'Erroneous ways of praying' that the attempt to 'fuse Christian meditation with that which is non-Christian' is not free from dangers and errors – though it later softened this with the assurance that these ways should not be 'rejected out of hand simply because they are not Christian'. Yet methods of meditation from Hinduism and Buddhism, Zen sitting, Transcendental Meditation and Yoga were now described as a 'problem'. The Vatican consulted no-one in India and its letter presented a purely Western view. It comes as no surprise to learn that it was badly received on the sub-continent, not least by the Indian bishops.

What were Catholics following these practices supposed to do? They were not finding fulfilment in their parish churches, nor were they encouraged to follow practices which they found renewed and deepened their Christian orthodoxy. But official documents have rarely stifled spiritual movement: the drift from the Churches continued, and interest in the East continued to grow.

Then, in September 2000, the CDF released its declaration on the unique salvific power of Jesus and the Church, *Dominus Iesus*. The document is critical of 'one-sided accentuations' which, for instance, are silent about Christ, on the grounds that he can only be understood by Christians, yet speak at length of the kingdom, because 'different people, cultures and religions are capable of finding common ground in the one divine reality'.[7] Similarly the document criticises people who say little on the mystery of redemption, but who stress the mystery of creation, reflected in the diversity of culture and beliefs. Surely this attempt to find common ground is a ray of light for interreligious dialogue? Should it not be encouraged rather than rejected?

Those charged with writing this document would have known that it was inflammatory and would be greeted with dismay both in ecumenical circles and the interfaith movement. The non-Catholic Churches were told that they 'suffer from defects' and could not be described as 'Churches in the proper sense'. While it was granted that they contained elements of sanctification and truth, the Church of Christ, *Dominus Iesus* said, 'continues to exist fully only in the Catholic Church', adding, with barely concealed triumphalism, that these Churches 'derive their efficacy from the very fullness of grace and truth entrusted to the Catholic Church'.

263

The same attempt to be even-handed, yet in the end to dismiss, was made in regard to the non-Christian religions. The personal equality of people in dialogue was acknowledged, but specifically in opposition to equality of doctrinal content: there was quite simply no question of that. It was granted that the various religious traditions contain 'elements which come from God ... Indeed, some prayers and rituals of the other religions assume a role of preparation for the Gospel.' However, hard on the heels of this morsel of encouragement comes the statement that this cannot be attributed to divine origin. Furthermore, the document goes on, 'other rituals, insofar as they depend on superstitions or other errors, constitute an obstacle to salvation'. The document states that the Church has sincere respect for the religions of the world. But this is followed by the line most cited in the weeks following the promulgation of *Dominus Iesus*:

> If it is true that the followers of other religions can receive divine grace, it is also certain that *objectively speaking* they are in a gravely deficient situation in comparison with those who, in the Church, have the fullness of the means of salvation.

There was an outcry. Jewish, Protestant, Buddhist and Muslim leaders were deeply hurt at what they understandably took to be a presumption of the inferiority of their faiths and Churches. There was also dismay on the part of other Christian Churches, who had been stung by a Note which accompanied the declaration making clear that it was not correct to refer to them as sister Churches because the Catholic Church was the 'mother' of all the Churches. A Lutheran bishop described the document as 'bullying' and the then Archbishop of Canterbury, Dr George Carey, said that the document did 'not reflect the deep comprehension that has been reached through ecumenical dialogue and cooperation'. The World Council of Churches warned that dialogue could be hindered by such a document. The World Alliance of Reformed Churches responded with 'disappointment and dismay'. A dialogue between Christians and Jews, due to take place at the Vatican, was cancelled as leaders dropped out in protest. Among many negative reactions by Catholic clergy, a cardinal said the document failed to reflect the ecumenical climate, while an Indian Jesuit described it as the equivalent of a fatwah.

Defences were offered. The CDF's secretary, Archbishop Tarcisio Bertone, stressed that the declaration had been been approved by the Pope. In an effort to steady the situation, a month later the Pope himself spoke out to make clear that salvation was not denied to non-Christians and that all who live a just life will be saved even if they do not believe in Jesus Christ and the Catholic Church. But the negative publicity caused by *Dominus Iesus* had done great harm. It was a tor-pedo in the hull of 30 years work in the field of interreligious dialogue. Members of other faiths could hardly be expected to be interested in a dialogue whose ultimate aim was conversion to Catholicism. The doors opened by *Nostra aetate* were clos-ing again, and the official position was hardening.

This may all seem rather remote from the wish of Catholics to practise Eastern meditation. It is not. The effects of such documents are felt even by Christians who would never read them, or read about them. They change the very climate in which the Church lives.

Calling Christianity to Be More Itself

So just what do people find in the East? They find a sense of the sacred, a respect for the earth, a search for the experience of unity. They find that God need not be claimed as the exclusive property of any one religion – though no faith is entirely free from this – but that the various religions have the same goal: that there are 'many ways up a mountain', as an Indian poem has it. They see no reason why Western Christianity should not draw on the infinite wisdom of Eastern spirituality – Hindu, Buddhist, Taoist and Confucian – just as there are certain aspects of Western life which could enrich the East: for instance that, as the East is strong on symbolism, so is the West strong on concepts.

So, too, many discover an understanding of different levels of consciousness, from the outer levels of activity to the still centre of peace. They find that the word 'God', which, through nobody's fault, has become associated with an external, judgemental concept of the divine, can be expressed by words such as 'illumination', 'enlightenment', the 'kingdom of Heaven within' or 'Nirvana'. Jesus called it 'the pearl of great price', and this is what they seek.

There is a genuine search for meaning, for an answer to the question 'Who am I?' There is even the beginning of an answer in the emphasis on the importance of simply *being*. Western society is concerned with *doing*, whereas the East is more content simply *to be*; yet 'being' is at the heart of the Judaeo-Christian tradition. In the Old Testament, God describes himself to Moses as 'I am that I am' and tells him that he must tell the children of Israel that 'I AM has sent me to you'. In the Fourth Gospel, Christ uses the same expression: 'Before Abraham was', he says, 'I am'. Today there is less concern with labels, whether we are Catholic, Methodist or Hindu, as with a yearning for the experience of being itself. As Murray Rogers, an Anglican priest who has spent many years in India, says: 'Our consciousness is an echo of the Consciousness of the Universe, of God.'[8]

In his spiritual diary, Abhishiktananda writes with impressive simplicity about the search for meaning, the longing simply 'to be'. It is a huge, all-encompassing vision, much influenced by his deep experience of advaitic Hinduism:

> The goal of the universe is consciousness of being, the final unveiling of the intuition that constitutes the human being. There were sages, there were seers, there were prophets, and each of them grasped something of the mystery within, the mystery within every being. And their intuitions are stars, beacons for their brothers. From the shore they send a signal, and on the rock they have lighted a flame. And this flame is a call.[9]

Perhaps most of all, these seekers, often poorly taught in the way of Christian prayer, welcome the practice of meditation; in particular two aspects of meditation that are not much taught in Christianity: method and posture. In the West such 'methods' tend to be criticised as elevating technique before grace, but we would do better to learn from them, giving them their due as helpful aids on the path of reflection and contemplation. In the *Bhagavad Gita,* one of the fundamental texts for Hindus, the Lord himself gives precise instructions on how to meditate. The meditator should sit, it is written there:

> with upright body, head and neck, which rest still and move not; with inner gaze which is not restless, but rests still between the eye-brows. With soul in peace, and all fear gone, and strong in the vow of holiness, let him rest with mind in harmony, his soul on me, his God supreme.[10]

Westerners also welcome the emphasis on direct experience rather than being encouraged to pray with concepts. Even if the experience is intermittent, occasional or slight, whether the experience is of boredom and restlessness, or, however briefly, the joy of simply 'being', it can be vouched for: it gives joy and confidence. Those who meditate regularly find their lives are enriched. They learn the value of silence and that silent meditation can lead to a sense of union, travelling beyond doctrine and dogma to a glimpse of the transcendental reality; though there are many methods of meditating, they all lead to the same place. This means more to today's seekers than dogmatic and doctrinal formulations of a religion, for they want to reach the source, the still point which every religion shares. The meditator is taken beyond the duality that pervades so much Western thinking.

Meditation, John Main used to say, 'verifies the truths of your faith in your own experience'. Christians who are drawn to Eastern spirituality do not – or rather, need not – pose a threat to the Church. If only the Church would act as celebrant, or at least as an eager participant, in the marriage of East and West, it would find its membership growing and its congregations more content. Those who look to the East for spiritual nourishment do not wish to reject Christianity – though many do – but instead feel the relationship between East and West could enlighten both; for not only could Christianity learn from the ancient wisdom of the *Upanishads* and from the great Chinese sages such as Lao Tsu, but also the East itself might be enriched by reading her rich and beautiful texts in the light of Christ. Most people long to stay with the faith of their childhood and their culture; few choose the wilderness when they have a warm and welcoming home.

That it is possible to practise Eastern meditation and to remain in the Catholic Church is seen in the life and work of people like Bede Griffiths and Abhishiktananda. Though Abhishiktananda struggled to reconcile Christianity with the deep knowledge of Hinduism that changed his life, both remained Catholics until the end of their lives. They neither became Hindus nor sought to convert Hindus. Of the many people making the journey from the East to the West the most spiritually charismatic, the Dalai Lama, has constantly advised people to practise in their own tradition rather than become Buddhists; he confirms what the Swami told John Main: that meditation will enrich their Christianity. Many people will testify to this.

The Dalai Lama has also brought science and meditation together, by encouraging scientists to examine advanced Tibetan spiritual practitioners. They discovered that:

> Mindfulness meditation strengthens the neurological circuits that calm a part of the brain that acts as a trigger for fear and anger. This raises the possibility that we have a way to create a kind of buffer between the brain's violent impulses and our actions. Experiments have already been carried out that show some practitioners can achieve a state of inner peace, even when facing extremely difficult circumstances.[11]

So, as the Dalai Lama's extraordinary ability to forgive his country's oppressors bears witness, meditation can play a powerful part in promoting world peace.

Future Paths

What can the Churches do? Curiously, as the official attitude coming from the Vatican hardens, so, in practice, there is evidence of a more encouraging environment. Many monks and priests go their own way, not allowing themselves to be too worried by Vatican injunctions. Laurence Freeman finds there is a growing awareness of meditation in the institutional

Church; he frequently receives encouragement from bishops to teach meditation.

As in so many ways we try to live as one world, so we should taste the wisdom of the East and be free to practise methods of meditation which come from her traditions. It is not entirely risk-free – but nor is any prayer. Some Christians suspect that meditation can lead to introspection rather than prayer; there are risks of self-aggrandisement or of falling into the *pax perniciosa* against which John Main warns. But cannot something be done to feed the hunger of those who want to devote more energy to the overriding part of our spiritual lives where we are one, for whom there is one truth, not exclusively owned by any particular faith? Could we not widen the goalposts enough to let Christians learn from the East? If this is too much to ask, could the priests and parishes not do more to revive Christian methods of silent prayer and encourage daily meditation, both in groups and individually?

If the resistance to anything savouring of what the Vatican documents refer to as 'other religions' is still too great to be overcome, could we not have more silence? Even at a Good Friday service there are rarely silences of longer than a few moments; many Sunday Masses allow no silence at all. Yet Meister Eckhart says – and who would argue with him? – that 'there is nothing closer to God than silence'.

Let the Christian Church have the humility to accept that there is a depth of wisdom in the East that can enrich our lives, and bring us more deeply into our own faith. Encourage the reading and absorption of ancient texts, many of them written 500 years before the Gospels. Learn from their practices of meditation. Read the ancient Hindu and Buddhist texts in the light of Christ, until one blazing, transcendent truth is revealed – a truth beyond all religious division. Let us fulfil the charge given to us in John 17:21, the ultimate call to non-duality: 'May they all be one. Father, may they be one in us, as you are in me and I am in you.'

Notes

1 Bede Griffiths, *The Marriage of East and West* (London: Collins, 1982), p. 8.
2 Abhishiktananda, letter to his sister, 29 May 1972, in James Stuart, *Swami Abhishiktananda: His Life through His Letters* (Delhi: ISPCK, 1989), p. 301.
3 Letter to Canon Lemarié 24 October 1960 in Stuart, *Swami Abhishiktananda*, p. 147.
4 This was written for a book that was banned by the Censor in 1954. Published in 1979 in *Initiations à la spiritualité de Upanishads* (Sisteron: Editions Présence), pp. 41–7.
5 Thomas Traherne, *Centuries* (London: The Faith Press, 1963), p. 14.
6 Quoted in *All India Seminar Church in India Today* (New Delhi: CBCI Centre, 1969).
7 Declaration *Dominus Iesus*: On the Unicity and Salvific Universality of Jesus Christ and the Church (Rome: Congregation for the Doctrine of the Faith), 6 August 2000.
8 In conversation with author, April 2003.
9 Abhishiktananda, *Ascent to the Depth of the Heart: The Spiritual Diary (1048–1973) of Swami Abhishiktananda (Dom H. Le Saux)* (New Delhi: ISPCK, 1998), 22 October 1966.
10 *The Bhagavad Gita,* trans. Juan Mascaro (Harmondsworth: Penguin Books, 1962), p. 70.
11 Tenzin Gyatso, 'The monk in the lab', *New York Times* (26 April 2003).

18

Oscar Romero, Bishop-Martyr and Model of Church

Julian Filochowski

The call from El Salvador woke me at 5 a.m. on 25 March 1980: Oscar Romero was dead, shot through the heart with a marksman's bullet as he raised the host at the offertory in a Mass he was celebrating in the hospital chapel where he lived.

I was shocked and sickened to lose a friend. But the sadness went deeper still: a light in the world had gone out. There are moments when one catches a fleeting glimpse of God at work in the world and of Christ's presence among us. The man we all knew as 'Monseñor' provided such a glimpse for me. Oscar Romero's three years as Archbishop of San Salvador had so many parallels with Jesus' own three-year public ministry – up to the violent death he could probably have avoided but knew in the end he had to face – that for a time those of us who loved him were as gutted as the disciples must have felt after the crucifixion.

Monseñor was a *Gaudium et spes* bishop in a feudal society. Trained in the Church of Popes Pius XI and XII, he was chosen to be archbishop because he was known to be bookish, timid and naturally inclined to the preservation of order. Through his courage to respond to the love and expectations of the poor he ended up the paradigm of a Vatican II bishop, one who is immersed in the joys and anxieties of his people and who empties himself for others. Romero presented a model of Church and of leadership which was as close to that of Christ as can be found in the twentieth century. This is why his memory remains so powerful, and grows greater as time passes.

And like the Jesus he followed, death has also been, in many ways, his victory. The death squads linked to the far Right and the security forces – and in particular to the former military intelligence officer Major Roberto D'Aubuisson – which planned and carried out his murder, sought to snuff out a prophetic voice. They wanted to obliterate not just his presence but his memory. Yet Archbishop Romero has not been an absent dead man. As a martyr who shed his blood for his suffering people he lives on in the hearts of hundreds of thousands of Salvadoreans and Latin American people struggling for survival. He is an icon, a symbol of holiness, a source of hope for the poor and oppressed, the patron of justice and peace and protector of the Church which everywhere chooses to place itself alongside the suffering poor.

His death did not end the violence. El Salvador's orgy of killing, which he worked so hard to prevent, if anything grew worse in the decade after his funeral: 60,000 non-combatants had died violently by the end of the 1980s. The repression which had been the constant backdrop to his ministry even followed him to the grave. His requiem Mass on Palm Sunday, 30 March 1980 – I was there with Bishop James O'Brien from Westminster; Peter Bottomley MP, who represented the British Council of Churches; and Bishop Eamon Casey from Ireland – was never allowed to finish. The mourners gathered in the cathedral plaza were bombed and fired on from the Ministry of Defence building, leaving more than 40 dead in the ensuing stampede and mayhem. I witnessed that massacre; 23 years on, it remains indelibly etched in my mind.

But Romero's legacy has grown stronger and stronger. There is a Hollywood film starring Raul Julia, an English operetta (written and performed by Worth Abbey school), as well as countless plays, poems, songs and hymns written in his memory. Several biographies, his homilies and his personal diary have been published in many languages. In Central America children named 'Oscar Arnulfo' are everywhere. Libraries, scholarships, prizes, trade unions, plazas and boulevards have been named in his honour. Even a little street in Brixton in south London, where the British Catholic aid agency Cafod has its home, was renamed 'Romero Close' in 1988. The West Door of Westminster Abbey carries a statue of Archbishop Romero, one of ten modern martyrs unveiled by the Archbishop of Canterbury in the presence of the Queen and Cardinal Hume at a magnificent ceremony during the Lambeth Conference in July 1998. A Romero tradition has grown up. People gather at his tomb daily; the place where he died and the place he lived have become hallowed. The day he died, 24 March, is Romero Day in the popular liturgical calendar of Latin America. His sanctity has been recognised by popular acclamation, and there is a movement for his canonisation which grows apace.

An Unlikely Martyr

Little of this could be seen in the man who was appointed Archbishop of San Salvador in 1977. Born 60 years earlier in Ciudad Barrios, Oscar Arnulfo Romero was ordained in Rome in 1942 and for nearly thirty years worked quietly as pastor, administrator and journalist. There followed four controversial years as auxiliary bishop of San Salvador, when he showed his conservative stances on social issues and the role of the Church after Vatican II, followed by three years as bishop of the rural diocese of Santiago de Maria. As both priest and bishop, he was a gifted communicator: he wrote articles, commented on the radio and edited three diocesan newspapers. But because his outlook was so cautious, his nomination – against a background of increasing repression – was for many a bitter disappointment. He was widely thought of as the candidate of the coffee barons; most priests and religious favoured Bishop Arturo Rivera Damas, who was strongly supportive of the Christian base communities and the peasant organisations emerging among the poor in the countryside.

But no-one had reckoned on Romero's damascene conversion following the brutal killing of his friend, the Jesuit Fr Rutilio Grande, by a death squad in March 1977. Now the repression reached directly into the heart of the newly appointed archbishop, and he responded dramatically. He closed Catholic schools for three days, and ordered all the churches in his diocese to suspend Mass the following Sunday. There would be only one Mass, in front of the cathedral, to which all were invited. The Mass would lament the death of Fr Grande and his two companion passengers who died with him in his car, and would draw attention to the barbarity which lay behind their deaths.

Not long after, I met him on a visit to San Salvador as Latin America education officer for the Catholic Institute for International Relations (CIIR) in London. He did not seem to be made of the stuff of twentieth-century martyrs: he was shy, retiring and self-effacing. He led a very simple and frugal life, living in a small room attached to the Divine Providence cancer hospital where he was looked after by the Carmelite sisters who ran it. In that room he had a small stereo, and his special treat was to listen to classical music. But he was too embarrassed to meet our small British delegation there (I was accompanying Lord Chitnis and the MPs Peter Bottomley and

Denis Canavan, representing the Parliamentary Human Rights Group) and so arranged to greet us in the dining room of the hospital. A humble, gentle and straightforward man, he was not well travelled, and was moved to hear that other bishops in South America and Africa were facing similar difficulties to his own.

He received all his visitors, whether they were high officials from the State Department in Washington or illiterate peasant farmers, with the same unfailing courtesy; his answers were always straightforward and direct. When I was in San Salvador, I saw the streams of *campesinos*, catechists, city workers, mothers and wives of prisoners who came to see him every day. He was very obviously and palpably close to them in their sufferings, their poverty and their sorrow. He loved them dearly.

I later spent time with Monseñor at the Council of Latin-American Bishops' Conference held in Puebla, Mexico, in 1979, which was when the 'option for the poor' entered church documents. I was there for CIIR working with some of the theologians and writing for the British Catholic press. Romero asked me to advise him on dealing with the media. He was always disarmingly open and frank with me and sought out information and advice about the foreign press and the news coverage of the crisis in El Salvador. He also wanted to know about Church personalities from overseas who had contacted him and about whom he knew little, and about European agencies which might be able to help his radio station, his printing press and other programmes. He would talk about his hopes and his fears of events in El Salvador, his pain over the continuing hostility of the papal nuncio (who had backed his appointment because he was sure Romero would not make waves) and some of his fellow bishops, and his gratitude for the unbelievable worldwide solidarity which had been demonstrated for the Church in San Salvador as it assumed the role of the voice of the voiceless. Puebla bolstered Romero, because it showed him he had support from fellow bishops in the wider Latin American Church.

It is easy to forget just how isolated Romero was at home. His fellow bishops resented him drawing attention to the repression, believing that any forthright criticism of the authorities would be incendiary. But Romero did not appear to resent them. He once told me about the Bishop of San Miguel, Alvarez, one of whose priests had been detained and tortured. Romero said to him: 'Now that they've tortured one of your priests, will you support my attempts to stop the persecution?' But the priest had not been tortured because he was a priest, the bishop had answered, but because he was a subversive. Monseñor told me the story with huge sadness but without a trace of anger.

Daring to Speak Out

Romero's preaching was legendary. If away from the pulpit he was self-effacing and bookish, in the pulpit he took on an utterly compelling fearlessness, directness and power. His cathedral was only half built, but as soon as he became archbishop he suspended the work on it. The cathedral was hot, humid and crammed with people who listened in total stillness, occasionally erupting into applause. He used to spend half the week praying over the gospel in preparation for Sunday. The homilies would last an hour or more; first, he broke open the gospel, then he proceeded to the news. His words went out live on the archdiocesan radio, and it seemed as if the whole of San Salvador was listening: Monseñor's voice rang out from radios in taxis, on the street, in the shanty towns. The National Guard made vain efforts to put the cork in the bottle: they entered cantinas in rural areas to force them to change stations, and repeatedly blew up the diocesan radio station itself (which was rebuilt with Cafod's help). But the opposition Monseñor roused only confirmed to the people his authenticity. Romero's own response to the bombing was to entreat his congregation themselves to become 'microphones of God' – spreading truth and hope.

Romero's courage in his preaching reached a pitch the day before he was killed: he had already called on US President Jimmy Carter to suspend arms shipments; this time he urged soldiers not to obey an unjust order: 'I beg you, I *order* you, *in the name of God*, stop the repression!' In speaking out like this, he knew he was marked. The threats and intimidation had grown more urgent and more intense, but he never wavered or drew back; like prophets down the ages, he continued to speak of the massacres, the persecution, the disappearances, the corruption and the calumnies, and nothing would cause him to stop.

He had many offers to leave El Salvador, but he knew he had to stay. Once he refused an invitation to visit Britain we had extended to him to speak about the repression and injustice. In a beautiful letter he explained that to speak truthfully outside the country could be interpreted as great provocation by the government. 'For the present,' he wrote, 'I believe the place from which to defend my people is from my own cathedral.' El Salvador was his home, and he knew it was also his Gethsemane.

Good News for the Poor

His preaching and teaching were entirely orthodox, as even those who have read and reread his sermons sniffing for heresy have had to admit. But besides the orthodoxy or 'right teaching' there was always the concomitant 'right action' or orthopraxis, as he sought that the Church in San Salvador live out the gospel message of love, truth, justice and freedom in a way that offered something real for the poor in their daily existence. Romero's closeness to the poor was a fact. He called them 'my people', and saw in their faces the disfigured countenance of God. With great affection they knew him in return simply as 'Monseñor'. In his life and in all his choices the poor came first; he in turn was evangelised by the poor, transformed by them.

Oscar Romero was a model 'evangeliser': he preached the gospel of Jesus Christ clearly and explicitly, in season and out of season. He brought the good news particularly to the poor, to those in distress, to the peasants living in near feudal helplessness, to the slum-dwellers in the shantytowns, to the prisoners and their families. But he also endeavoured at every stage – and this was crucial – to make the Word of God real and effective in the concrete situation of El Salvador, in the lives of the poor.

The gospel was not a book so much as a reality; it was Good News for the poor. It was the light with which to make a critical judgement on everything in society which was contrary to God's plan. In so far as they were unable to heed it, the Good News for the poor became bad news for the wealthy and powerful. He preached the God of Life and he denounced with the ferocity of the prophets of old all those things which brought death to his people – not only the torture and killing by the army but the exploitation on the plantations and in the factories, and the unjust land system which brought a slower but equally certain death through hunger and disease.

His challenge was always to conversion. The Word of God was addressed to all; while it was a challenge to the interests of the powerful, it was primarily for their change of heart. Romero pointed to the sinful systems and thence to the source of the sin which he described as the idols of his country and his time: riches and private property when they become absolutes, the idolatry of national security. He spoke out, too, against the idols of the Left: he warned the new mass organisations then forming of the idolatry of the 'organisation' or the 'party', and he consistently refuted violence on either side.

The gospel is known, in part, by the opposition that it produces. His appeal was so straightforwardly gospel-based that it produced fury in those who believed that the gospel could be made safe. His option for the poor was the demand not of ideology but simply of love. He said on one occasion:

> I would like to define the preferential option for the poor more precisely. When I say this I am reminded of the message from Puebla that we should not divide the Church – the poor on one side, the rich on the other – but (and this is important) a preferential option for the poor is calling without exception to all classes to become truly committed to the cause of the poor as if it were our own cause. That is the secret. Like Christ who said, 'whatsoever you do to the least of my brethren you do to me'.
>
> I offer you this by way of example. A building is burning and all are watching it burn with arms folded. But if one of them is told, 'Look here, I saw your mother and your sister go in and they still haven't come out', the situation changes. 'Your mother is burning' and you would go in even though you would get charred to rescue them. That is what it means to be truly committed.
>
> If we look at poverty from the outside as if we were looking at a fire, that is not to opt for the poor – no matter how well meaning we are. We should get inside as if it were our own mother and sister who are burning. Indeed it is Christ who is there, hungry, suffering.

The poor were oppressed; he defended them. He did so, first, by simply telling the truth about their oppression and the atrocities they suffered – by relaying and amplifying their voice and articulating their call for redress and justice. Second, he placed himself right alongside them and offered them all the services of the archdiocese – legal aid, shelter, advice. The poor were resigned; Romero gave them hope. He encouraged them to organise to defend their interests. He validated their struggles. So often those murdered were described as 'criminals' and 'subversives' by the powers of the State and their media. He called them 'martyrs', and reminded them that the blood of martyrs brings life and fruit. Most of all they saw he was really with them without any secret motive or hidden agenda but simply because he loved them and he restored dignity to them and hope for a better future.

A Saint for Our Time

Archbishop Romero was not, then, simply a great catechist who explained the Christian faith but also a great evangeliser and a tenacious advocate for fundamental human rights. The Church was persecuted and defamed for that preaching and that action: 'Be a Patriot; Kill a Priest' was a popular bumper sticker frequently seen on limousines in the rich suburbs of San Salvador. Six priests were killed before Romero. Many more would be killed after his death. In the end he too paid the ultimate price for his teaching and action.

In March 1980 the threats became feverish. Romero knew he was going to die. He accepted it with great equanimity, preparing himself, and even offering his own view of that death which came just days after he gave an interview with a Mexican newspaper.

I have frequently been threatened with death. I ought to say that, as a Christian, I do not believe in death without resurrection. If they kill me I will rise again in the people of El Salvador. I am not boasting, I say it with the greatest humility.

I am bound, as a pastor, by a divine command to give my life for those whom I love, and that is all Salvadoreans, even those who are going to kill me. If they manage to carry out their threats, from this moment I offer my blood for the redemption and resurrection of El Salvador.

Martyrdom is a grace from God which I do not believe I deserve. But if God accepts the sacrifice of my life, then may my blood be the seed of liberty, and a sign that hope will soon become a reality.

May my death, if it is accepted by God, be for the liberation of my people, and as a witness of hope in what is to come. Can you tell them, if they succeed in killing me, that I pardon and bless those who do it.

But I wish that they could realise that they are wasting their time. A bishop may die, but the Church of God, which is the people, will never die.

A week after Archbishop Romero was gunned down at the altar Cardinal Hume paid tribute to him at a memorial service in Westminster Cathedral. In his peroration he said, 'It would be wrong for me to anticipate the mind of the Church, but I personally believe that one day Oscar Romero will be declared a saint of the Church.' The cause for Romero's beatification was launched in San Salvador in 1990. In 1998 Basil Hume wrote to Rome in support of the beatification in the hope that Romero would be one of the martyrs recognised by the Church during the celebration of the Great Jubilee. His action was followed by similar letters from many other bishops, cardinals and episcopal conferences. Today, with little curial support, the cause languishes somewhere between the Vatican's Congregation for the Saints and the Congregation for the Doctrine of the Faith. Meanwhile, the poor of Latin America pray to 'San Romero', their beacon of hope, for support and intercession. In their hearts he was declared a saint a long time ago.

Oscar Romero's sanctity will be formally recognised in the course of the next ten years. He will be for the future a paradigm example of a Vatican II pastor who underwent personal conversion and with a profound, God-centred spiritual life, became a champion of the Christian gospel embodying love, truth and justice in himself and in his every action. In life he was known as the 'voice of the voiceless'; in death he has become the 'named of the nameless', the face of thousands of Central American martyrs who gave their lives, massacred or disappeared, because of their faith in the God of life who brings justice.

What does remembering Archbishop Romero mean? From a Christian point of view 'remembering' means something very different from a panegyric or a nostalgic speech. The fundamental Christian model of remembering is Jesus' command at the Last Supper, to 'do this in memory of me'. For the Church, to remember Archbishop Romero must first mean to continue his work and to imitate that option for the poor which he embraced and his whole ministry in San Salvador epitomised.

The chasm between rich and poor, North and South, in our world is widening. Globalisation has brought with it a process of globalised impoverishment. There are over 800 million people in our globalised world who are hungry all the time, malnourished, sometimes starving. Their simple aspiration is to be able to eat, something, three times a day. Yet we also perceive breathtaking and undreamed of wealth elsewhere in the global market world where material greed seems to know no bounds. Globalised poverty, globalised injustice demand globalised solidarity and prophetic witness to challenge the complacency and moral indifference. Oscar Romero would not be silent. It is the vocation of the whole Church today, as evangeliser, to be the voice of the voiceless poor. To speak out in the face of financial systems and choking debt, arms contracts, trade agreements and economic sanctions which are all too often structures impregnated with sin whenever they are death-dealing (rather than life-giving) contracts, systems and treaties.

Oscar Romero turned the world upside down for his poor. His life and martyrdom inspire not only Salvadoreans and Latin Americans – but that whole bread-sharing, justice-seeking, Christian people who reach into every corner of the earth intent on globalising compassion and globalising solidarity, precisely what *The Tablet* has championed this last 21 years.

Part IV

Postscript

19

John Wilkins: A Tribute

Hugo Young

Those of us who write for the British broadsheet press think we know the supreme value of journalistic independence. Even the editors of Rupert Murdoch's tabloids will go to their graves reciting with sincerity their lifelong defence of the freedom of the writer – the columnist, the reporter, scribes of every kind – to perform without interference from government. Proprietors may be another matter, but in the eyes of most British editors who work for powerful proprietors, the owner's instructions do not count as interference. So we all have our ways of wallowing in the pieties of the British way of journalism. We observe no official agendas. We think we have no constituency except our readers, otherwise known as markets. We can rattle off the canons of independence, even though in the grubby worlds of commerce and propaganda these may not always be perfectly observed.

Editing a paper that speaks out of, and to some extent into, an avowedly authoritarian institution such as the Roman Catholic Church is an altogether subtler task. The ground rules are different. The usual pieties cannot erase the context, or the sense that there is a particular constituency to be addressed. Independence requires a more scrupulous definition than is usually to be found in the self-serving clichés of the *Daily Mail*. *The Tablet* has not become arguably the most influential Catholic weekly in the world by flailing against all authority.

Such is the nature of its audience that it would not have survived had it taken that path. And yet, within its own context, it has retained, above all else, independence.

The genius of John Wilkins – I do not use the word lightly – in his two decades as editor of *The Tablet* is to have trodden a path between the traps that lie in wait for anyone in his position. He has preserved the paper's identity, embedded in the Catholic Christian tradition, as a loyal friend of the Church from which it grew. Yet he has insisted that neither loyalty nor friendship require servility or obedience. He has maintained the kind of independence that no journalism, whatever niche it occupies, can afford to sacrifice if it wishes serious readers to believe what it writes.

This definition of *The Tablet*'s role has not been as easily accepted within the Church as some of us had every reason to believe it should have been. John's time as editor, after all, began when the philosophy of Vatican II, which the paper had dedicated itself to serving ever since the end of the Council, still appeared to bathe the Roman Church – certainly the English branch of it – in the glow of openness and tolerance that is consistent, among other things, with the best kind of journalism. But old mindsets die hard. Not every bishop is a born Jeffersonian democrat, and by no means every strand of English Catholicism has foresworn the blind fealties of the pre-conciliar faith. While John was far too canny to engage in open battles with the hierarchy, there were vigilant eyes over his shoulder that still have only a shallow understanding of an editor's perspective. They assumed – still do, in some cases – that the task of *The Tablet* was to be the unquestioning voice of Rome.

Nowhere was this misunderstanding more palpable than in Rome itself. Throughout John's editorship, the very influence his paper acquired redoubled the complaints in the Vatican that its orthodoxy did not come up to muster. We witnessed the incapacity of the truly authoritarian mind to understand the most elementary meaning of journalistic independence. In certain corners of the Vatican *The Tablet* is criticised for its heterodoxy but more so, even after 20 years' evidence to the contrary, for the perception that it is itself an organ of the English branch of the Roman Church and therefore engaging in the heresy of criticism with official blessing. Some English bishops – a small minority perhaps – might like it to be more like that. Some Church leaders in John's time have thought nothing of calling him in for discussions that were not meant to be entirely collegial conversations between equals. But they knew, in the end, their limits. In Rome, the concept of a paper that is both truly Catholic and truly independent is literally beyond the comprehension of cardinals steeped in the culture of their own institutional power.

John has seen off these challenges thanks, in my opinion, to four great qualities he brought to the job of editing. He once told me he regarded the job as his vocation. I inferred this to mean it was the job above all others he was born to do, and to which he could bring the kind of commitment one might liken to that of a dedicated pastor.

This highlights his first virtue: an almost fanatical industry. He has cared about every word appearing in every issue of the paper he edited. He has been a hard-driving editor, not always easy for his small staff to work with. But great editors, especially of weekly papers, are often like that. They have to be. Their personal passions are what make their paper special, and their dedication to the details are usually what make it unique. There needs to be an element of benevolent dictatorship, which, rather like William Shawn, the legendary editor of the *New Yorker* for several decades in the mid-twentieth century, John duly supplied to *The Tablet*. Day and night, seven days a week, he toiled over the commissioning, the re-writing, the sub-editing, the correcting and – very necessary – the rejecting of what next week's paper might contain.

Personally I have never known him lose his cool or courtesy, though perhaps his staff have seen his collar get a little warm. But there was an iron rigour about his references and standards. He was a catholic as well as Catholic editor, but always clear that *The Tablet* should consist of pieces that passed his own subjective test of what was worth printing. *The Tablet* became his paper, as it had to be. John earned this right by giving his life to it, paying the costs as well as gaining the satisfactions of that degree of commitment.

This opens up his second great quality: the fact that he developed a vision of what *The Tablet* should become, and worked by slow degrees to make it happen. The formula proved an extraordinary success. He knew what his readers wanted, the tone that stimulated them, the range of subjects that would appeal. The circulation all but tripled in his time, without benefit of the massive marketing that pushed one of *The Tablet*'s contemporaries, the *Spectator*, at much expense, into a different league. The more interesting comparison is with the *New Statesman*, whose present circulation barely exceeds *The Tablet*'s. As *The Tablet*'s audience grew, the *New Statesman*'s shrank.

How did this happen? I think it owed much to a twin approach, subtly brought about, that has made John's *Tablet* distinctive. On the one hand, he eased it out of the Catholic, and even the religious, ghetto. It retained that special feel. But what it had to say about the politics and complications of the moment, especially when they were international, made it a mainstream presence. On the other hand, its agenda, like its perspective, remained its own. From the start, this was, of course, ecumenical. That was elementary, and added greatly to *The Tablet's* audience. But it amplified a wider journalistic point. Read down *The Tablet* index of contents in any week, and compare these with what its secular competitors announce, and you find, unfailingly, many fewer pieces that simply re-hash the issues the daily papers have incessantly chewed over. Time and again, its roots give it something else to say. For readers in search of fresh fields of controversy to graze, *The Tablet* offers much the largest diet of originality.

In the international field especially, there is no contest. The universal Church supplies not only a religious dimension to the discussion of global problems. It also guarantees a more universal agenda, and supplies a far-flung network of contributors, often people of unusual distinction outside journalism, the like of which is much harder for a secular weekly to establish. The core of this internationalism may be the Church in the World reporting at the back of the paper, a section to which John particularly applied his famous industry. But at the front, enlightening features regularly appear – whether about Latin America or Eastern Europe, especially – covering ground neglected throughout the rest of the British press. In a globalised world, John's unfailing resistance to parochialism has been a major explanation of his paper's steady success at home and abroad.

Thirdly, he knows his subject as well as he understands his audience. John, let's never forget, is a serious Catholic. He has read the encyclicals and the other texts. He has penetrated deep into the faith, as converts often do, putting us cradle Catholics to shame. He knows the post-conciliar history of the Church as well as any man alive.

He knows the back alleys of Rome and the Vatican, the safe houses where contacts may still be found by an editor not entirely approved of by Cardinal Ratzinger. No prudent bookie would fix odds on likely papal successors without touching base with John – even though he expressed as much sceptical uncertainty as anyone about how the forces in the consistory would in the end be ranged. His role in the Church nearer home has been just as sophisticated.

Though *The Tablet*'s readership is conspicuously global, its domestic voice matters. John's editorship coincided with a series of battles for supremacy between the Vatican and domestic hierarchies, especially over episcopal appointments. Under Cardinal Basil Hume, the English Church was remarkably free of the divisions that scarred its continental counterparts. The cardinal had his ways of pre-empting the imposition of bishops from what one can only call the hard Right. Himself personifying the English temperament of tolerance and moderation, Hume ensured for the most part that John Paul II was deflected from making appointments that would challenge if not insult that national characteristic. But *The Tablet* had a big role there too. As the main lay tone-setter for both intellectual and political Catholicism, it nurtured a climate in which Hume was able to defend his offshore outpost against the turbulence that some forces in Rome desired to unleash upon it. Without John's personal knowledge and watchfulness, and the respect in which he himself is held, this could not have happened to such benign effect.

Finally, though, one goes back to his grasp of the elusive quality that few other editors have to think about so carefully. In this, he would agree, he has been supported throughout his time by *The Tablet*'s owners. The paper is not a wholly, or even partly, owned subsidiary of the Church. The owners and the board have been as assiduous as the editor in sustaining that position, just as they have scrupulously avoided intervening, except sometimes on necessary budgetary matters, in the editorial decisions the editor makes. They, too, know what independence means.

But it is the editor who has to apply that easily stated philosophy in more complicated practice, and this is what John has been doing for 20 years. He is a friend of the Church but not its slave, an ally but not one subornable into believing that criticism amounts to disloyalty. Above all he has been a friend, through some taxing times, of *The Tablet*'s ever-expanding circle of readers. Without that bond, an editor will always fail. He must know how to challenge as well as satisfy them. In the challenge lies the satisfaction, for readers of a paper like *The Tablet*. Supplying both is what made John Wilkins a great editor.